THE COMPLETE BOOK OF
BAKING

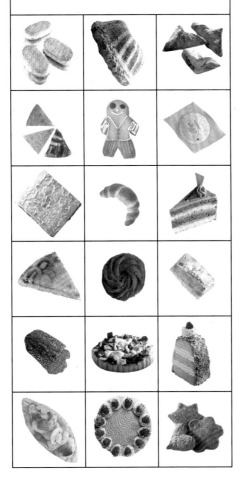

THE COMPLETE BOOK OF
BAKING

LONGMEADOW
PRESS

Author: Monika Schumacher

Translated and edited by Carole Fahy,
by arrangement with Bookdeals Translations
P.O. Box 263 Taunton, TA3 6RH, U.K.

Cover and recipe photography by Renate Krake
TLC-Foto-Studio GmbH, Germany
Introduction photography: Peter Barry, London, U.K.

3285
© 1994 English-language edition CLB Publishing,
Godalming, Surrey, England
Originally published in German as
Daß Große Bassermann Backbuch
© 1991 Falken Verlag GmbH
Niedernhausen/Ts., Germany
Published by Longmeadow Press
201 High Ridge Road, Stamford, CT 06904.

ISBN 0-681-00568-8
Printed in Singapore
First Longmeadow Press Edition 1994
0 9 8 7 6 5 4 3 2 1

CONTENTS

INTRODUCTION

Today, home baking represents the ultimate in sweet and savory temptation. Once regarded as sheer hard work, it has now become fun, and, although cakes, pastries, rolls, bread and all kinds of sweet, savory and spicy delicacies can now be bought in bakeries in almost unlimited variety, home baking is still very much alive. This is not really surprising, for home cooking these days is regarded as a very creative activity that gives plenty of scope for developing the cook's own ideas. Baking is fun twice over; firstly, there is that creative enjoyment and then the pleasure of seeing family and friends enjoy home-made cakes, delicious-smelling breads and spicy savories. And if home-made treats are also lovingly and imaginatively decorated, they will be doubly appreciated.

Success and praise are guaranteed by carefully following the instructions in this book. There are delicious recipes for all occasions: Christmas, Easter, family celebrations, afternoon teas and children's birthday parties.

The recipes are explained step by step, and the ingredients are listed in order of use. Just leafing through this book, with its mouthwatering illustrations, will lure the cook into the kitchen, and, with a little imagination, personal touches can be added to any recipe. We wish you lots of success in your baking, and of course in eating the delicious results!

MODERN BAKING TECHNOLOGY

Technological progress has helped to iron out the idiosyncrasies of individual ranges. Today, there is little difference between gas and electric ranges, for both work on the same principles, and are available using conventional radiated or fan-assisted heat. On the whole, all ranges these days give consistent heats, although slight variations may still occur in certain models, both gas and electric.

In order to achieve the best results, it is important to get to know the individual oven well by experimenting with small quantities before attempting to bake larger batches.

THE ELECTRIC OVEN

There are two different kinds of electric oven: conventional and fan-assisted.

In a conventional oven, the heat is radiated and will vary between the top and bottom of the oven. The oven's handbook will give the appropriate shelf heights for baking individual items.

Circofan or fan-assisted ovens work with hot air. The air is heated by elements in the back of the oven, blown in through a ventilator and circulated around the oven. This circulating heat gives even cooking throughout the oven, and it can save time as well as energy, if used properly.

THE GAS OVEN

Technology has now largely eliminated the dangers of gas, and all up-to-date gas ovens are fitted with modern safety equipment. Temperature in a gas oven can be regulated with a thermostat, as in an electric oven.

BAKING TEMPERATURES

Gas and electric oven temperatures in Fahrenheit are given in each recipe. For fan-assisted ovens and for shelf heights for individual items, always check your own oven handbook, as different models can vary. All temperatures given in the recipes are for ovens with top and bottom heat and assume the oven is pre-heated. For electric ovens, preheating to 400°F will take approximately 10-15 minutes. Gas ovens will reach an equivalent temperature in 5-10 minutes. Fan-assisted ovens do not need to be preheated.

OVENWARE

It is particularly difficult for the beginner to choose the right baking utensils from the vast choice on offer. Even experienced bakers and pastry cooks can get confused by the huge variety of sizes, shapes and materials available.

When choosing ovenware, bear in mind the particular oven for which it is intended. There are pans and dishes on the market specially designed for use either with gas or with electric ovens, and some which are suitable for both: read the manufacturer's instructions carefully, to avoid any unpleasant surprises!

The following is a list of the most common kinds of ovenware.

NON-STICK OVENWARE

Invented over thirty years ago, non-stick utensils are still as useful as ever today. The special plastic coating, known as PVC, that is used on pots and pans and dishes is sold under various brand names, such as Teflon. Being non-stick, the utensils are easy to clean, as well as facilitating the turning out of cakes. Non-stick pans can be used in gas, electric or fan assisted ovens, although, if the tin is coated with black PVC, it is advisable to reduce the stated

temperature slightly if using a gas oven.

HEAVY TIN OVENWARE

Heavy tin ovenware is less suitable for gas ovens than the light variety, as the pan is inclined to get too hot. However, it is very good for use in an electric oven. As with the light tin ovenware, the heavy variety should be "baked in" with salt before using for the first time.

LIGHT TIN OVENWARE

Light tin ovenware has been around a long time, and

is mainly recommended for gas cookers. Its only disadvantage is that the top of the cake browns before the rest, as light tin tends to resist heat. These pans should be sprinkled with salt before using for the first time and "baked in" at very high temperatures for 15-20 minutes.

ALUMINUM WARE

There is a wide variety of aluminium ware available; utensils with a matt finish are always preferable, as they conduct the heat better. There are aluminum utensils especially recommended for gas, electric and fan-assisted ovens. Variations also exist: some utensils are gold colored on the outside, or have coatings on the inside; these can be used in any kind of oven.

GLASS AND STONEWARE

Heat-resistant glass, such as Pyrex, or earthenware dishes are mainly used for those recipes which need to be baked at medium or lower temperatures, as they conduct heat very slowly, but achieve a constant, even heat successfully. Cooking temperatures for glass and stoneware should not be too high for too long a period, since both materials can overheat.

RECIPES AND INGREDIENTS

YEAST DOUGH

Yeast dough is the basis of many popular recipes. For tasty breakfast rolls and breads, snacks to grace a cold buffet or as the basis of sweet pastries, yeast dough is always a favorite. And for those who like a savory snack, yeast dough is particularly good with sausage and vegetable fillings. Recipes using yeast taste best when freshly baked. Storage is limited to a few days, for the cooked dough, unless frozen, dries out and goes stale very quickly.

Don't be put off by the fear that using yeast is very difficult — this is simply not true. Following our instructions and tips means that making yeast dough is as easy as any other form of cookery. As the name implies, the main ingredient of the dough is yeast. Yeast is a living substance that acts as a raising agent by aerating the dough and causing it to swell. However, yeast is only activated efficiently if given the right conditions, which means a temperature of around 98°F and recipe ingredients at the same temperature. When buying yeast, respect the "best before" date because sensitive yeast cultures have a relatively short effective lifespan. Yeast is sold in both dried, powdered form and fresh. Particularly good results can be achieved with fresh yeast.

When making yeast dough, it is important not only that all the ingredients are of even temperature but also that the yeast is given sufficient rising time at each stage. The recipes in this book differentiate between light, medium and heavy yeast dough. The higher the proportion of fat and other ingredients and the stronger the type of flour used, the more yeast will have to be added. Follow these guidelines: for a light dough, use ¾-1oz yeast; for a medium dough, 1oz yeast; and for a heavy dough, up to 2oz yeast.

1. Yeast dough should be kneaded on a lightly floured board, using a regular, rhythmic action. Fold the dough towards you and then use the heel of the hand to push the dough down and away. Give the dough a quarter turn with the other hand and then repeat the folding and pushing. A firm dough is easier to work with for a beginner.

2. Continue kneading the dough for about ten minutes until it is smooth and no longer sticky. Thorough kneading is essential to distribute the yeast throughout the dough and to strengthen the gluten in the flour, both of which mean that the dough will rise more easily and be much lighter in texture, once baked.

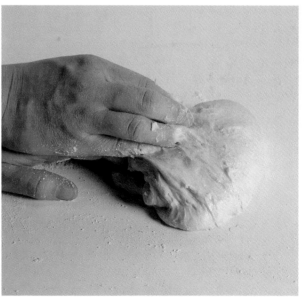

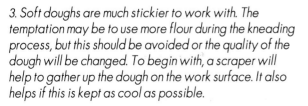

3. Soft doughs are much stickier to work with. The temptation may be to use more flour during the kneading process, but this should be avoided or the quality of the dough will be changed. To begin with, a scraper will help to gather up the dough on the work surface. It also helps if this is kept as cool as possible.

4. The kneading action is the same as for a firm dough and the aim is also to knead until the dough is smooth and has lost its stickiness, while remaining soft. A food processor or mixer with a dough hook attachment will take the hard work out of kneading and produce successful doughs, provided the manufacturers instructions are followed.

BASIC SPONGE MIXTURE

A sponge mixture is easy to make, and has a wide variety of applications, including fruit flans and sponge layers for other desserts. Typically, baking powder is used as the raising agent, and successful mixtures are the result of prolonged, smooth beating. All the ingredients have to be thoroughly mixed in until a homogeneous, glutinous consistency is achieved, and the mixture drops stiffly from the spoon. The amount of fluid used should be adjusted as necessary to achieve this consistency. The main ingredients of a sponge mixture are margarine, sugar, eggs, flour and, of course, baking powder. It is most important to add the ingredients in the order given. Soft margarine and sugar should be thoroughly beaten, either by hand or in a mixer, until the sugar is completely dissolved and the mixture light and fluffy. Eggs are added gradually, then the flour, which has been previously sifted together with the baking powder and a pinch of salt. This is added to the mixture alternately with the liquid. Finally, any remaining ingredients are added. If the mixture curdles, possibly because ingredients are at different temperatures, the bowl should be placed over hot water and the mixture beaten again. If the recipe uses whisked egg whites, these will be added last, and should be folded very carefully into the mixture. Sponge cakes will keep fresh for a few days, and are especially suitable for freezing.

STRUDEL PASTRY

Hot apple strudel is a popular dessert, particularly in Austria and southern Germany, where it appears on every menu and is still made at home as a treat on Sundays in most households. The art of making strudel pastry is to roll it out until almost transparent, without allowing it to tear. Clever and practiced hands can do this in a flash, and even beginners can achieve paper-thin results using the following little trick. Put a cloth on a kitchen table; sprinkle the cloth with flour and spread the partially rolled-out strudel

1. Using a hand-held electric beater makes light work of sponge mixtures, which require prolonged, smooth beating for the best results. After creaming together the margarine and sugar until light and fluffy, the eggs are added gradually, beating either continuously or after each addition, until they are fully incorporated.

dough on it. Now the dough can be pulled evenly in all directions, or rolled out further with a rolling pin. The sweet or savory filling is then spread on top and the dough rolled up. Strudel dough tastes equally good hot or cold, and it is not difficult to make. Flour, oil or margarine, eggs, lukewarm water and a pinch of salt are mixed together at room temperature, and the dough beaten and kneaded until it is smooth and shiny. The more the dough is worked, the easier it is to pull. After pulling, it must rest for at least an hour in the refrigerator, during which time the filling can be prepared.

2. Baking pans should always be prepared in advance, so that the finished sponge mixture can be poured in gently and transferred to the oven as quickly as possible, to retain all the mixture's lightness. Sprinkling the greased tin with breadcrumbs or a little flour or lining with wax paper are further protections against sticking.

3. Occasionally a sponge mixture may curdle. Using eggs at room temperature and beating them in thoroughly after each addition will minimise the risk of this happening. If, however, a mixture does curdle, it can be restored by placing the bowl over a pot of hot water and beating the mixture again until it regains the correct consistency.

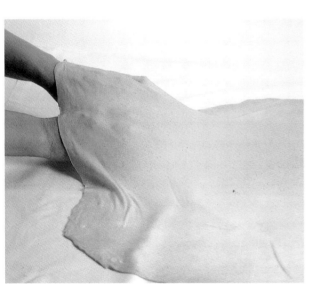

1. Strudel dough must be properly kneaded to achieve the necessary elasticity and should be allowed to rest for at least an hour before rolling out. Once the dough has been partially rolled out, place it on a cloth and use the hands to stretch it to almost transparent thinness, working gently and evenly from the centre outwards.

2. The cloth can be used to help roll up the strudel, once the filling has been spread over the pastry. The cloth acts as a support to roll the dough around the filling, jelly roll style, thus minimising the danger of tearing the pastry at this stage. Although a spiced apple filling is traditional, other fruits can be used for deliciously different variations.

SHORT PASTRY AND CRUMB TOPPINGS

Short pastry is the basis for numerous flans, tarts and pies. It is quickly and easily made, and has both savory and sweet applications. Crumb topping is a variation on short pastry; it is not kneaded and has a higher proportion of fat to flour. The higher the proportion of fat, the crumblier the topping will be and the richer the taste. Short dough should stand, covered, for some time after kneading, either in a cool kitchen or in the refrigerator. (For crumb toppings as used in fruit crumbles, ingredients are mixed in equal parts. Crumb toppings must be mixed very quickly so they stay cool, otherwise the mixture becomes sticky and unappetizing.) The flour is sifted, together with the baking powder where required, and a well made in the middle. Into this are put the sugar and lightly beaten eggs, while the margarine is spread in pieces around the edge of the flour. Working, with the hands, from the outside to the middle, the ingredients are thoroughly combined. The dough is covered after mixing. If it is to be used to line a flan dish or baking pan, only a little flour should be sprinkled on the bottom of this, or the usual consistency of short pastry will be lost. Before baking, the dough should be pricked several times to stop air bubbles forming.

1. Use the fingertips only to rub the fat into the flour for the lightest and crispiest short pastry. It is often easier to work directly on a pastry board or work surface.

4. Use the rolling pin to transfer the rolled pastry to the tin. This method minimises the risk of the pastry tearing as it is lifted from the board into the tin.

1. For crumb mixtures, use the fingertips to rub the fat quickly but lightly into the flour. The mixture will resemble fine breadcrumbs, when the fat has been well rubbed in.

2. Once the sugar has been stirred in, the crumb topping is spooned over the prepared fruit. A wide variety of fruits can be used to make delicious desserts.

2. Light kneading will give a firm, smooth dough and a better result. Always work on a cool, lightly floured surface and flour your hands to avoid stickiness.

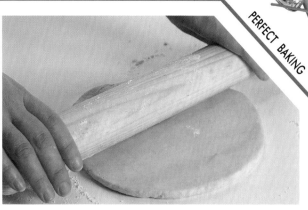

3. Rolling out is easier on a floured surface, using a floured rolling pin. A cool surface is also important to prevent sticking — marble is ideal.

5. Once the pastry circle has been positioned centrally over the pan ease it gently in without stretching, and leave a slight overhang.

6. Remove the excess pastry and give a neat, even edge to the pastry case by rolling the pin over the top of the pan and gathering up the trimmings.

7. Press the pastry gently into the ridges of the pan. Using a wedge of the excess pastry makes this easier to do without stretching the dough or making it sticky.

8. When baking blind, prick the base all over with a fork first. Then line the pastry case with wax paper and weigh this down with a layer of ceramic "beans."

FAT-FREE SPONGE

This mixture starts as a creamy mass of eggs, sugar and flour. Since no fat is added, these sponge cakes are light and easily digested. As with other mixtures, there are many methods of preparation and numerous combinations of ingredients according to personal preference and eventual use. However, one thing is absolutely fundamental: the more the eggs are beaten, the more voluminous the cake will be. For this reason, the use of an electric mixer is recommended, as the right consistency will be achieved in a very short time and with very little effort. The remaining ingredients then have only to be folded carefully into the mixture. The flour must be sifted very finely before it is folded in. This mixture should go into the oven as quickly as possible, since it will collapse, if left standing for long. Use a loose-bottomed cake pan, the base of which must either be greased well or lined with wax paper. After baking, brush the paper with cold water to remove easily. Wrapping the cooled cake in foil or cling film and leaving it for a day will bring out its full flavor. For flan cases or cake layers, cut a round cake into several horizontal layers. This is easily done by inserting a long, sharp knife into the cake, holding the knife steady and turning the cake through 360 degrees with the other hand. A strong piece of thread can also be used to slice as many layers as required quickly and easily; the different layers can be lifted apart with the aid of a palette knife.

PUFF PASTRY

Puff pastry is delicious and versatile, tasting as delicious with sweet fillings as with meat, cheese or vegetables. Ready-made puff pastry is very convenient, as making it from scratch is a difficult and time-consuming process. When rolling out the dough, remember to roll it in two different directions alternately. Use only a little flour when rolling out, or the pastry will become tough and dry instead of light and flaky. When cutting into shape, use a sharp

1 A fat-free sponge relies on lengthy whisking to achieve the best results. To cut down on the time involved, an electric mixer is recommended. The eggs and sugar must be whisked until they are thick, creamy and doubled in volume. The ideal consistency has been reached when the whisk leaves a thin trail in the mixture, if lifted.

knife or the individual layers may stick together and fail to puff up during baking. The high fat content of puff pastry means that the baking sheet is not greased but simply rinsed with cold water. Since puff pastry does not contain any sugar, it browns slowly and can stand high baking temperatures. For a golden finish, lightly beat an egg yolk with a little water and brush the pastry with this before baking, to glaze.

WAFFLE MIXTURE

In grandmother's day, waffles were cooked in heavy, cast-iron pans that were placed either on top of the stove or in the oven. Today, electric waffle irons are easy to use and spread the heat evenly. Many recipes and secret tricks for making delicious waffles have been handed down from mother to daughter, and experienced cooks still swear by their own little idiosyncrasies, such as only using fresh farm eggs

2. If the egg whites are to be added separately, they should be whisked until stiff but not dry. A metal spoon should be used to fold them gently but thoroughly into the rest of the ingredients, so that the whites are fully incorporated without losing any of their lightness or volume. It is important to work quite quickly.

3. The flour must be sifted very finely before being folded in, to retain as much lightness as possible in the mixture. Fold the flour in carefully, using a metal spoon. Then transfer the mixture to pre-prepared tins. This sponge mixture should go into the oven as quickly as possible, to prevent it collapsing.

or spring water. The waffle iron should be greased with oil or margarine. Waffles taste best fresh, eaten either with cream or a mixture of cinnamon and sugar. They also freeze well. When freezing, keep the waffles separate between sheets of wax paper. It is important that the basic waffle mixture is beaten until light and airy; this is achieved more easily using an electric mixer. The flour is then added, spoonful by spoonful, until the mixture is glutinous.

CREAMED COTTAGE CHEESE DOUGH

This dough is easily and quickly made. It is suitable for many different recipes, and can be shaped and filled as desired. The addition of creamed cottage cheese makes deliciously light pastries which should be eaten on the day of baking.

CHOUX PASTRY

Doughnuts, cream buns and the famous éclair make quick and easy surprises for afternoon tea. Be careful not to let a draught near the choux pastries while they are still hot, however, or these delicate treats will collapse. This is really the only point to watch when making and using choux pastry. In Switzerland it is known as "boiled pastry," because flour is simply stirred into margarine and water that has been heated to boiling point. When the mixture has formed a ball, it is "burned off," i.e: stirred until a white layer has formed at the bottom of the pan, indicating that all superfluous liquid has evaporated. The mixture is then taken off the heat and one egg is beaten in immediately; stirring continuously, the remaining eggs are beaten in gradually. The right consistency has been reached when the mixture hangs from the spoon. The mixture must be cooled before adding baking powder, otherwise this will lose its raising power. Choux pastry cannot be rolled or shaped by hand. It is piped from an icing bag in rosettes, strips, letters etc. onto a baking sheet which has been lightly greased and floured. Leave cooked items to cool down very slowly to keep them light. With cream buns and éclairs a "hat" must be cut off the top immediately, using scissors, to let the steam escape. Choux pastry must be eaten the day it is made or it becomes tough and rubbery.

1. The flour is beaten into the boiled water and fat until it comes smoothly away from the sides and base of the pan in a ball. Once this stage has been reached, stop beating or the mixture will become fatty.

PIZZA DOUGH

The popularity of pizza has spread from its native Italy throughout the world. There is a huge range of ingredients that are suitable for toppings, so why not design your own combinations? The pizza base is a flat circle of one of several possible doughs, the most common of which is a yeast dough. Different flours can be used, and all pizza doughs can be prepared quickly and easily.

1. Pizza dough should be rolled out to a circle slightly larger than required and placed on a greased and floured baking sheet. The excess dough is then folded in and pressed down gently to give a slightly raised edge.

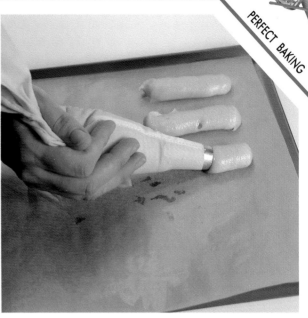

2. Beat in the eggs gradually. They may either be lightly beaten in advance and added a little at a time, or added whole, one by one. In both cases, the mixture must be well beaten after each addition, to incorporate the egg fully.

3. Choux pastry is too soft to be rolled out and is either piped or spooned onto the prepared baking sheet. For éclairs, it is piped out in strips about 3-inches long. Choux pastry can also be deep-fried.

2. The raised edge helps to contain the topping and makes it easier to spread this over the base. Although a tomato mixture is the basis of most toppings, the variations, using extra ingredients, are almost limitless.

BAKING TIPS

Get all ingredients and utensils ready before starting. Weigh out all the required ingredients in advance and, if necessary, bring them to room temperature. If baking pans have rust marks, sprinkle these with salt, rub down with salad oil and wipe off with paper. Spring-release or loose-bottomed pans don't always fit together exactly, so line the base with a circle of wax paper cut slightly larger than necessary and folded up the edge of the pan, so the cake mixture can't leak out. One-piece cake pans can also be lined with wax paper, in which case the pan should be greased well first, as should the lining paper, to prevent it sticking either to the pan or to the cake. Remove the paper as soon as the cooked cake has been turned out to cool. When making sponge-cake layers, only grease the base of the cake pan. As a general rule, all pans, except the non-stick variety, should be lightly greased with margarine before use. Never use strong-smelling fats such as lard or bacon fat.

• Cakes will turn out of the pan more easily if the pan is placed in the refrigerator for about 15 minutes after greasing, or if it is sprinkled with breadcrumbs or flour before the cake mixture is put in.

• Margarine straight from the refrigerator is normally too hard to work with, except when making short pastry and puff paste. To make smooth beating easier, rinse the mixing bowl with hot water first.

• Always break eggs into a cup first to check they are fresh.

• Traces of yolk in egg white impair the whisking/stiffening process.

• Egg whites are sometimes difficult to beat to a stiff consistency. A few drops of water added at the start can help, but it is important to watch continuously in case the water separates from the egg foam.

The addition of a few drops of lemon juice or a pinch of salt may save the day.

• Always sift flour, baking powder and powdered sugar before use, as any small lumps may not dissolve later.

• Always slide the mixture slowly into the baking pan, and fill to an inch or more below the rim of the pan to give the cake room to rise.

• Always wipe off any drops of mixture from the rim or the outside of the pan, as otherwise they will burn during baking and damage the pan.

• It is easier to roll out kneaded dough and puff pastry between two sheets of wax paper.

• Cutting out shapes is easier if the pastry cutter is first dipped in flour.

• If you want to open the oven door to check on progress, kitchen windows and doors must be closed to avoid draughts, otherwise the cake may collapse. If, after testing, a cake needs more baking time, but is already becoming too dark, cover the top with wax paper. Never reduce the temperature significantly as this may cause the cake to collapse.

• At the end of baking time, turn the oven off and leave the cake inside, with the door closed, for 5 minutes before removing.

• Generally, turn the cake out of the pan while still warm, although there are a few exceptions that prove this rule. Place a wire rack on top of the cake and, holding the pan with a kitchen towel, turn it and the wire rack over.

• Leave cakes to cool before working further on them. If possible, leave, covered with a dish towel, overnight.

1. Kneaded doughs and puff pastry are easier to roll out between two sheets of wax paper. This method is also useful for some of the softer biscuit or cookie doughs. Keeping the doughs cool also makes the process easier.

2. Cutting out shapes is much easier if the cutters are dipped in flour first. This also gives a cleaner, more distinct edge to the shapes. Cutters are now available in many different shapes and sizes.

• Always soak sheet gelatine in cold water.

• If gelatine is lumpy after dissolving, heat slightly and then strain before use.

• Sliced fruit, particularly apples, pears and bananas, turn dark very quickly. To avoid this, keep the slices in water with a piece of lemon added.

• If the top of a cake is too dark, rub it over with a cheese grater and then cover thickly with icing, or powdered sugar.

• Trim uneven surfaces of cake layers with a sharp knife and turn over.

• When making fruit flans and cakes, make sure the fruit for the filling is quite dry, as any juice will soak in and cause sogginess. To avoid this, bake flan cases blind.

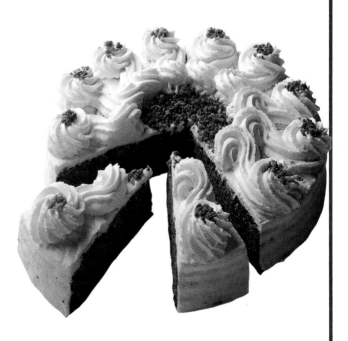

BASIC SHORT PASTRY

Suitable for:
Sweet or savory flans
Sweet or savory tarts
(Exclude sugar for savory items)

Ingredients:
2 cups flour
2½oz sugar
Pinch of salt
½ cup margarine, chilled
1 egg

1.

Method:
1 Sift the flour and baking powder onto a pastry board and add the sugar and salt. Dot the margarine over the top in small pieces and dredge more flour over.
2 Using a palette knife, cut the fat into the flour until the mixture resembles fine breadcrumbs.
3 Make a well in the middle, drop in the egg with a little flour and mix in well.
4 Work the mixture to a smooth dough by hand. Leave to stand in a cool place before using.

2.

Quick Method:
On low speed, mix all the ingredients together using an electric mixer or the pastry hook attachment of a handmixer. Increase the speed to knead thoroughly. Leave to stand as above before using.

3.

4.

Tips for Short Pastry:
● Using powdered sugar instead of sugar gives a smoother finish to your pastry.
● Wrap the rolled-out pastry around a rolling pin to lift it off the board and over the prepared baking pan.

BASIC SPONGE

Suitable for:
Large and small cakes
Sponge flan cases

Ingredients:
½ cup margarine
½ cup sugar
Pinch of salt
2 eggs
2 cups flour
2 tsps baking powder
¼ pint milk

1.

Method:
1 Beat the margarine in electric mixer until smooth and creamy, then gradually add sugar and eggs, and continue to beat until the sugar is dissolved and mixture is light and fluffy.
2 Sift together the flour and baking powder, and fold this into the mixture alternately with the milk. The baking powder should not be lumpy or it will create large air pockets in the mixture.
3 The mixture is ready when it drops slowly and stickily from the spoon.
4 Grease the cake pan and sprinkle breadcrumbs on the base. Turn the mixture into the tin and bake as instructed.

2.

Variation:
If the recipe requires the egg yolk and white to be added separately, beat the egg with the margarine and sugar until the mixture is light and fluffy, and fold in the stiffly beaten egg white at the end.

3.

Quick Method:
Beat all the ingredients together using an electric whisk, beginning on a low setting and then beating for 1½ minutes on the highest setting.

4.

Variation

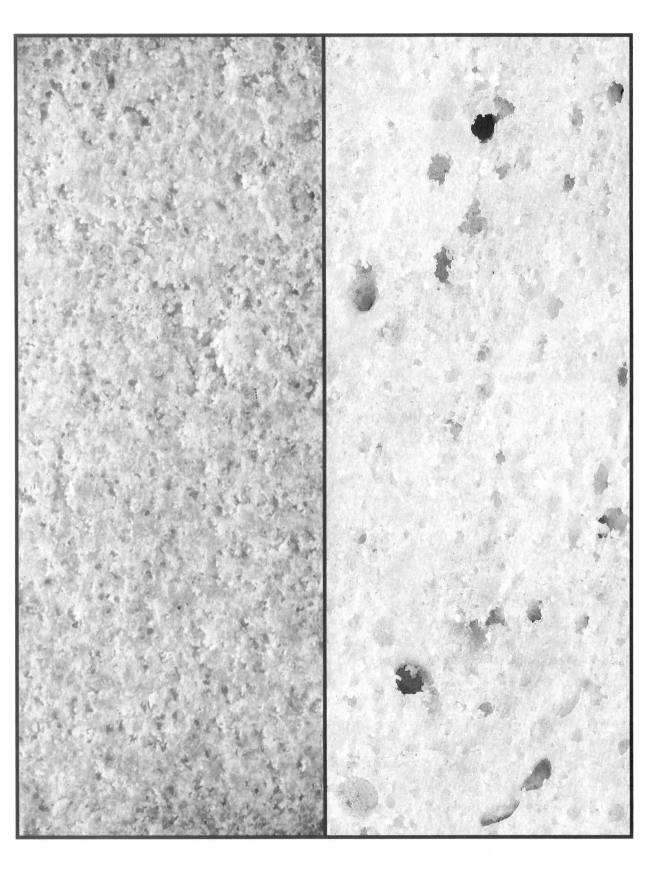

BASIC YEAST DOUGH

Suitable for:

Sugar cakes
Sponge with crumb topping
Almond slices
Yeast cakes
Fruit cakes
Fruit loaf
Yeast Rings
Savory biscuits (use only a pinch of sugar to help the yeast work)
Bread
Rolls
Pizza dough

Ingredients:

1oz yeast
1 cup lukewarm milk
1 pinch of salt
2½oz margarine
4 cups all purpose flour
¼ cup sugar
1 pinch salt (savory biscuits: 1 tsp)
1-2 eggs

Method:

1 Crumble the yeast into the lukewarm milk, add pinch of sugar, cover and leave to work for 5-10 minutes in a warm place.
2 Melt margarine and leave to cool.
3 Put flour, sugar, salt and margarine into a bowl. Break in eggs, add dissolved yeast and mix well together.
4 Knock down and knead dough until you have a homogeneous mixture which is smooth and supple.
5 Cover with tin foil or a cloth and leave to rise until doubled in volume (20-30 minutes).
6 Knead thoroughly once more.

1.

2.

3.

4.

5.

6.

Quick Method:

Put all the ingredients except milk into an electric mixer bowl. Mix and then knead using kneading hook, first on low speed and then on high until dough is smooth and soft. Add milk only after mixer is running. Leave to rise to double original volume – approximately 1 hour as yeast has been crumbled straight into dough mixture.

Tips for Yeast Dough:

Ensure yeast dough does not become more than luke-warm. Yeast develops best at 98.6°F and at 140°F it dies.
● When dough is prepared and shaped to your requirements it should be left again to rise. This applies to both dried and fresh yeast.
● Yeast dough can be kept frozen for up to 3 months. For dough which is to be frozen use only half the quantity of yeast and add a little more sugar. Allow to rise for a short time only before freezing. After defrosting proceed with preparation as before.

BASIC COTTAGE CHEE DOUGH

Suitable for:

Pizza dough
Vegetable tarts
Yeast cakes

Ingredients:

1¾ cups cottage cheese
1 pinch of salt
7 tbsps milk
8½ tbsps oil
1-2 eggs
1 pinch baking powder
3 cups flour

Method:

1 Mix cottage cheese, salt, milk, oil and eggs well together.
2 Mix flour and baking powder. Put half into food mixer bowl and, using the kneading hook attachment, mix into the cheese mixture.
3 Turn dough out onto a floured board and knead in the remaining flour by hand.

1.

2.

3.

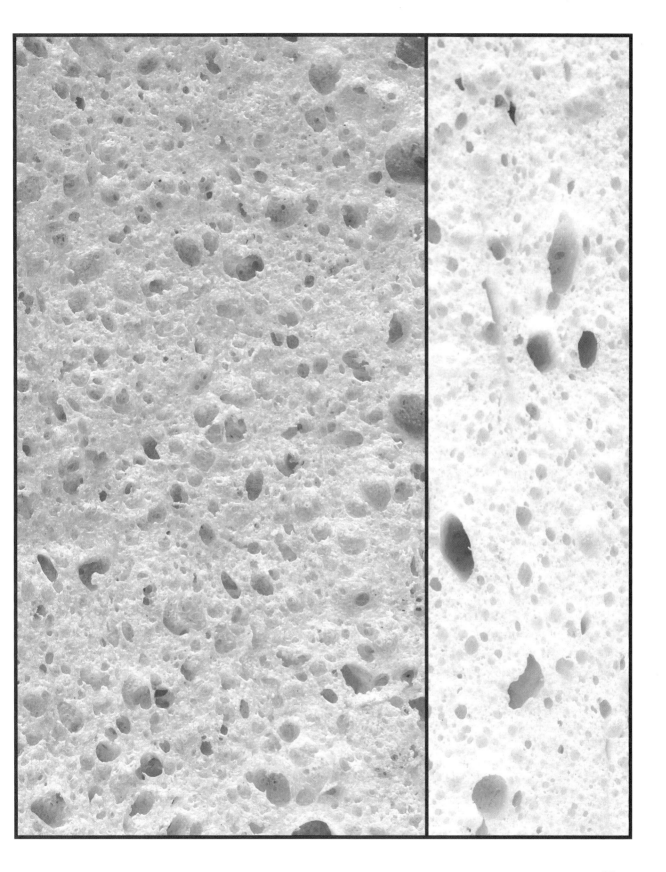

BASIC WHISKED SPONGE

Suitable For:
Cakes
Cream cakes

Ingredients:
4 eggs, separated
5 tbsps water
½ cup sugar
Pinch of salt
Margarine, where specified
¾ cup flour
Pinch of baking powder

Method:

1 Using either a balloon whisk or an electric mixer with whisk attachment, beat the egg yolks, water, sugar and salt together in a bowl until the mixture is thick and creamy.

2 If the recipe specifies margarine, melt this, allow it to cool, then beat it into the mixture in a thin trickle.

3 Beat the egg whites until stiff, and fold into the egg yolk mixture. Mix the flour, cornstarch and baking powder together and sift onto the egg mixture.

4 Fold the flour carefully into the egg mixture; do not stir or the air beaten into the mixture will be lost and the cake will be heavy.

5 For a sponge cake, grease the base of a spring-release pan and line it with wax paper. Turn the cake mixture into this, and bake according to recipe. Once cooked, leave the cake to stand in the pan for about 20 minutes. Turn out and remove the wax paper.

6 When completely cold, slice the cake into layers as required using strong cotton thread.

1.

2.

3.

4.

5.

6.

BASIC CHOUX PASTRY

Suitable For:
Cream Puffs
Crullers

Ingredients:
1 cup water
¼ cup margarine
1 tsp sugar (if required)
Pinch of salt
1¼ cups flour
4-5 eggs
1 tsp baking powder

Method:

1 In a saucepan, bring the water, margarine, sugar and salt to the boil. Remove from the heat and add all the flour at once, beating the mixture until smooth.

2 Replace on a medium heat and stir the mixture until it comes away from the sides of the pan to form a ball in the center. Remove from the heat.

3 Beat in one egg immediately and turn the mixture into a bowl. Gradually beat in the remaining eggs one by one, incorporating them well into the mixture.

4 Finally, add the baking powder as per the recipe's instructions.

1.

2.

3.

4.

Choux Pastry Tips
● Choux pastry is not suitabl for freezing.
● For baking, the pan mu either be greased or lined wit wax paper.
● As soon as choux pastry is re moved from the oven after ba ing, it should be pierced so th steam can escape. This pre vents the finished pastries be coming rubbery.

THE
MAGIC OF
CAKES

This delicious collection of recipes begins with
unusual Continental ring cakes and other popular
favorites. These are followed by mouthwatering tarts
and pies that no one can resist.

LEMON CAKE

Makes approximately 8 servings

½ cup margarine
Grated zest of ¼ lemon
⅜ cup sugar
2 eggs
4 tbsps milk
1¾ cups flour
½ cup cornstarch
½ tsp baking powder
Margarine, for greasing

To Moisten
4 tbsps lemon juice
¼ cup sugar
2 tbsps water
1 tbsp brandy

Icing
⅔ cup powdered sugar
1¼ tbsp lemon juice
Zest of 1 lemon

1 Beat the margarine with grated lemon zest, sugar, eggs and milk until fluffy. Mix together the flour, cornstarch and baking powder and gradually fold this into the margarine mixture.

2 Grease an 8-inch decorative baking pan, e.g. cloverleaf shape. Turn the mixture into this and bake in a preheated oven, 350°F for 45-50 minutes. Leave to cool.

3 Boil the lemon juice with the sugar and water, add the brandy and sprinkle liberally over the cake to moisten.

4 Mix the powdered sugar with the lemon juice and spread over top and sides of cake. Decorate with finely cut strips of lemon zest.

GRANDMOTHER'S CHOCOLATE CAKE

Makes approximately 20 servings

1 cup margarine
1 cup sugar
4 tsps vanilla sugar
4 eggs
Pinch of salt
½ cup cocoa powder
1 tsp instant coffee
4 cups flour
4 tsps baking powder
½ cup milk
½ cup cocktail cherries
¼ cup chopped walnuts
Margarine for greasing

Icing

1½ cup powdered sugar
2½-3½ tbsps water
½ cup walnut kernels

1 Beat the margarine until creamy, then gradually add the sugar, vanilla sugar and, finally, the eggs one by one. Continue beating until the sugar has dissolved. Add the salt, cocoa powder and coffee powder. Sift together the flour and baking powder and fold into the mixture, alternating with the milk.
2 Halve the cocktail cherries, roll them in flour and fold them into the mixture together with the walnuts.
3 Grease an 8½-inch tube pan, pour in the mixture and bake in a preheated oven, 375°F for about 1 hour 15 minutes.
4 Mix the water and powdered sugar together and spread onto the cake while this is still warm. Decorate with the walnuts.

COTTAGE CHEESE CAKE

Makes 20 servings

1 cup margarine
1 cup sugar
4 eggs
Juice and grated zest of 1 lemon
1½ cups low fat creamed cottage cheese
4 cups flour
4 tsps baking powder
½ cup raisins
½ cup chopped almonds
4 tbsps rum
Margarine for greasing
Breadcrumbs

1 Beat the margarine until pale and fluffy. One by one, beat in the sugar, eggs, lemon juice and grated zest.
2 Wrap the low fat creamed cottage cheese in a cloth, and squeeze to remove any moisture. Incorporate the cheese into the mixture. Sift together the flour and baking powder and gradually fold into the mixture. Finally stir in the raisins, chopped almonds and rum.
3 Grease an 8½-inch tube pan and sprinkle with breadcrumbs. Pour in the mixture and bake in preheated oven, 400°F for 60-70 minutes.

Note: This cake only works with very dry creamed cottage cheese.

MANDARIN CAKE

Makes approximately 20 servings

6oz can mandarin oranges
1 packet lemon cake mix
½ cup ground hazelnuts or filberts
Margarine for greasing

Icing

1½ cups powdered sugar
6 tbsps orange juice
2½ tbsps coconut oil
Grated zest of 1 orange

1 Strain the mandarins. Make up the cake mixture according to the instructions on the packet. Halve the mandarin segments and fold them into the mixture, together with the hazelnuts or filberts.
2 Turn the mixture into a greased 8½-inch tube pan. Bake for 50 minutes in a preheated oven, 340°F.
3 Mix the powdered sugar to a smooth consistency with the orange juice and coconut oil. Set one third aside. Mix the remainder with the orange zest and spread over the cooled cake. Leave to harden. Spread the remaining icing over the cake, to form a second layer.

PINEAPPLE CAKE

Makes approximately 20 servings

1 cup margarine
1¼ cups sugar
7 tsps vanilla sugar
Pinch of salt
6 eggs
Grated zest of 1 lemon
4 tbsps lemon juice
4 cups flour
2 tbsps baking powder
8oz fresh or canned pineapple slices, cut into chunks
Margarine for greasing
Breadcrumbs

1 Make a basic sponge mixture using the margarine, sugar, vanilla sugar, salt, eggs, flour, baking powder, lemon juice and zest.
2 Dust the well-drained pineapple chunks lightly with a little flour and fold them into the mixture.
3 Grease an 8½-inch tube pan. Sprinkle with breadcrumbs and turn the mixture into this. Bake for 65-70 minutes in a preheated oven, 300-325°F.

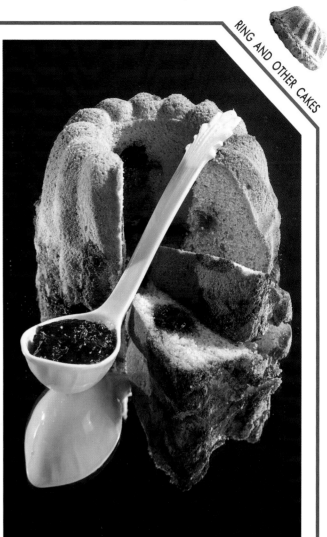

WALNUT CAKE

Makes approximately 20 servings

1½ cups margarine
1¼ cups sugar
Pinch of salt
7½ tsps vanilla sugar
4 tsps baking powder
3 cups flour
6 eggs
1 cup walnuts, ground
5 tbsps brandy
Fine breadcrumbs
Margarine for greasing
Powdered sugar

1 Beat the margarine, sugar, salt, vanilla sugar and eggs until light and fluffy. Mix together the nuts, baking powder and flour and incorporate them gradually into the mixture, together with the brandy.
2 Grease an 8½-inch tube pan and sprinkle with breadcrumbs. Turn the mixture into this. Bake for 50 minutes in a preheated oven, 340°F.
3 When cool, dust the walnut cake with powdered sugar.

GRANNY'S RED JAM CAKE

Makes approximately 20 servings

1 cup margarine
1 cup sugar
4 tsps vanilla sugar
Pinch of salt
4 eggs
3 tbsps rum
4 tsps baking powder
4 cups flour
⅝ cup thick red-fruit jam
Margarine for greasing
Breadcrumbs

1 Beat together the margarine, sugar, vanilla sugar, salt and eggs until light and fluffy, then add the rum. Sift together the flour and baking powder and incorporate them gradually to make a fairly solid sponge mixture.
2 Turn half the sponge mixture into an 8½-inch tube pan which has been greased and sprinkled with breadcrumbs, and use the back of a spoon to create a hollow in the middle of the mixture.
3 Pile the jam into the hollow, and cover with the remaining sponge mixture. Swirl a fork through the mixture, to create a marble effect.
4 Bake for about 60 minutes in a preheated oven, 340°F.

the instant coffee and vanilla sugar, and mix together well.

2 Sift together the flour and baking powder, and gradually fold into the cake mixture. Stir in the milk; the dough should be of a sticky consistency.

3 Beat the egg whites stiffly and fold them gently into the mixture.

4 Line a 12-inch square cake pan with buttered wax paper and turn the mixture into this. Bake for about 50 minutes in a preheated oven, 350°F.

FRUIT RING

Makes approximately 20 servings

1 cup margarine
1 cup sugar
4 eggs
Grated zest of 1 lemon
5 tbsps lemon juice
4 cups flour
3 tsps baking powder
½ cup milk
½ cup raisins
½ cup currants
¾ cup almonds
Margarine for greasing

1 Beat the margarine and sugar until light and fluffy. Beat in the eggs one at a time, then add the lemon zest and juice.

2 Sift together the flour and baking powder, and fold into the mixture, alternating with the milk.

3 Sprinkle the raisins and currants with a little flour and stir these into the mixture together with the almonds.

4 Grease an ½-inch tube pan with margarine, turn the mixture into this and bake for about 60 minutes in a preheated oven, 350°F.

MOCHA CAKE

Makes approximately 20 servings

⅝ cup margarine
⅞ cup sugar
Pinch of salt
4 eggs, separated
2½ tbsps instant coffee
3 tsps vanilla sugar
2 cups flour
2 tsps baking powder
8 tbsps milk
Margarine for greasing

1 Beat the margarine until creamy; one by one, beat in the sugar, salt and egg yolks. Stir in

KING'S CAKE

Makes approximately 16 servings

7/8 cup margarine
5/8 cups sugar
Pinch of salt
3 eggs
Grated zest of 1 lemon
5 tbsps lemon juice
2 1/2 tbsps rum
1/2 cup marzipan, chopped

3 cups flour
3 tsps baking powder
1/2 cup milk
1/2 cup raisins
1/2 cup currants
1/4 cup glacé cherries
1/4 cup mixed orange and lemon peel
Margarine for greasing

Icing
7/8 cup powdered sugar
7 tbsps rum
2 1/2 tbsps coconut oil, warmed
1/2 cup flaked almonds, toasted

1 Beat the margarine with the sugar and salt until light and fluffy. Gradually beat in the eggs, lemon peel and juice, rum and marzipan.

2 Sift together three-quarters of the flour and the baking powder and fold into the mixture, alternating with the milk.

3 Add the raisins, currants, halved cherries and peel to the remaining flour, mix well and stir into the cake mixture.

4 Turn the mixture into a greased loaf pan and bake for approximately 70 minutes in a preheated oven, 350°F. Turn out and leave to cool.

5 Mix together the powdered sugar, rum and coconut oil. Spread over the cooled cake and sprinkle with the flaked almonds.

ORANGE LOAF CAKE

Makes approximately 16 servings

1 cup margarine
1 cup sugar
Pinch of salt
3 eggs
4 egg yolks
1 cup flour
2½ tbsps orange liqueur
Grated zest of 1 orange and 1 lemon
1 cup cornstarch
2½ tbsps orange juice
1 tbsp lemon juice
½ cup ground almonds
½ cup candied orange peel, chopped
Margarine for greasing
Breadcrumbs

Icing

¼ cup clear marmalade
1½ cups powdered sugar
4 tbsps orange juice
⅛ cup candied orange peel, chopped

1 Beat the margarine, sugar and salt until light and fluffy, then gradually blend in the eggs and egg yolks adding a little flour as you work. Stir in the orange liqueur and grated orange and lemon zest. Add the remaining flour, cornstarch, orange and lemon juice, almonds and candied orange peel.

2 Grease a loaf pan and sprinkle with breadcrumbs. Turn the mixture into this and bake for 75-90 minutes in a preheated oven, 350°F.

3 Heat the marmalade and spread over the cold cake. Mix the powdered sugar and orange juice to a smooth paste and spread over the top and sides of cake. Decorate with the chopped candied orange peel.

MARBLE CAKE

Makes approximately 20 servings

1 cup margarine
1⅛ cups sugar
4 tsps vanilla sugar
4 eggs
2½ tbsps rum
Pinch of salt
1 cup flour
4 tsps baking powder
½ cup milk + 2 tbsps milk
2 tbsps cocoa
⅛ cup chopped almonds
Margarine for greasing

1 Cream together the margarine, 1 cup of the sugar and the vanilla sugar. Beat in the eggs one at a time, then add the rum and salt. Sift together the flour and baking powder, and add gradually to the mixture, alternating with the ½ cup milk. Divide into servings of one-third and two-thirds.

2 Mix the one-third portion with the cocoa, almonds, remaining sugar and 2 tbsps milk. Set aside.

3 Grease a 12-inch tube or loaf pan and spoon the two mixtures alternately into this. Swirl a fork through the layers, to create the marbled effect.

4 Bake the cake for 60-70 minutes in a preheated oven, 350°F.

SPICY CAKE

Makes approximately 20 servings

4 eggs
⅞ cup sugar
½ cup margarine, softened
Grated zest of ½ lemon
2½ heaped tsps cinnamon
¼ heaped tsp ground cloves
1¼ level tsp cardamom
½ tsp aniseed
½ tsp ginger
Pinch of nutmeg
2 cups flour
2½ tsps baking powder
⅛ cup chopped almonds
¼ cup grated chocolate
¼ cup finely sliced candied peel
¼ cup maraschino cherries, chopped
Margarine for greasing
Powdered sugar for dusting.

1 Beat the eggs until foamy, then gradually beat in the sugar. Stir in the softened margarine, then, one by one, the grated lemon peel, spices, the flour sifted together with the baking powder, the almonds, chocolate, lemon zest and cherries.
2 Grease a 10-inch loaf pan, and line with wax paper. Turn the cake mixture into this and bake for about 50 minutes in a preheated oven, 375°-400°F.

YEAST RING

Makes approximately 20 servings

1 tbsp fresh yeast
¼ pt lukewarm milk
1 cup margarine
4 cups flour
Pinch of salt
1 cup sugar
⅝ cup chopped almonds
Grated zest of 1 lemon
5 tbsps lemon juice
4 eggs
¼ cup candied peel
⅞ cup raisins
Margarine for greasing
Powdered sugar for dusting

1 Crumble the yeast into the lukewarm milk, and leave in a warm place until frothy. Soften the margarine.
2 Mix together the flour, salt, sugar and ½ cup of the almonds in a bowl. Add the yeast mixture, the softened margarine, the lemon zest and juice and the eggs. In a mixer, work to a smooth dough. Add the candied peel and raisins.
3 Grease a loaf tin or 8½-inch tube pan. Sprinkle with the remaining almonds and turn the cake mixture into this. Leave to rise in a warm place.
4 Bake for approximately 75 minutes in a preheated oven, 350°F.
5 Turn out and leave to cool before dusting with powdered sugar.

CHOCOLATE SPONGE CAKE

Makes Approximately 20 servings

1-¾ cups flour
1½ tsps baking powder
2 tbsps cocoa powder
2 tbsps chopped almonds
⅝ cup sugar
Pinch of salt
3 tsps vanilla sugar
⅝ cup margarine, softened
3 eggs
5 tbsps milk
Margarine for greasing

Icing

2½ tbsps apricot jam
3½oz chocolate icing
1 tbsp white frosting
1 tbsp pink frosting
Sugar pearls, etc. to decorate

1 Sift together the flour, baking powder, and cocoa. Add the almonds, sugar, salt, vanilla sugar, margarine, eggs and milk, and mix together well either by hand or in an electric mixer.

2 Grease an 8½-inch star-shaped pan and turn the mixture into this. Bake for about 50 minutes in a preheated oven, 350°F.

3 Spread the cooled cake thinly with the jam, and cover with the chocolate icing. Decorate with sugar pearls, etc.

Note: This chocolate cake makes an attractive gift presented in a decorative box.

RUM SANDCAKE

Makes approximately 20 servings

1 cup margarine
1 cup sugar
Grated zest of ½ lemon
2½ tbsps rum
Pinch of salt
4 eggs
1 cup all-purpose flour
1 cup cornstarch
Margarine for greasing

NOUGAT CAKE

Makes approximately 16 servings

⁵⁄₈ cup margarine
⁵⁄₈ cup sugar
3 tsps vanilla sugar
Pinch of salt
3 eggs
2 cups flour
3 tsps baking powder
4 tbsps rum
4 tbsps milk
¼ cup chopped almonds
3½ ounces nougat
Margarine for greasing

1 Beat the margarine with the sugar, vanilla sugar and salt until light and fluffy. Beat in the eggs one at a time. Sift together the flour and baking powder and fold into the mixture, alternating with the rum, milk and almonds.

2 Turn two-thirds of the mixture into a greased 8-inch tube pan. Melt the nougat in a double boiler over a pan of hot water, leave to cool, then stir into the remaining mixture. Spread this over the mixture in the tube pan, and swirl a fork through both layers to give a partly marbled effect.

3 Bake for about 60 minutes in a preheated oven, 350°F.

1 Cream the margarine until light. One by one, beat in the sugar, vanilla sugar, grated lemon zest, rum, salt and eggs. Continue to stir until the sugar has dissolved.

2 Sift together the flour and cornstarch and fold gradually into the mixture.

3 Grease a 10-inch loaf pan and line with wax paper. Turn the mixture into this and bake for about 60 minutes in a preheated oven, 350°F.

MARZIPAN SPONGE SLICES

Makes approximately 40 servings

Short Pastry
1⅞ cups flour	
½ cup margarine	
¼ cup sugar	
1 egg	
Pinch of salt	
Margarine for greasing	

Sponge Mixture
1 cup margarine	
1 cup sugar	
Pinch of salt	
4 eggs	
Grated zest of 2 lemons	
½ cup marzipan	
4 cups all-purpose flour	
Scant ¾ cup milk	

Decoration
¼ cup red jam	
¾ cup powdered sugar	
4 tbsps water	
½ cup almond slivers	

1 Use the flour, sugar, margarine and salt to make a basic short pastry. Knead and chill for 30 minutes. Roll out to fit a greased baking sheet, and bake for 15 minutes in a preheated oven, 400°F. Remove and leave to cool.

2 Meanwhile, beat the margarine with the sugar and salt, until light and fluffy. Beat in the eggs, one at a time, then add the lemon zest and the marzipan, worked to a paste. Sift together the flour and baking powder and fold gradually into mixture, alternating with the milk.

3 Spread the cooled pastry with the jam, spoon over the sponge mixture and return to the oven for a further 30 minutes.

4 Mix the powdered sugar and water to a smooth paste and spread over the warm cake. Sprinkle almond slivers on top, and cut the cake into small squares immediately.

SPICY CHOCOLATE CAKE

Makes approximately 20 servings

1 cup margarine
1¼ cups brown sugar
3 tsps vanilla sugar
3 eggs
5 tbsps crème fraîche
3 tbsps karo syrup
Pinch of ground cloves
2 tbsps cinnamon
Pinch of nutmeg
3½ ounces semi-sweet chocolate, grated
4 tbsps cocoa
2 tsps baking powder
1¾ cups flour
⅞ cup ground almonds
⅝ cup ground walnuts
2½ tbsps rum
Margarine for greasing

Filling

8 ounces plain chocolate
⅝ cup margarine
1 cup powdered sugar
1¼ tbsp almond liqueur
1¼ tbsp instant coffee

To Decorate

Chocolate icing
Cocoa beans

1 Beat the margarine until creamy, gradually adding the sugar, vanilla sugar, crème fraîche, karo syrup, spices, grated chocolate, the flour and baking powder sifted together, and the cocoa, almonds, nuts and rum, in that order.

2 Spread the mixture into a greased square or rectangular baking pan and bake for 25 minutes in a preheated oven, 400°F. Turn out and leave to cool.

3 Melt the chocolate in a bowl over a pan of hot water. Beat the margarine and powdered sugar until light and fluffy, then stir in, one by one, the liqueur, coffee and melted chocolate.

4 Slice the cooled cake in half horizontally. Spread the bottom layer with the chocolate filling and replace the top layer.

5 Decorate with the chocolate icing and cocoa beans.

GRANDMOTHER'S CRUMB CAKE

Makes approximately 30 servings

1½oz fresh yeast
1 cup lukewarm milk
1½ cups sugar
1¾ cups margarine
8 cups flour
Salt
2 eggs
2 vanilla pods
Margarine for greasing

1 Crumble the yeast into the lukewarm milk, add a pinch of sugar and leave, covered, in a warm place until frothy. Melt ½ cup of the margarine and leave to cool.
2 Mix 2 cups of the flour, a pinch of salt, ½ cup of the sugar, the eggs, the softened margarine and the yeast mixture. Using an electric mixer, mix and knead to a smooth dough. Cover and set aside in a warm place to rise.
3 Meanwhile, mix the remaining flour with a pinch of salt, the vanilla pith, and the remaining sugar. Rub in the remaining margarine to make a coarse crumb mixture.
4 Knead the risen yeast dough briefly. Place on a greased baking sheet and use a spatula to flatten the dough out. Sprinkle the crumb mixture on top and leave to stand for a short while.
5 Bake for about 20 minutes in a preheated oven, 375°-400°F.

CHOCOLATE CAKE

Makes approximately 24 servings

1¾ cups margarine
1¾ cups sugar
7 eggs
1¼ cups chocolate, grated
3¼ cups all-purpose flour
⅔ cup ground almonds
Margarine for greasing

Topping

⅔ cup marzipan paste
5 tbsps water
1½ cups powdered sugar

1 Beat the margarine until creamy. Gradually beat in the sugar. Beat in the eggs one by one. Add the grated chocolate, flour and ground almonds.
2 Turn the mixture into a greased baking pan and bake for 40 minutes in a preheated oven, 350°F.

Turn out and leave to cool.
3 Mix the marzipan paste with the powdered sugar and water, roll it out between two sheets of wax paper, then spread over the cooled cake. Cut into squares.

MARZIPAN CAKE

Makes approximately 24 servings

1 cup margarine
1 cup sugar
Pinch of salt
4 eggs
2 cups all-purpose flour
Margarine for greasing

Topping

7 tbsps raspberry jam
1¾ cups marzipan
Egg white

1 Beat the margarine, sugar and salt until light and fluffy. Beat in the eggs, one by one. Fold in the flour thoroughly.
2 Turn the mixture into a greased baking pan and bake for 30 minutes in a preheated oven, 350°F. Turn out and leave to cool.
3 Spread the jam over the cooled cake. Mix the marzipan paste with the powdered sugar and water and roll the mixture out between two sheets of wax paper. Cover the top of cake with the marzipan and brush with a little beaten egg white.

HONEY SLICES

Makes approximately 24 slices

4 cups flour
2/3 cup hazelnuts or filberts, chopped
1 tsp cinnamon
Pinch ground cloves
Grated zest of 1/2 lemon
1/4 cup ground almonds
2/3 cup clear honey
1/2 cup sugar
1/2 tsp bicarbonate of soda
1/2 tsp potash
1 tbsp rose water
1 egg
Margarine for the pan

Icing

11/2 cups powdered sugar
3 tbs water
1/2 cup almonds, flaked

1 Mix flour, nuts, cinnamon, cloves, grated lemon zest and almonds in a bowl. Heat the honey and sugar together, stirring until sugar is dissolved. Leave to cool and stir into mixture. Dissolve bicarbonate of soda and potash in the rosewater. Beat in the egg and add to the cake mixture.

2 Knead the cake mixture into a smooth dough and roll out to a thickness of 1/2 inch. Turn into a greased baking pan and bake for 40 minutes in a preheated oven, 350°F.

3 Cut the cake into squares while still warm. Mix the powdered sugar with the water and use to ice the squares. Sprinkle with flaked almonds.

DUTCH ALMOND CAKE

Makes approximately 24 servings

Pastry Base

5 cups flour
1 cup margarine
2/3 cup sugar
Pinch of salt
2 eggs
4 tbsps milk
Margarine for greasing

Cake Topping

2/3 cup margarine
3/4 cup sugar
7 tsps vanilla sugar
6 eggs
Grated zest of 1 lemon
11/3 cups ground almonds
1/2 cup flour
1 tsp baking powder
3 tbsps heavy cream
3 tbsps apricot jam

1 Make the pastry base by mixing the flour, margarine, sugar, salt, eggs and milk to a smooth dough. Chill for 30 minutes.

2 Roll out the dough, and use to line a greased baking sheet 12 inches x 16 inches. Prick the pastry all over with a fork and bake blind for 15 minutes in a preheated oven, 425°F. Remove the pastry base and reduce the heat to 350°F.

3 Meanwhile, beat together the margarine, sugar, vanilla sugar, eggs, grated lemon zest and almonds until light and fluffy. Sift together the flour and baking powder and fold into the cake mixture. Stir in the cream.

4 Spread the apricot jam over the cooked pastry base, pour over the cake mixture and bake for about 40 minutes at the reduced heat.

ORANGE CAKE

Makes approximately 32 servings

Coconut Mixture
2 cups flour
1/4 cup sugar
Pinch of salt
1/2 cup margarine
2 tbsps shredded coconut
Margarine for greasing

Sponge Mixture
1 cup margarine
1 cup sugar
4 eggs
Grated zest of 1 orange
2 cups flour
2 1/2 tsps baking powder
3-4 tbsps orange juice

Glaze
4 tbsps clear marmalade
2 1/2 tbsps orange juice

BEE STINGS

Makes approximately 24

1 1/2 oz fresh yeast
1 cup lukewarm milk
1/2 cup sugar
4 cups flour
Pinch of salt
1 egg
Grated zest of 1 lemon
1/2 cup margarine, melted
Margarine for greasing

Topping
2/3 cup margarine
2/3 cup brown sugar
2/3 cup flaked almonds
1 1/4 tbsp flour
2 1/2 tbsps whipping cream
1 1/4 tbsp clear honey

Filling
1 packet vanilla pudding

1 Crumble the yeast into the lukewarm milk and leave in a warm place until frothy. Mix the sugar, flour, salt, margarine, lemon zest and frothy yeast mixture into a dough. Leave in a warm place to rise. Spread out onto a baking sheet.
2 Put all the ingredients for the topping into a saucepan, bring to the boil, stirring, then remove from the heat and leave to cool. Spread the cooled topping over the dough base. Leave in a warm place to rise again. Bake for about 20 minutes in a pre-heated oven, 400°F.
3 Make up the vanilla pudding according to the instructions on the packet and set aside.
4 Once cooled, cut the cake into squares. Cut each slice in half and sandwich together with pudding.

To Moisten

½ cup orange juice
2½ tbsps lemon juice
2½ tbsps orange liqueur
1 level tbsp powdered sugar

To Decorate

Peel of 2 thinly pared oranges
Sugar water
⅔ cup powdered sugar
3-4 tbsps orange juice

1 To make the coconut mixture, mix the flour, sugar and salt on a pastry board. Using a palette knife, cut in the chilled margarine in small pieces. Mix well together. Add the coconut, quickly mix in and knead to a smooth dough. Chill.

2 Roll out the dough and use to line a greased baking sheet 12 inches x 16 inches. Prick the dough all over with a fork and bake for about 10 minutes in a preheated oven, 400°F.

3 Beat together the margarine and sugar until light and fluffy. Gradually beat in the eggs and orange zest. Sift together the flour and baking powder and fold into the sponge mixture, together with the orange juice.

4 Combine the orange juice and marmalade and brush over the warm coconut dough. Pour over the sponge mixture, and bake for a further 15-20 minutes.

5 Mix together the orange juice, lemon juice, orange liqueur and powdered sugar and use to moisten the warm cake. Set aside to cool.

6 Cut the orange zest into thin strips, bring to the boil in the sugar water and then drain. Mix the powdered sugar with the orange juice, and use to ice the cake. Sprinkle orange zest on top.

PLUM FLAN

Makes approximately 24 servings

½oz fresh yeast
1 cup lukewarm milk
½ cup sugar
2 cups flour
Pinch of salt
½ cup margarine
1 egg
Margarine for greasing

Topping

3lbs plums, stoned
2 eggs
½ cup sugar
Cinnamon to taste
1 cup sour cream

1 Crumble the yeast into the lukewarm milk, add a pinch of sugar and leave in a warm place until frothy. Mix together the flour, sugar, salt and melted margarine, then add the yeast mixture and the egg. Knead together well. Cover with foil and leave to rise in warm place.
2 Use the dough to line a greased baking pan. Arrange the plums on top and bake for about 20 minutes in a pre-heated oven, 400-425°F.
3 Meanwhile, stir together the eggs, sugar, cinnamon and sour cream. Spread over the flan and return to the oven for a further 30 minutes.

APRICOT MERINGUE CAKE

Makes approximately 12 servings

Topping

1½lbs apricots
⅓ cup sugar

Sponge Flan

½ cup margarine
½ cup sugar
3 tsps vanilla sugar
Pinch of salt
Grated zest of 1 lemon
3 eggs
2½ tsps baking powder
1¾ cups flour
2½ tbsps heavy cream
2½ tbsps rum
Margarine for greasing

Meringue

2 egg whites
½ cup sugar
¼ cup shredded or flaked coconut/ground almonds

1 Pour boiling water over the apricots, then skin, halve and stone them. Cover the fruit with the sugar and set aside.
2 Beat the margarine until fluffy. Gradually beat in the sugar, vanilla sugar, salt, grated lemon zest and the eggs, one by one. Sift together the flour and baking powder and fold into the mixture, alternating with the cream and rum.

3 Grease and line a 10-inch loose-bottomed pan and turn the mixture into it. Arrange the apricots on top and bake for about 50 minutes in a pre-heated oven, 350°F.

4 Meanwhile, make the meringue. Whisk the egg whites until stiff, and gradually fold in the sugar and coconut/almonds. Using a piping bag, decorate the hot cake with the meringue mixture, and return to the oven for a further 10 minutes.

COTTAGE CHEESE AND PLUM FLAN

Makes approximately 24 servings

1 cup low fat creamed cottage cheese

7 tbsps milk

1 egg

3½ tbsps vegetable oil

½ cup sugar

3 tsps vanilla sugar

Salt

3¼ cups flour

3 tsps baking powder

Margarine for greasing

Topping

3lbs plums, stoned

2 eggs

½ cup sugar

Cinnamon to taste

1 cup thick sour cream

1 Mix together the cheese, milk, egg, vegetable oil, sugar, vanilla sugar and salt. Sift together the flour and baking powder and stir one half into the mixture. Knead in the second half. Roll out the dough and use to line a greased baking pan.

2 Arrange the plums on top of the dough. Bake for 20 minutes in a preheated oven, 400°F.

3 Meanwhile, beat together the eggs, sugar, cinnamon and sour cream. Pour over the flan and return to the oven for a further 30 minutes.

BLUEBERRY FLAN WITH CRUMB TOPPING

Makes approximately 24 servings

1oz fresh yeast
1 cup lukewarm milk
Pinch of sugar
4 cups flour
½ cup sugar
Pinch of salt
½ cup margarine
2 eggs
Margarine for greasing

Crumb Topping

4 cups flour
1 cup sugar
1 vanilla pod
1¼ cups margarine
2 teaspoons cinnamon

Topping

4 cups blueberries

1 Crumble the yeast into the lukewarm milk with a pinch of sugar, stir, cover and leave for 20 minutes in a warm place until frothy.

2 Mix together the flour, sugar, salt and melted margarine. Stir in the yeast mixture. Knead the dough well. Cover and leave in a warm place until it has doubled in size.

3 Use the crumb ingredients to make a basic crumb mixture. Set aside. Wash and pick over the blueberries.

4 Roll out the dough and use to line a greased baking sheet. Spread half the crumb mixture evenly on top, followed by the drained blueberries and then the remaining crumb mixture.

5 Bake for 20-25 minutes in a preheated oven, 400°F.

Note: Packet yeast dough may be substituted in this recipe.

APPLE DUMPLINGS

Makes 8 dumplings

Pastry
2 cups flour
½ cup margarine
½ cup sugar
Pinch of salt
Grated zest of 1 lemon
1 egg
Margarine for greasing

Filling
8 small apples
1 tpsb raisins
1 tbsp chopped walnuts
2 tbsps rum
1 tbsp sugar

Glaze
1 egg yolk, beaten
Powdered sugar to dust

1 Use the pastry ingredients to make a basic short pastry, knead and chill.
2 Peel and core the apples. Fill the centers with the raisins, walnuts, rum and sugar.
3 Roll out the pastry and cut out 8 circles large enough to cover the apples. Place an apple in the middle of each pastry circle. Pull the pastry up around each apple, pinch the edges together firmly to seal and decorate with pastry shapes made from the trimmings.

4 Brush the beaten egg yolk over the pastry to glaze. Place the apple dumplings on a greased baking sheet and bake for 45 minutes at 425°F.
5 Before serving, dust the apple dumplings with powdered sugar.

GOOSEBERRY FLAN WITH CRUMB TOPPING

Makes approximately 24 servings

Pastry
3 cups flour
1 tsp baking powder
¾ cup margarine
½ cup sugar
2 eggs
1 tbsp milk
Margarine for greasing
Breadcrumbs

Filling
2¼ cups milk
2 packets junket
½ cup water
1 egg yolk
3 cups low fat creamed cottage cheese
1¼ cups sugar
7 tsps vanilla sugar
1 egg white, beaten
3 cups gooseberries

Crumble
¾ cup flour
½ cup margarine
½ cup sugar

1 Mix the pastry ingredients to a firm dough, knead and chill.
2 Mix the milk, junket powder, water and egg yolk and cook until thick, following the instructions on packet. Stir in the cheese, sugar, vanilla sugar and beaten egg white.
3 Grease a baking pan and sprinkle with breadcrumbs. Roll out the pastry and use to line the pan. Spread the junket mixture evenly over and top with the gooseberries.
4 Make a crumb topping with the flour, margarine and sugar and sprinkle this over the gooseberries. Bake for approximately 45 minutes in a preheated oven, 425°F.

CHERRY PIE

Makes approximately 24 servings

1½oz fresh yeast
1 cup lukewarm milk
Pinch of salt
6 cups flour
½ cup sugar
Pinch of salt
Grated zest of ½ lemon
½ cup margarine
Margarine for greasing

Filling

2 eggs
8 cups sweet cherries, stoned
¾ cup ground almonds
½ cup sugar
1-2 teaspoons cinnamon
Powdered sugar

1 Crumble the yeast into the lukewarm milk, add a pinch of sugar and a little flour and leave in a warm place until frothy.

2 Mix together the flour, sugar salt and grated lemon zest. Alternately add the frothy yeast, melted margarine and eggs, mixing well after each addition. Knead the dough well and leave to rise in a warm place.

3 Roll out half the dough, and use to line a greased baking sheet, pulling the dough up the sides of the sheet. Sprinkle over the gound almonds and spread cherries on top.

4 Mix together the sugar and cinnamon and sprinkle over the cherries. Roll out the remaining dough and use to cover the pie. Wet the edges and press together firmly to seal.

5 Cover the pie with foil and leave to rise in a warm place. Bake for approximately 30 minutes in a preheated oven, 400°F. When cold, dredge with powdered sugar.

UPSIDE DOWN APPLE CAKE

Makes approximately 12 servings

Filling

¾ tbsp margarine
1½ tbsps chopped walnuts
1 tbsp sugar

1lb cooking apples
½ cup margarine
¾ cup sugar
Grated zest of 1 lemon
Pinch of salt
2 eggs
4 tbsps lemon juice
2 cups flour
2½ tsps baking powder

1 Line a shallow 10-inch spring-release pan with wax paper. Melt the margarine and spread over the paper.

2 Mix together the chopped walnuts and sugar. Peel and core the apples, cut them into thick slices and arrange these over the bottom of the pan. Sprinkle over the nut mixture.

COCONUT SPONGE WITH PLUMS

Makes approximately 12 servings

½ cup margarine
½ cup sugar
3 tsps vanilla sugar
Pinch of salt
2 eggs
2½ tbsps rum
1½ cups flour
1¼ tsps baking powder

½ cup shredded coconut
4 cups plums, stoned
Powdered sugar
Margarine for greasing
Breadcrumbs

1 Beat together the margarine, sugar, vanilla sugar, salt, eggs and rum until light and fluffy. Sift together the flour and baking powder and fold into the mixture, together with the coconut.

2 Grease a shallow 10-inch cake pan with a removable base. Sprinkle with bread-crumbs. Turn the mixture into the pan, mounding it up slightly at the edges.

3 Arrange the plums close together on top of the cake mixture.

4 Bake the cake for approximately 60 minutes in a preheated oven, 350°F. Before serving, dust with powdered sugar.

3 Beat the margarine, sugar, grated lemon zest and salt until light and fluffy. Gradually beat in the eggs and lemon juice. Sift together the flour and baking powder and incorporate gradually into mixture. Spread the cake mixture over the apples.

4 Bake for approximately 45 minutes in a preheated oven, 400°F.

5 Remove from the oven and leave to cool for approximately 10 minutes after baking. Release the pan. Place a serving plate over the cake, turn it up-side down and remove the pan's base and the wax paper.

WINTER STRAWBERRY PIE

Makes 12 portions

2 cups flour
1¼ tsps baking powder
½ cup margarine
¼ cup sugar
2 egg yolks
Margarine for greasing

Filling

2 egg whites
1 tbsp ground almonds
1 tbsp candied orange peel
1 tbsp candied lemon peel
¼ cup powdered sugar
1-2 tbsps fine breadcrumbs
3 cups frozen strawberries, thawed

1 Sift together the flour and baking powder. Cut in the margarine, then work in the sugar and egg yolks quickly and thoroughly to make a smooth dough. Grease a 10-inch flan pan with a removable base. Roll out the dough and use to line the base and sides of the pan. Prick the pastry case several times with a fork. Bake for approximately 15-20 minutes in a preheated oven, 400°F. Remove from the oven and raise the heat to 450°F.

2 Whisk the egg whites until stiff, then fold in the almonds, finely chopped orange and lemon peel and powdered sugar.

3 Sprinkle the cooled pastry case with breadcrumbs, fill with the strawberries and pile the meringue mixture on top.

4 Return to the oven for about 10 minutes, until the meringue is a pale gold color. Leave to cool slightly, then serve immediately.

APRICOT BEIGNETS

Makes approximately 18

½ cup margarine
¼ cup sugar
3 tsps vanilla sugar
2 eggs
5 tbsps sour cream
3 cups flour
2½ tsps baking powder

Filling

1 8oz can apricots
1 tbsp shredded coconut
1 egg yolk
Vegetable oil for deep-frying
Powdered sugar to dredge

1 Beat together the margarine, sugar, vanilla sugar, salt and eggs until light and fluffy. Add the cream. Sift together the flour and baking powder, stir a little into the mixture, then mix in the remainder by hand. Knead, then leave to stand. Roll out the dough to a thickness of ¼ inch.
2 Drain the apricots, roll them in coconut and arrange on one half of the dough, well spaced out.
3 Beat the egg yolk and brush it around the apricots. Fold the second half of the pastry over the apricots. Press the two layers together well around each apricot half.
4 Cut out the apricot beignets with a pastry cutter. Make sure the edges are firmly sealed.
5 Heat the vegetable oil in a large saucepan or deep frying pan to approximately 350°F. Fry the apricot beignets a few at a time for about 4 minutes. Drain on paper towels and dust with powdered sugar.

GOOSEBERRY AND YOGHURT TARTLETS

Makes 8

1½ cups flour
Pinch of salt
3 tsp vanilla sugar
1 tbsp anisette
¾ cup margarine
¾ cup low fat creamed cottage cheese
Margarine for greasing

Filling

3 cups canned gooseberries
1½ tbsps sugar
2 eggs
½ cup full fat plain yoghurt
1 tbsp anisette
Sugar for sprinkling

1 Working quickly, mix the flour, salt, vanilla sugar, anisette, margarine and cheese to a dough and set aside in the refrigerator to chill.
2 Drain the gooseberries. Add sugar to taste if desired. Toast the coconut with 2 tablespoons sugar until golden brown.
3 Roll out dough and use to line 8 greased 4-inch tartlet pans. Sprinkle each pan with the toasted coconut and fill with the gooseberries. Beat together the eggs, yoghurt, anisette and remaining sugar and pour this over the gooseberries.
4 Bake the tartlets for about 25 minutes in a preheated oven, 400°F. Turn the tartlets out immediately, and sprinkle with sugar before serving.

PLUM FLAN

Makes approximately 24 servings

1½oz fresh yeast
1 cup lukewarm milk
½ cup sugar
4 cups flour
Pinch of salt
½ cup margarine, melted
1 egg
Margarine for greasing

Topping

3lbs plums, stoned
½ cup soft brown sugar
Cinnamon
¼ cup almonds, chopped

1 Crumble the yeast into the milk, stir in a pinch of both sugar and flour. Cover, and leave for 5-10 minutes in a warm place until frothy.
2 Put the flour, sugar, salt, the cooled margarine and the beaten egg into a bowl. Add the frothy yeast, mix well and thoroughly knead the dough, using an electric mixer if possible. Cover with foil and leave in a warm place until doubled in size. Knead again and use to line a greased baking pan.
3 Arrange the plums on top of the dough. Leave in warm place to rise again, then bake for 25-30 minutes in a preheated oven, 425°F.
4 Mix the soft brown sugar with the cinnamon and sprinkle over the warm cake. Dust with the almonds.

RHUBARB FLAN BOURBON

Makes approximately 12 servings

Filling

1½lb rhubarb

Flan base

½ cup margarine
1 cup sugar
3 tsps vanilla sugar
Pinch of salt
2 eggs
1½ cups flour
2½ tsps baking powder
2-3 tbsps heavy cream

Margarine for greasing

Topping

1 tbsp sugar
1 packet junket, vanilla flavor
2 cups milk
1 egg

1 Wash and trim the rhubarb and cut into 3-inch pieces.
2 Beat the margarine with the sugar, vanilla sugar and salt until light and fluffy, then beat in the eggs, one by one. Sift together the flour and baking powder and fold into the mixture, alternating with the cream.
3 Grease a 9-inch flan pan with a removable base. Spread the flan mixture into it and top with the rhubarb. Bake for about 40 minutes in a preheated oven, 350°F.
4 Mix the sugar and the junket powder with a little milk, then add the egg. Bring the remaining milk to the boil and stir in the junket mixture. Stirring continuously, bring back to the boil. Remove from the heat, leave to cool, then spread over the rhubarb.

STRAWBERRY SUMMER DREAM

Makes 12 servings

1 x 9-inch sponge flan base

Topping

1 cup creamed cottage cheese
1/2 cup sugar
3 teaspoons vanilla sugar
Grated zest of 1 lemon
3 tablespoons lemon juice
3 sheets gelatine
1/2 cup whipping cream
2lbs strawberries

Glaze

1/2 cup apple juice
1/2 cup red wine
2 1/2 tbsps lemon juice
1 tbsp sugar
1 packet quick-setting gelatine, strawberry flavor

1 Place the sponge flan base on a serving dish.
2 Mix the cheese with the sugar, vanilla sugar, lemon juice and grated lemon zest. Stir in the dissolved sheet gelatine; set aside in the refrigerator. Whip the cream until stiff, and mix into the half-set cheese and gelatine.
3 Pile the mixture onto the flan base and arrange the drained and halved strawberries on top.
4 Mix the apple juice, red wine, lemon juice and sugar with the quick-setting gelatine, following the instructions on the packet, and drizzle carefully over the strawberries. Allow to set.

TYROLEAN APPLE STRUDEL

Makes 4-6 servings

2 cups flour, ½ tsp salt
½ cup lukewarm water
1½ tbsps margarine, melted
1 tbsp fine breadcrumbs

Filling

2lbs apples
½ cup sugar
½ tsp cinnamon
3 tsps vanilla sugar
⅓ cup raisins and currants, mixed
¼ cup chopped almonds
Margarine for greasing
⅓ cup powdered sugar to dredge

1 Mix the flour, salt, water and margarine to a firm dough and knead until smooth and elastic. Brush with warm water and leave to stand in a warmed pan for 30 minutes.

2 Roll out the pastry on a floured cloth and carefully pull until very thin, using the backs of the hands, and working from the center to the outside: you should be able to see the cloth through the pastry. Trim to form a rectangle and sprinkle with the breadcrumbs.

3 Slice the peeled apples very thinly, and mix with the sugar, cinnamon, raisins, vanilla sugar and almonds. Arrange this mixture over the pastry, leaving 2 inches clear all around the edge. Fold these edges inwards over the apple mixture. Use the cloth to roll the strudel up fairly loosely, patting it into shape occasionally. Brush with melted margarine and bake for 50-60 minutes in a preheated oven, 400°-425°F. Once or twice during cooking, brush the strudel with more melted margarine.

4 Dust the strudel with powdered sugar, slice and serve warm as a dessert or cold for afternoon tea.

GOOSEBERRY FLAN

Makes approximately 16 servings

1/3 packet yellow cake mix

Filling

4 cups gooseberries
1/2 cup sugar
1/2 cup cornstarch

Topping

1/4 cup marzipan paste
1/4 cup sugar
1 egg white

1 Wash and pick over the gooseberries, then cook them in a little water for a few minutes without allowing them to soften. Make a paste with the cornstarch and a little cold water and stir this into the gooseberries to thicken. Leave to cool.

2 Make up the cake mixture according to the instructions. Turn the mixture into a greased 11-inch pie pan, heaping the mixture upwards slightly around the outside edgs.

3 Pile the gooseberries onto the cake and bake for 20-25 minutes in a preheated oven, 400°F.

4 Cream the marzipan paste with the sugar and egg white. Fill an icing bag with the marzipan mixture and use to decorate the cooked flan. Pop under a preheated broiler for a few minutes, until the marzipan turns golden brown.

RHUBARB RING

Makes approximately 20 servings

1 cup margarine
1 cup sugar
7 tsps vanilla sugar
Pinch of salt
5 eggs, separated
1/2 cup ground almonds
12oz rhubarb
2 cups flour
3 1/2 tsps baking powder
Margarine for greasing
Breadcrumbs
Powdered sugar for dusting

1 Beat the margarine with the sugar, vanilla sugar, salt and egg yolks until light and fluffy. Cut the rhubarb into small pieces, and add to the mixture with the almonds. Sift together the flour and baking powder, then fold into the mixture. Whisk the egg whites until stiff, then carefully fold into the cake mixture.

2 Grease a 10-inch ring mold, and sprinkle with breadcrumbs. Turn the mixture into this and bake for 60 minutes in a preheated oven, 350°F.

3 When cooked, turn the rhubarb ring out of the mould, and dust with powdered sugar before serving.

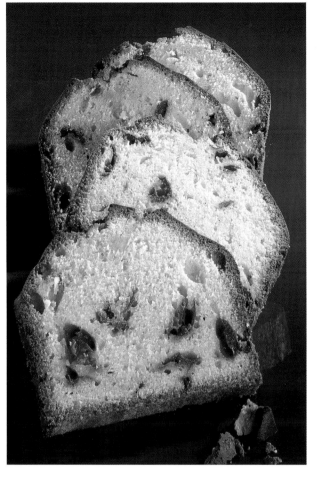

CHERRY MARZIPAN CAKE

Makes approximately 20 servings

½ cup margarine
1 cup sugar
7 tsps vanilla sugar
4 eggs
Pinch of salt
Grated zest of 1 lemon
2½ cups flour
1 tsp baking powder
1 cup marzipan paste, crumbled
7oz bottle or can morello cherries
Margarine for greasing
Breadcrumbs
⅔ cup frosting, if desired

1 Beat together the margarine, sugar and vanilla sugar until light and fluffy, then beat in the eggs, salt and lemon zest. Sift together the flour and baking powder and gradually fold into the mixture. Stir in the crumbled marzipan paste. Lastly, carefully fold in the well-drained cherries.
2 Grease an 11-inch loaf pan, and sprinkle with breadcrumbs. Turn the mixture into this and bake for 70-80 minutes in a pre-heated oven, 300°-325°F. Leave to cool slightly before turning out. Frost, if desired.

BLUEBERRY FLAN

Makes approximately 12 servings

2 cups flour
½ cup margarine
½ cup sugar
Pinch of salt
2 egg yolks
Grated zest of ½ lemon
Margarine for greasing

Filling

2 cups blueberries
4 egg whites
⅔ cup sugar
1¼ tbsps cornstarch

1 Mix the flour, margarine, sugar, salt, egg yolks and lemon zest to a dough. Chill for 30 minutes. Roll out, and use to line a 10-inch flan pan with a remov-able base. Bake for 20-30 minutes in a preheated oven, 400°F. Remove the cooked flan base and reduce the heat to 300°-325°F.
2 Wash and pick over the blueberries, draining them well.
3 Whisk the egg whites until very stiff, fold in the sugar and cornstarch and whisk for a further 5 minutes. Fold the blueberies carefully into the egg white mixture and pile onto the flan base.
4 Return the blueberry flan to the oven for about 40 minutes.

BLACKBERRY SLICES

Makes approximately 24 slices

2 cups flour
2/3 cup sugar
Pinch of salt
2/3 cup margarine, chilled
1 egg
1 1/2 tsps ground almonds
2 1/2 tbsps rum
Margarine for greasing

Filling

6 tablespoons blackberry jam
1 tablespoon maraschino
2 cups blackberries
3/4 tbsp shredded coconut
2 1/2 tsps sugar

Topping

2 cups creamed cottage cheese
1/2 cup sugar
3 tsps vanilla sugar
Grated rind of 1 lemon
7 tbsps lemon juice
7 sheets gelatine
1 cup cream, whipped

Glaze

2 1/2 tbsps blackberry jam
Scant cup blackberry juice
3 sheets gelatine

1 Mix together the flour, sugar and salt on a pastry board, then dot with the chilled margarine cut into small pieces. Cut in with a pastry knife. Make a well in the mixture and put in the egg, almonds and rum. Working quickly, mix to a dough with your hands. Chill for 30 minutes.

2 Roll out the dough twice. Use to line a rectangular baking pan. Prick the base several times with a fork and bake for 10-15 minutes in a preheated oven, 400°-425°F.

3 Mix the blackberry jam and maraschino together. Spread onto the warm pastry base and arrange the blackberries on top. Toast the coconut and sugar under the broiler until golden, then sprinkle over the blackberries.

4 Mix together the cheese, sugar, vanilla sugar, lemon zest and juice. Soak the gelatine and dissolve in a little water over a low heat. Stir into the cheese mixture. When this is half set, fold in the whipped cream and spread evenly over the blackberries.

5 Stir together the blackberry jam and a little of the blackberry juice, then make up to 8 fl oz with the remaining blackberry juice. Soak the gelatine, dissolve it in a little water over a low heat and add to the blackberry juice and jam mixture. Leave until lightly set, then spread over the topping. Leave to chill in the refrigerator. Cut into squares before serving.

CALVADOS APPLECAKE

Makes 16 servings

Pastry

6 cups flour
¾ cup sugar
6 tsps vanilla sugar
1½ cups margarine
3 eggs
Margarine for greasing

Filling

5lbs cooking apples
1½ cups white wine
1½ cups water
Grated zest of 1 lemon
½ cup sugar
⅓ cup chopped almonds
⅔ cup raisins
2¼ cups apple juice from cooking
1 heaped tbsp cornstarch

Icing

1¼ cups powdered sugar
7 tbsps calvados
2½ tsps coconut oil

1 Mix the pastry ingredients to a dough and chill, covered, in the refrigerator.

2 Meanwhile, peel and core the apples and cut them into thick slices. Bring the white wine, water, grated lemon peel and sugar to the boil and stew the apples in this until part-cooked but still firm. Drain in a colander.

3 Roll out half the pastry and use to line a greased baking sheet. Sprinkle over the almonds. Spread the cooled apple on top and sprinkle the raisins over. Thicken the apple juice with the cornstarch, adding a little extra liquid, if necessary, and spread over the apples.

4 Roll out the remaining pastry, and lay it over the apples. Press the edges together to seal, and prick the top all over with a fork. Bake for about 30 minutes in a preheated oven, 425°F.

5 Mix together the powdered sugar, calvados and coconut oil. Brush this icing over the cooled cake. Cut into slices.

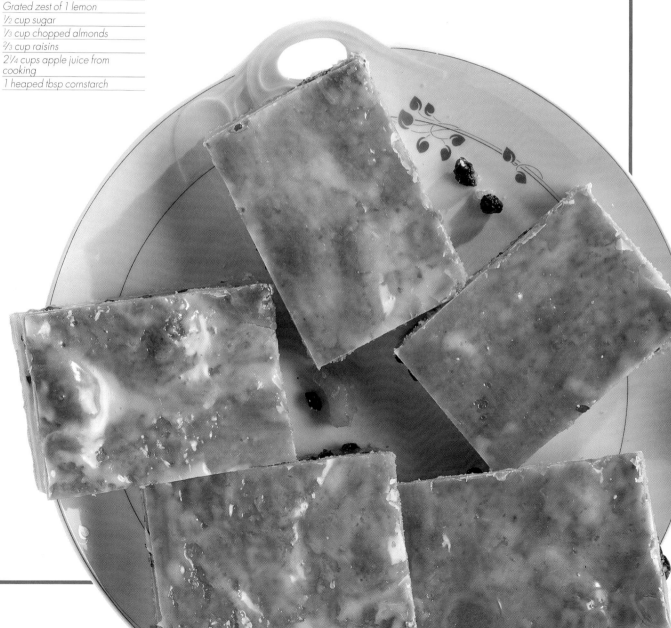

CAKES FOR THE GOURMET

A dream come true: you don't need to be a brilliant cook to spoil yourself and your family with these tempting and exotically decorated cakes. Just follow the simple recipes in this chapter for certain success.

CHOCOLATE WINDMILL CAKE

Makes approximately 12 servings

1 cup margarine
1 cup sugar
Pinch of salt
5 eggs
2½ cups flour
2 tsps baking powder
1¼ tbsps instant coffee
4 tbsps warm water
Margarine for greasing
2 tbsps cocoa
1¼ tbsps warm water
1¼ tbsps crème de cacao liqueur

Filling

2¼ cups milk
1 packet chocolate flavor filling
⅔ cup sugar
¾ tbsp cocoa
¾ cup margarine

Decoration

Grated chocolate
Wafer-thin chocolate leaves

1 Make a sponge mixture with the margarine, sugar, salt, eggs, flour and baking powder. Dissolve the coffee in the 4 tbsps warm water and stir into the sponge mixture.
2 Turn half the mixture into a greased 9-inch pan with a removable base and bake for about 35 minutes at 350°F.
3 Meanwhile, mix the cocoa with the remaining warm water and the crème de cacao and stir into the reserved sponge mixture.
4 Leave the first sponge layer to cool. Cut it in half horizontally. Bake and slice the second batch of mixture in the same way.
5 Spread the cake layers with the chocolate filling and stack together, alternating light and dark layers of sponge. Reserve a little of the filling to pipe a windmill design on the top of the cake and fill in the shapes with grated chocolate. Decorate the outer edge of cake with wafer-thin chocolate leaves.

CINNAMON CAKE

Makes approximately 12 servings

4 eggs, separated
3¾ tbsps warm water
½ cup sugar
3 tsps vanilla sugar
Pinch of salt
2½ tbsps cinnamon
¾ cup flour
½ cup cornstarch
Margarine for greasing

Filling

2¼ cups milk
1 packet vanilla flavor filling
2 egg yolks
½ cup sugar
4 tbsps white rum
3 tbsps cinnamon
1 cup margarine

Icing

½ cup powdered sugar
3 tbsps white rum
Grated chocolate to decorate

2½ tbsps rum

1 cup whipping cream

1 tbsp margarine

2½ tbsps sugar

½ cup crushed glazed nuts

1 Strain the chestnuts and set aside 6 for decoration. Purée the remainder in an electric blender. Bring the purée to the boil with the milk, sugar and vanilla pod. Season with salt and simmer for about 40 minutes, stirring continuously. Remove the vanilla pod and leave the mixture to cool. Stir in the softened margarine, the cocoa and 1 tbsp rum.

2 Crumble the macaroons into a bowl, moisten with the rum and leave to soak.

3 Line a 7-inch pan with a removable base with damp wax paper. Spread a layer of chestnut cream in the bottom, sprinkle over half the soaked macaroons, add a second layer of chestnut cream, followed by the remaining soaked macaroons and a final layer of chestnut cream. Place the

1 Beat the egg yolks with the water, sugar, vanilla sugar and salt until light and foamy. Stir in the cinnamon. Whisk the egg whites until stiff, and fold them into the yolk mixture. Sift the flour, cornstarch and baking powder over the mixture, then fold in very gently using a balloon whisk. Turn the mixture into a greased 9-inch pan with a removable base and bake for about 40 minutes in a preheated oven, 400°F.

2 Make up the milk, vanilla filling and sugar, egg yolks, rum

and cinnamon into a thick custard. Melt the margarine, let it cool, then stir it slowly into the warm custard.

3 Slice the cake base in three horizontally and sandwich the layers together with the filling.

4 Mix the powdered sugar with the rum and use to ice the cake. Decorate with grated chocolate.

CHILLED CHESTNUT CAKE

Makes 8 servings

3½ cups canned whole chestnuts

1½ cups milk

½ cup sugar

1 vanilla pod

Pinch of salt

½ cup margarine, softened

⅓ cup cocoa

1 tbsp rum

⅔-¾ cup macaroons

cake in the freezer for about 8 minutes.

4 Whip the cream until stiff, then use to cover the top and sides of the chilled cake.

5 Melt the 1 tbsp margarine in a frying pan, toss the 6 reserved chestnuts in this and then add the 2½ tbsps sugar to glaze. Sprinkle the cake with the crushed glazed nuts, decorate with the chestnuts and serve immediately.

COFFEE AND MERINGUE CAKE

Makes 12 servings

3 eggs, separated
4 tbsps lukewarm water
Pinch of salt
²/₃ cup sugar
¼ cup margarine, melted and cooled
¾ cup cornstarch
1¼ tsp baking powder
Margarine for greasing

Meringue
1 egg white
¼ cup sugar

Filling
½ cup egg flip
1¼ tsps instant coffee
1¼ tsps cocoa
⅓ cup powdered sugar
5 sheets gelatine
2¼ cups whipping cream

1 Beat the egg yolks, water, salt and sugar until light and foamy, and add the melted and cooled margarine. Whisk the egg whites until stiff, and spoon onto the mixture. Sift the flour, cornstarch and baking powder over the egg whites. Gently fold everything together.

2 Grease the bottom of a 9-inch cake pan with a removable base, turn the mixture into this and bake for 25-30 minutes in a preheated oven, 350°F.

Remove the cake and reduce the heat to 225°F.

3 Cut out a sheet of wax paper the size of the pan. Mark out 12 wedges on this to act as a guide. Grease the paper and place on a baking sheet. Whisk the egg white until stiff, gradually whisking in the sugar. Spoon the meringue into an icing bag and pipe decorations onto the wax paper guide. Dry the meringue out for 40 minutes in the oven, leaving the door slightly open.

4 Slice the cake in two horizontally. Mix together the egg flip, coffee, cocoa and powdered sugar. Soak the gelatine, dissolve it in a little water over a low heat and mix into the coffee mixture. Whip the cream until stiff and fold into coffee mixture as it begins to set.

5 Place one cake layer in ring of cake pan. Spread half the filling over this layer. Place the second cake layer on top and spread with the remaining filling. Arrange the meringue decorations on top and chill the finished cake.

Note: This cake may also be served semi chilled.

PEACH CAKE WITH ALMOND CREAM

Makes approximately 12 servings

1/3 cup margarine
1/3 cup sugar
Pinch of salt
3 eggs
1/4 cup ground almonds
1 1/4 cups flour
1/4 tsp baking powder
Margarine for greasing
1 large can peach halves

Cream

1 packet vanilla pudding powder
1 cup milk
1/4 cup sugar
2 eggs
1 cup whipping cream

Topping

3 kiwi fruit
5 tbsps apricot jam
Toasted flaked almonds

1 Beat the margarine, sugar, salt and eggs until light and fluffy. Add the almonds and the flour sifted together with the baking powder. Turn the mixture into a greased 9-inch cake pan with a removable base and bake for about 25 minutes in a preheated oven, 350-375°F. Leave to cool, before turning out.

2 Mix the vanilla pudding powder with a little milk, the sugar and eggs. Bring the whipping cream and the remaining milk to the boil, stir in the pudding mix and boil for 1 minute. Leave to cool, stirring occasionally.

3 Replace the cooled sponge in the cake pan ring, without the base, and pour the almost set cream on top. Leave to set in the refrigerator.

4 Peel and slice the kiwi fruit. Drain the peaches and arrange both fruits on top of the cream.

5 Heat the apricot jam, rub through a strainer and brush over the fruit. Sprinkle the toasted almonds on top and decorate with whipped cream, if desired.

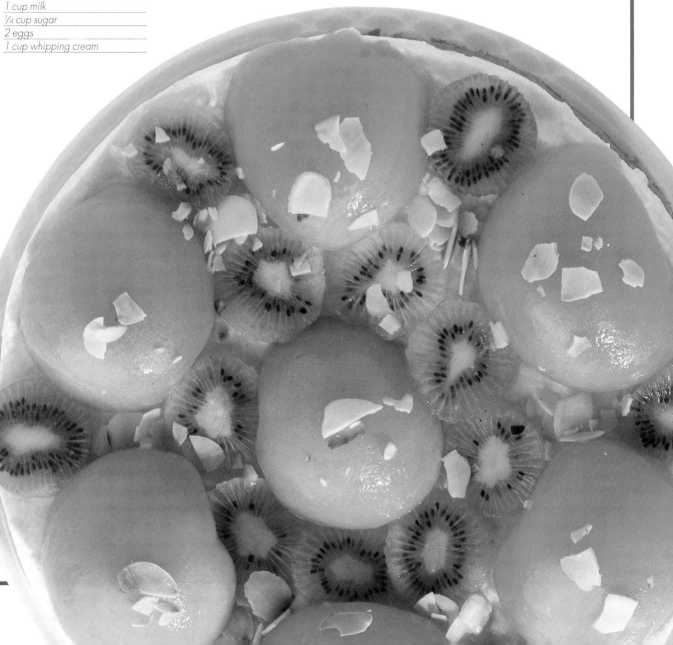

PINEAPPLE MARZIPAN CAKE

Makes approximately 12 servings

½ cup marzipan paste
¾ cup margarine
¾ cup sugar
3 tsps vanilla sugar
3 eggs
2½ cups flour
2½ tbsps baking powder
¼ cup ground almonds
4 slices fresh pineapple or
7oz can pineapple chunks

Decoration
¼ cup marzipan paste
¼ cup powdered sugar
Red and green coloring
1 packet chocolate icing

1 Cream the marzipan paste and margarine to a soft consistency by hand. Gradually beat in the sugar, vanilla sugar and eggs. Sift together the flour and baking powder, and fold into the mixture, a spoonful at a time. Add the almonds. Drain the pineapple well, cut into small pieces, and add to mixture.
2 Line a 10-inch cake pan with a removable base with wax paper. Turn the mixture into this and bake for 60-70 minutes in the center of a preheated oven, 350°F.
3 For the decoration, mix the marzipan paste to a smooth paste with the powdered sugar. Color half red and a quarter green, and leave the rest white.
4 Make up the chocolate icing and spread over the top and sides of the cake.

5 Roll out the white marzipan paste thinly and cut out 2 hearts. Roll out the green paste and cut out a few leaf shapes. Draw veins on the leaves with the back of a knife blade.

6 To make the roses, firstly shape some of the red paste into cones, about ¾ inch high. Roll out the remaining red paste and cut out a number of small circles 1¼ inches in diameter. Cut the circles in half.
7 Press the semicircles around the cones in layers, shaping the top edges to form petals. Press the layers firmly together at the base. Arrange the roses, leaves and hearts attractively on top of the cake.

MARZIPAN CAKE

Makes approximately 12 servings

Mixture

4 eggs, separated
3-4 tbsps warm water
½ cup sugar
3 tsps vanilla sugar
Pinch of salt
⅓ cup margarine, melted
¾ cup flour
¾ cup cornstarch
Pinch of baking powder
Margarine for greasing

Filling

3 tbsps clear marmalade
1½ cups marzipan paste

2½ tbsps rum
2 cups whipping cream
1 tbsp sugar
3 tsps vanilla sugar
¾ cup ground almonds
5 tsps chocolate powder
⅔ cup hazelnuts

1 Whisk the egg yolks with the water, sugar, vanilla sugar and salt until light and foamy, then whisk in the cooled margarine. whisk the egg whites until stiff and pile on top of the mixture. Sift the flour, cornstarch and baking powder over the egg whites and gently fold everything together.
2 Turn the mixture into a greased 10-inch cake pan with a removable base and bake for 35-40 minutes in a preheated oven, 425°F. Turn out and leave to cool.
3 When cold, cut in half horizontally and spread the marmalade over one layer.
4 Mix the marzipan paste with the rum and roll out into two circles to fit the cake layers. Place one layer of marzipan on top of the marmalade-covered cake base.
5 Whip the cream with the sugar and vanilla sugar, and stir in the hazelnuts and chocolate powder. Divide into three equal servings.
6 Spread one-third of the cream over the marzipan. Cover with the second layer of cake. Spread the second portion of cream on top of this. Use the remaining cream to cover the sides of the cake, reserving a little for decoration if desired. Place the second marzipan layer on top of the cake.
7 Knead the marzipan trimmings together. Roll out and cut into decorative shapes, then put them under a preheated broiler to brown. Decorate the cake with piped cream, if desired, and with the marzipan shapes.

ORANGE MONT BLANC

Makes 12 servings

⅓ cup margarine

2 eggs

½ cup sugar

3 tsps vanilla sugar

Pinch of salt

¾ cup flour

1¾ tsps baking powder

2-3 tbsps whipping cream

Margarine for greasing

Breadcrumbs

Topping

5 tbsps apricot brandy

5 sheets gelatine

3 oranges

2 cups whipping cream

1 tbsp sugar

3 tsps vanilla sugar

1¼ tbsps grated orange zest

Icing

½ cup orange juice

¼ cup sugar

1 packet quick-setting gelatine

Pistachios for decorating

1 Melt the margarine and leave to cool. Whisk the eggs, sugar, vanilla sugar and salt until light and foamy. Whisk in the margarine. Sift together the flour and baking powder. Fold into the mixture, together with the whipping cream.

2 Grease a 10-inch flan ring and sprinkle with breadcrumbs. Turn the mixture into this and bake for 20-25 minutes in a preheated oven, 350°F. Leave to cool.

3 Moisten the flan base with the apricot brandy. Soak the gelatine sheets.

4 Peel and slice the oranges. Drain, reserving the juice. Whip the cream with the sugar, vanilla sugar and grated orange zest until stiff.

5 Drain the gelatine, dissolve over a low heat and mix with the cream mixture. Put a little cream into an icing bag and use to decorate the edge of the cake. Pile the remaining cream onto the flan base. Arrange the orange slices on top.

6 Using additional unsweetened orange juice if necessary, make up the reserved orange juice to ½ cup. Add the sugar. Use this liquid to make up the quick-setting gelatine according to the instructions on the packet. Spoon over the oranges. Decorate the piped edge of the cake with chopped pistachios.

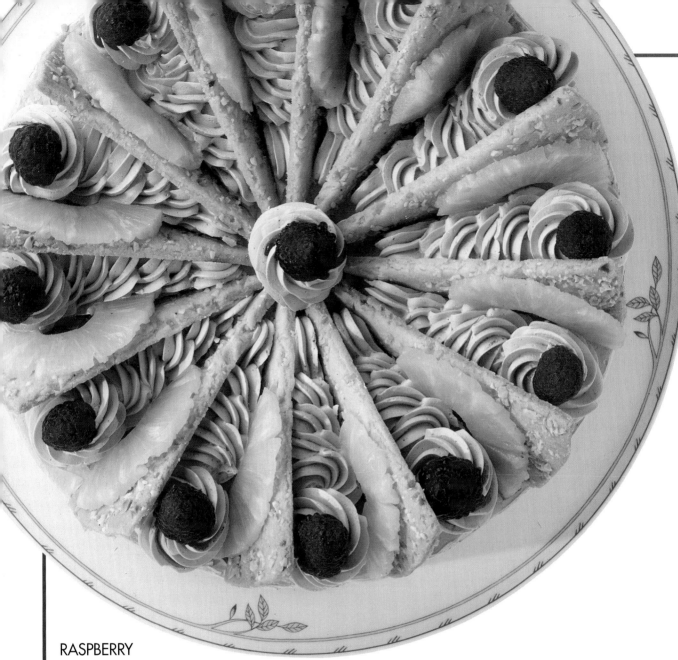

RASPBERRY CREAM CAKE WITH PINEAPPLE

Makes approximately 12 servings

¾ cup margarine
⅔ cup sugar
3 tsps vanilla sugar
5 eggs
Pinch of salt
Grated zest of 1 lemon
2½ cups flour
2½ tsps baking powder
⅓ cup finely chopped walnuts
Margarine for greasing

Filling

1 cup raspberries
1 tbsp sugar
3½ cups whipping cream
3 tbsps vanilla sugar
12 slices fresh pineapple

1 Make a basic sponge mixture using the margarine, ½ cup of the sugar, the vanilla sugar, eggs, salt, grated lemon zest, flour and baking powder. Mix together the walnuts and the remaining sugar.

2 Divide the mixture into six servings. Turn one portion into a greased 10-inch cake or pie pan with a removable base. Sprinkle with a little of the walnut/sugar mixture and bake for 8-10 minutes in a preheated oven, 400°F, until golden brown. Immediately after baking, slide the sponge layer carefully onto wax paper and leave to cool. Bake five more layers in the same way. While still warm, cut one layer into twelve wedge-shaped pieces.

3 Sprinkle the raspberries with the sugar. Reserve a few for decoration and purée the rest. Whip the cream with the vanilla sugar, and fold in the raspberry purée. Reserve some of the raspberry cream for piping.

4 Sandwich the layers together with raspberry cream. Arrange the twelve cake wedges in a fan shape on top of the cake (see illustration) and pipe the reserved cream between them. Decorate with the pineapple slices and the reserved raspberries.

CARIBBEAN FRUIT CAKE

Makes approximately 12 servings

1 cup flour
1/2 cup powdered sugar
Pinch of salt
1/3 cup ground almonds
1/3 cup margarine
Margarine for greasing

Topping

1 tin creamed coconut
6 sheets gelatine
1 cup whipping cream
2 cups pineapple slices, canned
2 bananas
Lemon juice
3 kiwi fruit
2 cups canned mandarin oranges

Glaze

1/2 cup pineapple juice
1 1/4 tsps sugar
1 packet quick-setting gelatine

1 Make a firm dough using the flour, powdered sugar, salt, ground almonds and margarine. Roll out and use to line a greased 10-inch cake pan with a removable base. Bake for 12-15 minutes in a preheated oven, 400°F. Leave to cool, then remove the base and place the cake back in the cake ring.

2 Soak the gelatine according to the instructions. Put 1 cup of the creamed coconut into a bowl and stir in the prepared gelatine. Whip the cream until stiff and fold into the partly-set coconut cream. Spread evenly over the cake base.

3 Drain the pineapple slices and cut them into semicircles. Slice the bananas and brush them with a little lemon juice. Peel and slice the kiwi fruit, halving them if necessary, and drain the mandarins.

4 Arrange the fruit on the cake base, lightly pressing them into the cream. Make up the glaze using the pineapple juice, sugar and quick-setting gelatine, according to the instructions on the gelatine packet. Spoon evenly over the fruit.

Note: You can store any remaining creamed coconut for a short time in a screw-top jar in the refrigerator. It is. good in fruit salads, summer drinks, etc.

PEAR CAKE

Makes approximately 12 servings

Pastry
1¼ cups flour
¾ tsp baking powder
¼ cup sugar
⅓ cup margarine
1 small egg

Fruit Filling
1lb can pears, or approximately
1¼lb fresh dessert pears

Sponge Filling
3 large eggs, separated
2-3 tbsps pear brandy
⅔ cup sugar
¾ cup flour
⅓ cup ground almonds
⅔ cup cocoa
3 tsps baking powder

Decoration
2 pears, cut in half
Chocolate icing
1 packet lemon or chocolate icing
Crushed, glazed nuts

1 Make a firm dough from the pastry ingredients and chill for 30 minutes. Roll out, and use to line a greased deep pie pan, 10 inches in diameter. Bake blind for 10 minutes in a preheated oven, 400°F.
2 Arrange the well-drained fruit filling on the pastry case, cut edge downwards.
3 To make the sponge filling, whisk the egg yolks with the brandy until light and foamy. Whisk in the sugar and continue whisking until it has dissolved. Whisk the egg whites until stiff. Pile on top of mixture. Sift the flour, cornstarch, almonds, cocoa and baking powder over the egg whites. Using a balloon whisk, very gently fold everything together.
4 Pour the sponge filling over the pears and bake for about 50 minutes in a preheated oven, 350°-400°F.
5 Coat the pear halves with chocolate icing. Spread lemon or chocolate icing over the cake, sprinkle the crushed glazed nuts

round the edge and arrange the chocolate pears on top.

TROPICAL TART

Makes approximately 12 servings

Pastry Base
½ cup margarine
⅔ cup powdered sugar
3 tsps vanilla sugar
1 egg
Pinch of salt
2 cups flour
½ bottle rum flavoring
Margarine for greasing

Filling
¾ cup dates
½ cup margarine
½ cup brown sugar
⅔ cup coco-crisps
1 14oz can pineapple slices
2 packets quick-setting gelatine
4 rum-flavored chocolate truffles

SACHERTORTE

Makes approximately 12 servings

½ cup semi-sweet chocolate, grated
¼ cup almonds, unskinned
½ cup margarine
½ cup sugar
5 eggs, separated
1 cup flour
1 heaped tsp baking powder
Margarine for greasing

Icing

½ cup brandy
7 tbsps apricot jam
½ cup chocolate icing

1 Grate the chocolate and grind the almonds. Beat the margarine, sugar, egg yolks and chocolate until light and fluffy. Sift together the flour and baking powder, and fold in first this mixture, then the ground almonds and finally the stiffly-beaten egg whites.
2 Grease the bottom of a 9-inch cake pan with a removable base. Turn the mixture into this and bake for 40-45 minutes in a preheated oven, 400°F.
3 Slice the cake in half horizontally. Sprinkle brandy over both layers and leave to cool.
4 Sandwich the layers together with some of the jam. Spread the remaining jam all over the cake. Prepare the chocolate icing and coat the cake with it.

1 Cream the margarine until fluffy, then beat in the powdered sugar and vanilla sugar. Add the egg, salt, flour and rum flavoring and mix to make a light dough. Chill.
2 Use to line a greased 10-inch pie pan and bake for 15-20 minutes in a preheated oven, 400°F. Leave to cool.
3 Stone and dice the dates. Heat the margarine in a saucepan, put in the dates and cook them slowly until soft. Stir in the sugar and lastly the coco-crisps.
4 Spread the above mixture evenly into the pastry case, pressing it down well. Arrange the pineapple slices on top and coat with the quick-setting gelatine, prepared according to the packet instructions. Decorate with the rum truffles.

BLACK FOREST CAKE

Makes approximately 12 servings

⅓ cup margarine
⅓ cup sugar
Pinch of salt
4 eggs, separated
2½ tbsps kirsch
⅓ cup ground almonds
¾ cup flour
1 heaped tsp baking powder
Margarine for greasing

Filling and Decoration

½ cup sour cherries, canned or preserved
5 tbsps kirsch
4 sheets gelatine
2¼ cups sweetened cream, whipped
1 tbsp semi-sweet chocolate, coarsely grated

1 Beat the margarine, sugar, vanilla sugar, salt, and egg yolks until light and fluffy. Break the chocolate into small pieces, pour hot water over and leave to stand. Drain, retaining about 2½ tbsps of water. Beat the chocolate until smooth, then fold it into the sponge mixture, together with the kirsch and almonds.

2 Whisk the egg whites until stiff, and pile on top of the cake mixture. Sift the flour and baking powder over the egg whites. Carefully fold everything together.

3 Grease a 9-inch cake pan with a removable base. Turn the mixture into this and bake for about 50 minutes in a preheated oven, 350°F.

4 Drain the cherries. Slice the cooled sponge in half horizontally and sprinkle liberally with kirsch. Soak the gelatine, dissolve over a low heat and incorporate well into the whipped cream.

5 Spread the cream over the first sponge layer. Arrange the cherries on top, cover with the second sponge layer and spread the remaining cream all over and round the cake. Decorate with coarsely-grated chocolate.

SOUTH SEAS CAKE

Makes approximately 12 servings

Pastry

1 cup flour
¼ cup sugar
1 tbsp shredded coconut
⅓ cup margarine
Margarine for greasing

Sponge Mixture

2 eggs, separated
2½ tbsps water
¼ cup sugar
½ cup flour
1 heaped tbsp cornstarch

Filling

1lb apples
½ cup white wine
¼ cup sugar
Grated zest of 1 lemon
1 8oz can pawpaw cubes
approximately 5 tbsps white wine
5 kiwi fruits
2½ tbsps lemon juice
3 packets quick-setting gelatine

Meringue

2 egg whites
⅓ cup sugar
Pinch of cinnamon
1 tbsp shredded coconut

Glaze

1 tbsp apricot jam

1 Make a dough from the pastry ingredients. Leave to stand for 1 hour. Roll out and use to line a shallow 9-inch cake pan with a removable base. Prick the base in several places with a fork and bake for about 10 minutes in a preheated oven, 425°F.

2 Meanwhile, whisk the egg yolks, water and sugar until light and foamy. Whisk the egg whites until stiff, spoon onto the sugar mixture. Sift the flour and cornstarch over the egg whites, and carefully fold everything together.

3 Brush the jam over the hot pastry base, diluting it with a little water if it is too thick. Spread the sponge mixture on top and bake for a further 10-15 minutes. Leave to cool, then remove from the pan.

4 Peel and core the apples, and cut each apple into eight pieces. Simmer gently for about 5 minutes in the white wine with the sugar and grated lemon zest. Drain, reserving the liquid.

5 Drain the pawpaw cubes, reserving the juice. Make up the reserved liquids to 2¼ cups. Add lemon juice to taste and use to make up the quick-setting gelatine, according to the instructions on the packet.

6 Place the cake on a heat-proof dish and place the ring of the cake pan over it again. Spread a little of the gelatine mixture over and arrange the fruit on it, covering the cake right up to the edge of the ring. Spoon over the remaining gelatine mixture. Leave until almost set.

7 Whisk the egg whites until stiff, whisk in the sugar and fold in the cinnamon and coconut. Spread this over the cake and put under a preheated low broiler until lightly colored. Remove cake pan ring and leave the cake to cool.

ALMOND CAKE

Makes 12 servings

⅔ cup ground almonds
⅔ cup sugar
3 tsps vanilla sugar
2 eggs
5 eggs, separated
½ cup flour
½ cup cornstarch
Grated zest of 1 lemon
Margarine for greasing

To Moisten

2½ tbsps brandy

Filling

1 cup margarine
4 egg yolks
1¼ cups powdered sugar
7½ tbsps strong, cold coffee
1 cup crushed glazed nuts

Decoration

2 egg whites
Powdered sugar
Food coloring
½ cup marzipan
Icing flowers, if desired

1 Whisk the almonds, sugar, vanilla sugar, eggs and egg yolks until light and thick. Sift over the flour, cornstarch and grated lemon zest and fold in carefully with a balloon whisk. Whisk the egg whites until stiff and fold in.

2 Turn the mixture in a greased 10-inch cake pan with a removable base, and bake for about 50 minutes in a preheated oven, 350°F.

3 Slice the cooled cake horizontally into three layers, sprinkle each layer with brandy and leave to soak in.

4 Cream the margarine until light and fluffy, then beat in the egg yolks, powdered sugar and coffee one after the other. Continue beating until mixture is of a thick, foamy consistency. Stir in the nuts. Use this coffee cream to sandwich together the cake layers.

5 Whisk the remaining egg whites until light and foamy. Stir in the powdered sugar to make a thick, hard icing. Use to ice the top and sides of the cake.

6 Color the marzipan as required and shape into flowers, leaves and stems. Decorate the cake, adding ready-made icing flowers if desired.

ALASKA SPONGE

Makes approximately 7 servings

Sponge
1 egg, separated
1/4 cup sugar
3 tsps vanilla sugar
1 1/4 tbsps water
1/3 cup flour
Margarine for greasing

Filling
1/3 cup raisins
6 tbsps rum
1 1/2 cups whipping cream
1 tbsp sugar
1/4 cup chocolate, coarsely grated
1 packet chocolate ice cream
1 packet lemon ice cream

Decoration
Chocolate, coarsely grated

1 Use the sponge ingredients to make up a basic sponge mixture. Line a loaf pan with a 4 1/2-inch-wide strip of foil or wax paper. Grease with margarine and turn the sponge mixture into this. Lay another strip of foil or wax paper on top, to cover the sponge. Bake for 12-15 minutes in a preheated oven, 425°F. Remove the top foil or wax paper, turn out the sponge, pull off the second piece of foil or paper and leave the sponge to cool. Cut into two 6-inch-long rectangles.

2 In a saucepan, heat the raisins with the rum, then remove from the heat and allow to cool. If the raisins do not absorb all the rum, sprinkle the sponge with remainder. Whip the cream until stiff, adding sugar to taste. Divide into two servings, adding the grated chocolate and rum raisins to one portion.

3 Build up the cake as follows: a layer of sponge, a layer of raisin cream, a layer of chocolate ice cream, another layer of raisin cream, a layer of lemon ice cream, another layer of raisin cream and a final layer of sponge.

4 Spread the plain whipped cream all around the cake, decorate with coarsely grated chocolate and put into the freezer for at least 3 hours. Slice before serving.

STRAWBERRY AND LEMON CREAM CAKE

Makes approximately 12 servings

2 cups flour
¼ cup sugar
Pinch of salt
Grated zest of 1 lemon
½ cup margarine
1 egg

Topping

1½lb strawberries
¼ cup sugar
2½ tbsps syrup of pomegranate
2 packets quick-setting gelatine, strawberry flavor
1 packet lemon trifle topping mix
½ cup white wine
¾ cup sugar
1 cup full fat cream cheese
7½ tbsps vanilla sugar
5 tbsps lemon juice
2 cups whipping cream
Lemon slices, to decorate

1 Mix the flour, sugar, salt, lemon zest and egg together well. Knead to a light dough. Leave to stand in a cool place.

2 Meanwhile, wash, hull and halve the strawberries and sprinkle with sugar.

3 Roll out the dough. Line the base and sides of a 10-inch cake pan with a removable base with wax paper. Line with the pastry and bake for about 20 minutes in a preheated oven, 400°F. Leave to cool in the pan.

4 Drain the strawberries, and make up the liquid to 2¼ cups with water. Add the syrup of pomegranate. Arrange half the strawberries over the cake base. Make up 1 packet of quick-setting gelatine with 2¼ cups of the strawberry juice, according to the packet instructions. Spread over the strawberries.

5 Mix the trifle topping with the white wine and leave to soak for 10 minutes. Add the sugar and dissolve over a low heat, stirring constantly. Leave to cool.

6 Mix the cheese with the vanilla sugar and lemon juice, then stir in the topping. Whip the cream until stiff and fold it into the half-set mixture. Spread over the strawberries, smoothing the top. Leave to set. Arrange the remaining strawberries on top.

7 Make up the second packet of quick-setting gelatine with the remaining strawberry juice and spoon over the cake. Carefully remove the wax paper from the sides and bottom of the cake. Decorate with the lemon slices.

BANANA TOWER

Makes approximately 12 servings

Mixture

5 eggs
1 cup sugar
Pinch of salt
7½ tbsps light cream
½ cup margarine, melted and cooled
2 cups flour
3¾ tsps baking powder

4 Whisk the egg yolks, sugar and vanilla sugar until light, then add the wine. Peel and slice the bananas, purée them with the lemon juice and stir into the mixture. Soak and then dissolve the gelatine and beat it into the mixture.

5 When the mixture is half set, carefully fold in first the whipped cream and then the stiffly beaten egg whites. Divide into two servings.

6 Replace the cake pan ring around one of the larger cake layers and cover thickly with one portion of cream.

7 Divide the second portion of cream in two. Spread one half over the second large cake layer. Place this second layer on top of first. Use the remaining cream to sandwich together the two smaller cake layers and place these on top of the larger ones.

8 Make up the chocolate couverture according to the instructions, add the coconut oil and cover the cake with it. Decorate with whipped cream.

Filling

5 eggs, separated
¾ cup sugar
3 tsps vanilla sugar
Grated zest of 1 lemon
3-4 tbsps white wine
3 cups ripe bananas
8-9 tbsps lemon juice
8 sheets gelatine
1 cup whipped cream
6¼ tbsps maraschino

Icing

7oz chocolate couverture
1 tbsp coconut oil

For Decoration

1 cup whipping cream

1 Whisk the eggs, sugar and salt until light and foamy, then gradually whisk in the cream and margarine. Sift together the flour and baking powder, and fold into the mixture.

2 Grease two cake pans with removable bases, one 6 inches in diameter and the other 9 inches in diameter. Divide the mixture between these and bake for 20-25 minutes in a preheated oven, 400-425°F. Leave to cool.

3 Slice each cake in half horizontally and moisten liberally with maraschino.

AN INVITATION TO AFTERNOON TEA

Do you enjoy a good, old-fashioned tea? Then why not invite a few friends around and treat them to delicious, crunchy cookies, and three different kinds of cake, made from one basic mixture.

ALMOND TRIANGLES

*Makes approximately
45 triangles*

2 cups flour
½ cup margarine
1 egg
⅓ cup sugar
Margarine for greasing

Filling
½ cup ground almonds
⅔ cup sugar
1 egg, separated

Icing
1 tbsp coconut oil
½ cup powdered sugar
3 tsps cocoa powder
1-2 tbsps rum

1 Make a dough from the flour, margarine, egg and sugar. Knead lightly and leave to stand in a cold place for 30 minutes.
2 Mix the almonds, sugar and egg white to a firm consistency.
3 Roll out the dough thinly. Cut out 2½-inch rounds and arrange them on a greased baking sheet. Place a ball of almond mixture on top of each round. Brush the pastry edges with beaten egg yolk. Fold the pastry inwards on three sides and press the edges lightly into the almond filling.
4 Bake in a preheated oven, 400°F for 10-15 minutes.
5 Meanwhile mix the coconut oil with the powdered sugar, cocoa and rum. Ice the warm triangles at the point where the folded edges meet.

RUM RINGS

Makes approximately 40 rings

2½ cups flour
¼ cup cocoa powder
Pinch of salt
½ cup sugar
1 cup margarine
2½ tbsps rum
Margarine for greasing
1 egg
1 tbsp chopped almonds

1 Make a dough from the flour, cocoa, salt, sugar, margarine and rum. Knead lightly and leave to stand in a cold place for at least 60 minutes.
2 Roll small pieces of the dough into thin coils. Twist two coils together to form a ring. Make about 40 rings in this way.
3 Arrange the rings on a greased baking sheet, brush with beaten egg and sprinkle with chopped almonds.
4 Bake in a preheated oven, 400-425°F. for 12-14 minutes. When cooked, they should be golden brown in color.

DUTCH SHORTBREAD

Makes approximately 25 cookies

1 cup margarine
½ cup sugar
7½ tsps vanilla sugar
Pinch of salt
2½ tbsps rum
½ cup ground almonds
2½ cups flour
Good pinch of baking powder
Margarine for greasing

1 Beat the margarine, sugar, vanilla sugar and salt until light and fluffy. Add the rum, almonds and the flour, sifted together with the baking powder.
2 Using an icing bag, pipe wide strips onto a greased baking sheet.
3 Bake the shortbread in a preheated oven, 425°F for 10-15 minutes.

SWEET CARAWAY COOKIES

Makes approximately 40 cookies

2 cups flour
½ cup margarine
½ cup sugar
1¼ tbsps caraway seeds
Pinch of ground nutmeg
Grated zest of 1 lemon
1 small egg
1¼ tbsps sherry
Sugar

LEMON HEARTS

Makes approximately 40 hearts

2 cups flour
½ cup margarine
⅔ cup sugar
3 egg yolks
Grated zest of 1 lemon
Good pinch of baking powder

Margarine for greasing
⅓ cup powdered sugar
1 tbsp lemon juice
Approximately 1 tbsp water

1 Make a dough from the flour, margarine, sugar, egg yolks, grated lemon zest and baking powder, working the ingredients together quickly but thoroughly. Leave to stand in a cold place for a short time.

2 Roll out the dough fairly thickly. Using a heart-shaped cutter, cut out cookies and arrange on a greased baking sheet. Bake in a preheated oven, 425°F for about 12 minutes, until golden brown.

3 Mix the powdered sugar, lemon juice and water and use to frost the hearts.

1 Make a dough from the flour, margarine, sugar, caraway seeds, nutmeg, grated lemon zest, egg and sherry and chill.

2 Roll out the dough to ⅜ inch thick, and cut out various shapes using cookie cutters.

3 Line a baking sheet with wax paper, arrange the cookies on it and bake in a preheated oven, 400°F for 10-15 minutes.

4 While they are still hot, sprinkle the cookies with sugar.

HALF-'N-HALVES

Makes approximately 25 cookies

2 cups flour
½ cup margarine
½ cup sugar
7½ tsps vanilla sugar
1 egg
1 tbsp ground hazelnuts or filberts
Margarine for greasing
1⅓ cups powdered sugar
2-3 tbsps raspberry syrup

1 Make a dough from the flour, margarine, sugar, vanilla sugar, egg and nuts. Leave in a cold place for 15 minutes.

2 Roll out the dough to the thickness of a knife blade, and cut out 1½-inch rounds. Arrange the rounds on a greased baking sheet and bake in a preheated oven, 425°F for about 12 minutes until golden brown.

3 Mix half the powdered sugar to a thick consistency with the raspberry syrup and 1 tsp water. Mix the remaining powdered sugar with plain water.

4 Frost each cookie half in red icing and half in white, and leave to set.

COCONUT DROPS

Makes approximately 60 cookies

1 cup margarine
1 cup sugar
¾ tsps vanilla sugar
Pinch of salt
4 egg whites
1¾ cups flour
½ tsp baking powder
1 cup shredded coconut
Margarine for greasing

1 Beat the margarine, sugar, vanilla sugar, salt and egg whites until light and fluffy. Sift together the flour and baking powder and fold into the mixture alternately with the coconut.
2 Using an icing bag fitted with a plain nozzle, pipe out small amounts of the mixture onto a greased baking sheet. Bake in a preheated oven, 400°F for about 10 minutes.

Note: A teaspoon may also be used to drop the mixture onto the sheet.

CREAM COOKIES

Makes approximately 40 cookies

4 cups flour
½ tsp baking powder
Pinch of salt
Pith of 2 vanilla pods
1½ cups margarine
¾-1 cup sour cream
Brown sugar

FRUIT COOKIES

Makes approximately 80 cookies

1 cup margarine
1 cup sugar
Pinch of salt
1 egg
1 cup raisins
2¾ cups flour
1¼ tsps bicarbonate of soda
1¼ tsps water
Margarine for greasing

1 Beat the margarine, sugar, salt and egg until light and fluffy. Dissolve the bicarbonate of soda in the water, and stir in, together with two-thirds of the flour and the raisins. Mix in the remaining flour, kneading lightly.

2 Chill the dough in the refrigerator. Roll out with a little flour and cut out into 1½-inch rounds. Arrange on a greased baking sheet and bake in a preheated oven, 400-425°F for about 10 minutes.

1 Make a dough from the first six ingredients and leave overnight in the refrigerator.

2 Roll out to a thickness of about ⅛ inch. Cut out shapes as desired, sprinkle these with brown sugar and arrange them on a baking sheet lined with wax paper. Bake in a preheated oven, 400°F for about 10 minutes.

ALMOND FLAKES

Makes approximately 15 cookies

½ cup flaked almonds
1¼ tbsps clear honey
3 tsps vanilla sugar
⅓ cup chocolate, coarsely grated
1 tbsp coconut oil
5 tbsps whipped cream

1 Toast the flaked almonds with the honey and vanilla sugar until golden brown, then leave to cool.
2 Melt the grated chocolate with the coconut oil in a bowl over a pan of hot water. Stir in the flaked almonds. Leave the mixture to cool slightly, then fold in the whipped cream. Line a baking sheet with greased foil or wax paper. Arrange dollops of the mixture on this.
3 Place in the refrigerator to set.

SPANISH CINNAMON BUNS

Makes approximately 12 buns

1 cup margarine
1 cup sugar
Pinch of salt
6 eggs
3-4 tsps cinnamon
2 cups flour
Margarine for greasing

1 Beat the margarine, sugar, salt and eggs until light and fluffy, then fold in the cinnamon and flour.
2 Divide the mixture between twelve greased muffin pans and bake on the lowest shelf in a pre-heated oven, 400°-425°F for about 15 minutes.

CHOCOLATE RINGS

Makes approximately 50 cookies

¾ cup margarine
1 cup powdered sugar
1 egg yolk
3 tsps vanilla sugar
2½ tbsps cocoa powder
1¼ tsps instant coffee
2 cups flour
Margarine for greasing

1 Beat the margarine, powdered sugar, egg yolk, vanilla sugar, cocoa and coffee until light and fluffy. Fold in the sifted flour.
2 Using an icing bag fitted with a star nozzle, pipe out rings of the mixture onto a baking sheet lined with greased foil or wax paper.
3 Bake in a preheated oven, 400°-425°F for about 8-10 minutes.

CHOCOLATE ALMOND TREATS

Makes approximately 45 cookies

1 cup almonds
½ cup semi-sweet chocolate
1 cup sugar
3-4 level tsps cinnamon
3 eggs
Margarine for greasing

1 Grind the almonds and grate the chocolate. Mix together with the sugar, cinnamon, flour and eggs to make a dough.
2 Using two teaspoons, drop spoonfuls of the mixture onto a greased and floured baking sheet.
3 Bake the cookies in a preheated oven, 350°F for about 20 minutes.

SWISS COOKIES

Makes approximately 50 cookies

1½ cups flour
⅓ cup margarine
⅓ cup sugar
3-4 tsps vanilla sugar
1 egg
Pinch of salt
¼ cup raisins
¼ cup hazelnut or filbert kernels
Margarine for greasing

1 Make a dough from the flour, margarine, sugar, vanilla sugar, egg and salt. Stir in the raisins and hazelnut kernels.
2 Shape into rolls about 1½ inches thick and either put into the freezer or leave for 24 hours in a very cold place. Cut the rolls into ¼-inch-thick slices. Arrange the cookies on a greased baking sheet and bake in a preheated oven, 400°-425°F for 15-20 minutes, until golden brown.

GREEK WALNUT TRIANGLES

Makes approximately 40 triangles

1 cup margarine
2/3 cup powdered sugar
Pinch of salt
2½ cups flour
2 tsps baking powder
¼ cup walnuts, chopped
Margarine for greasing
Powdered sugar for dredging

1 Stir together the margarine, powdered sugar and salt, without beating. Sift together the flour and baking powder and add to the mixture, together with the walnuts.
2 Shape the dough into rolls the thickness of a finger, and cut into 6-inch lengths.
3 Bend each length into a triangle, place on a greased baking sheet and bake in a preheated oven, 400°F for 10-12 minutes.
4 When cold, dredge with powdered sugar.

MINI ROCK CAKES

Makes approximately 80 cakes

3¾ cups flour
3¾ tsps baking powder
2/3 cup sugar
1 cup margarine
2/3 cup raisins
2 eggs
5 tbsps milk
Margarine for greasing

1 Mix the flour, baking powder and sugar on a pastry board. Dot with the cold margarine cut into small pieces. Cut the margarine into the flour with a palette knife. Add the raisins.
2 Beat the eggs with the milk. Make a well in the flour mixture, pour in the egg mixture, and quickly work the two together to make a soft dough.
3 Using a teaspoon, drop spoonfuls of the mixture onto a greased baking sheet and bake in a preheated oven, 400°F for 20-25 minutes.

CRUMBLE COOKIES

Makes approximately 40 cookies

2 cups flour
1¼ tsps baking powder
1 cup margarine
3¾ tbsps whipping cream
3¾ tsps vanilla sugar
Egg yolk
Brown sugar
Margarine for greasing

1 Sift together the flour and baking powder. Make a smooth dough from this, the margarine, cream and vanilla sugar. Chill.
2 Roll out the dough, cut out hearts or stars, brush thinly with egg yolk and sprinkle with brown sugar.
3 Arrange the cookies on a greased baking sheet and bake in a preheated oven, 400-425°F for about 8 minutes until just golden.

ALMOND SNAPS

Makes approximately 50 cookies

⅓ cup margarine
½ cup sugar
¼ cup karo syrup
1¼ tsps cinnamon
¼ cup chopped almonds
1¼ cups flour
2½ tbsps whipping cream
½ cup chocolate couverture

1 Beat the margarine, sugar and syrup until light and fluffy. Fold in the cinnamon, almonds, flour and cream.
2 Bake the mixture in batches. Place four teaspoonfuls of the mixture at a time on a greased baking sheet, leaving large gaps in between. Dip a knife in hot water and flatten each spoonful of mixture.
3 Bake in a preheated oven, 400°-425°F. for 3-5 minutes.
4 Leave to cool slightly. While still warm, take each cookie carefully off the tray and shape by bending round a rolling pin.
5 Coat half of each cookie by dipping in the chocolate couverture.

93

CHOCOLATE PRALINES

Makes approximately 20 cookies

½ cup sugar
½ cup chopped almonds
1 cup whipping cream
¼ cup candied lemon zest
1 tbsp margarine
6¼ tbsps orange liqueur
Vegetable oil for greasing
Semi-sweet chocolate couverture
Strips of orange zest

1 Melt the sugar in a saucepan, without allowing it to color. Stir in the almonds, cream and lemon zest, and bring to the boil, stirring constantly until the mixture starts to thicken. Add the margarine and orange liqueur and continue to boil until the mixture shrinks away from the bottom of the saucepan and the spoon leaves a mark. Pour the mixture quickly into an oiled baking pan.
2 When the mixture has hardened, cut it into small squares, using a knife dipped in water.
3 Leave to go quite cold, then coat thinly with the melted chocolate couverture and leave to harden.
4 When the chocolate is almost hard, decorate the pralines with paper-thin strips of orange zest.

CHOCOLATE CHIP COOKIES

Makes approximately 30 cookies

½ cup margarine
⅓ cup sugar
½ cup brown sugar
1 tsp vanilla sugar
Pinch of salt
1 egg
1¼ tbsps water
1½ cups flour
½ cup semi-sweet chocolate
¼ cup hazelnut or filbert kernels
Margarine for greasing

1 Beat the margarine, sugar, brown sugar and vanilla sugar until light and fluffy. Add the salt, egg and water and mix together well. Fold in the sifted flour. Cut the chocolate into small cubes, chop the nut kernels roughly and stir both into the mixture.

2 Drop teaspoonfuls of the mixture onto a greased baking sheet and flatten each one lightly. Bake in a preheated oven, 400°F for about 12 minutes.

GINGER COOKIES

Makes approximately 30 cookies

2 cups flour
Pinch of salt
1/4 cup ground almonds
1 1/4 tsps ground ginger
1 1/4 tsps cinnamon
3/4 tbsp fresh ginger, grated
1/2 cup sugar
1/2 cup margarine
1 egg, beaten
Margarine for greasing
1 egg yolk for brushing
Almonds, glacé cherries or crystallized ginger to decorate

1 Mix together the flour, salt, ground almonds, ginger, cinnamon, grated ginger and sugar on a pastry board. Dot with flakes of margarine and cut these in using a palette knife. Make a well in the mixture, drop in the beaten egg and mix together well with the palette knife. Knead quickly to a smooth dough. Cover and chill.
2 Roll out the dough and cut into shapes. Arrange on a baking sheet lined with a sheet of wax paper. Mix the egg yolk with a little water and brush over the cookies to glaze. Bake in a preheated oven, 400°F for about 8 minutes.

SWISS BISCUIT SQUARES

Makes approximately 50 cookies

2 cups flour
1 cup sugar
Pinch of salt
2 1/2 tsps cinnamon
1/2 cup ground almonds
1/2 cup margarine
1 egg, beaten
Margarine for greasing
1 egg yolk

1 Mix together the flour, sugar, salt, cinnamon and almonds on a pastry board. Using a palette knife, cut in the margarine. Add the beaten egg, mix and knead together well.
2 Roll out the dough on a greased baking sheet to a thickness of 3/4 inch. Mix the egg yolk with a little water and brush over the dough. Use a fork to mark a criss-cross pattern on top.

3 Bake in a preheated oven, 350°-400°F for about 20 minutes. Cut into 1 1/2-inch squares whilst still hot.

CHOCOLATE DROPS

Makes approximately 40 cookies

7 tbsps margarine
2 cups flour
½ cup cornstarch
½ cup sugar
3-4 tsps vanilla sugar
1½ tbsps cocoa powder
2½ level tsps baking powder
Flour
Almond halves

1 Melt the margarine and set aside to cool. Mix together the flour, cornstarch, sugar, vanilla sugar, cocoa powder, baking powder and liquid margarine to a smooth dough.
2 Roll walnut-sized pieces of the dough into balls and arrange them on a floured baking sheet.
3 Press an almond half onto each cookie. Bake in a pre-heated oven, 400°F for about 20 minutes.

Note: These chocolate drops may also be frosted if desired.

FLORENTINES

Makes approximately 30 cookies

1 cup flaked almonds
½ cup candied orange peel, roughly chopped
¼ cup margarine
½ cup whipping cream
1 cup sugar
1¾ cups flour
Margarine for greasing
Flour
4oz cup semi-sweet chocolate couverture

1 Put the almonds, orange peel, margarine, cream, sugar and flour into a saucepan and bring to the boil, stirring continuously.

2 Grease and flour a baking sheet. Drop teaspoonfuls of the mixture onto the sheet, leaving large gaps between. Using the back of a teaspoon, press each cookie flat.

3 Bake in a preheated oven, 400°-425°F for 7-10 minutes.

4 Melt the chocolate couverture in a bowl over a pot of hot water. Coat the undersides of the florentines with the couverture, and pattern with a fork if desired.

THREE-IN-ONE LOW FAT SPONGES

Basic Low Fat Sponge Mixture

⅓ cup margarine, softened
6 eggs, separated
7½ tbsps warm water
1 cup sugar
Pinch of salt
1 cup flour
¾ cup cornstarch
1¼ tsps baking powder

1 Whisk the egg yolks with the water, sugar and salt until light and foamy. Carefully incorporate the margarine.
2 Whisk the egg whites until stiff and fold into the mixture.
3 Sift the flour, cornstarch and baking powder over the mixture. Using a balloon whisk, carefully fold everything together.
5 Divide the sponge cake mixture into three equal servings.

CRANBERRY CREAM SPONGE

Makes 8 servings

1 portion low fat sponge cake mixture
1 cup whipping cream
1¼ tbsps sugar
½ cup cranberries
Margarine for greasing
Powdered sugar

1 Grease an 8-inch cake pan and turn the sponge mixture into it. Bake for 20-25 minutes in a preheated oven, 400°F. Turn out and leave to cool.
2 Whip the cream until stiff. Lightly crush the cranberries with a fork and fold them into the cream.
3 Slice the cooled sponge cake in half horizontally. Sandwich together again with the cream and cranberry mixture. Dust the cake with powdered sugar. Slice.

COFFEE SPONGE

Makes approximately 6 servings

1 portion low fat sponge cake mixture
1 cup whipping cream
2½ tbsps sugar
1¼ tbsps coffee powder
Margarine for greasing

1 Grease a 6-inch spring-release cake pan and turn the sponge mixture into it. Bake for 20-25 minutes in a preheated oven, 400°F. Turn out and leave to cool.
2 Whip the cream and sugar together until stiff. Mix in the coffee powder.
3 Slice the cake in half horizontally. Sandwich together again with the coffee cream, reserving enough for decoration. Using an icing bag, decorate the cake with the remaining cream.

PEACH CAKE

Makes approximately 6 servings

1 portion low fat sponge cake mixture
1 13oz can peaches
5 tbsps apricot jam
1¼ tbsps gin
1 cup whipping cream
1¼ tbsps sugar
Margarine for greasing
Peach slices to decorate

1 Grease a 7-inch spring-release cake pan and turn the sponge mixture into it. Bake for 20-25 minutes in a preheated oven 400°F. Turn out and leave to cool.
2 Put the peaches in a colander to drain. Heat the apricot jam and stir in the gin.
3 Cut the cooled sponge cake in half horizontally. Arrange the drained peach slices on the bottom sponge layer and spread the apricot jam over them. Replace the top sponge layer.
4 Whip the cream and sugar until stiff, then spread over the top and sides of the cake. Decorate with the additional peach slices.

THREE-IN-ONE YEAST-DOUGH DELIGHTS

Basic Yeast Dough Mixture

1 packet yeast
1 cup lukewarm milk
1/3 cup sugar
5 cups flour

Pinch of salt
2/3 cups margarine, melted
1 egg

1 Crumble the yeast into the milk, add a little sugar, cover and leave in a warm place until frothy.

2 Put the flour, remaining sugar and salt into a bowl. Add the frothy yeast, margarine and egg. Mix to a dough then knead well, using an electric mixer if possible. Cover and leave to rise in a warm place.

3 Knead the risen dough well and divide into three equal servings.

ROSE BUN ROUND

Makes 8 servings

1 portion yeast dough
3/4 tbsp margarine, melted
1 tbsp cinnamon sugar
1 tbsp crushed glazed nuts
Margarine for greasing

Roll out the dough to an 8-inch x 10-inch rectangle. Brush with the melted margarine and sprinkle over the cinnamon sugar and nut brittle.

Roll up along the long side, and slice into eight equal rounds. Grease a shallow 6-in cake pan with a removable base. Arrange the slices, cut edges upwards, in a circle in the tin, with one slice in the center. Cover and leave to rise in a warm place. See Yeast Plait for cooking instructions.

GUGELHUPF

Makes approximately 4 servings

1 portion yeast dough
3/4 tbsp sugar
Grated lemon zest
1 tbsp raisins
1 tbsp candied lemon peel
1 tbsp glacé cherries, quartered
3 3/4 tbsps lukewarm milk
Margarine for greasing
Powdered sugar for dusting

YEAST PLAIT

Makes approximately 8 servings

1 portion yeast dough
Margarine for greasing
Milk for glazing
Brown sugar and flaked almonds

1 Divide the dough into three, make each portion into a roll of equal length and thickness, and plait them together. Place on a small, greased baking sheet, cover and leave to rise in a warm place. Before baking, brush with milk, then sprinkle with flaked almonds and brown sugar.

2 All three recipes are baked in a preheated oven, 400°–425°F. The Plait should be baked for about 20 minutes, whilst the Rose cake and Gugelhupf need about 30-40 minutes. Dust the Gugelhupf with powdered sugar, before serving.

Note: All three recipes are suitable for freezing.

Add the sugar, lemon zest, raisins, candied lemon peel, glacé cherries and lukewarm milk to the yeast dough. Mix together well. Press the dough into a greased 6-inch tube pan, cover and leave to rise in a warm place. See Yeast Plait for cooking instructions.

THREE-IN-ONE PLAIN SPONGES

Basic Sponge Mixture

1½ cups margarine	
1½ cups sugar	
7 eggs	
3 cups flour	
2 tsps baking powder	
Breadcrumbs	

Beat the margarine, sugar and eggs until light and fluffy. Sift together the flour and baking powder, and fold into the mixture. Divide the mixture between three bowls.

HAZELNUT SPONGE

Makes approximately 4 servings

1 portion sponge mixture
¼ cup toasted hazelnuts or filberts, ground
2 tbsps rum
Margarine for greasing
Breadcrumbs
Powdered sugar

Stir the nuts and rum into one portion of the sponge mixture. Turn into a 6-inch tube pan, which has been greased and sprinkled with breadcrumbs. See Orange Cake for baking instructions.

SPICY SPONGE

Makes approximately 8 servings

1 portion sponge mixture
5 tbsps mixed spice
1¼ tbsp rum
2½ tbsps semi-sweet chocolate morsels
Margarine for greasing
Breadcrumbs
⅔ cup chocolate couverture, melted
Candied fruit

Stir the mixed spice and rum into the second portion of sponge mixture. Fold in the chocolate morsels. Grease an 8-inch loaf pan and sprinkle with breadcrumbs. Turn the mixture into this. See Orange Cake for baking instructions.

ORANGE CAKE

Makes approximately 8 servings

1 portion sponge mixture
Grated zest of ½ orange
2½ tbsps orange liqueur
Margarine for greasing
Breadcrumbs
⅔ cup powdered sugar
2½ tbsps orange juice
1¼ tsp coconut oil
Candied fruit to decorate

1 Stir the grated orange zest and orange liqueur into the third portion of sponge mixture. Grease a 6-inch tube pan, sprinkle with breadcrumbs and turn the mixture into it.

2 Bake all three cakes in a preheated oven, 400°-425°F. The Orange Cake requires 40 minutes and the Spicy Cake and Filbert Sponge require about 50 minutes.

3 Dust the Hazelnut sponge with powdered sugar before serving. Cover the cooled Spicy Cake with the melted chocolate couverture and decorate with candied fruit. For the Orange Cake, mix the powdered sugar with the orange juice and coconut oil and use to frost the cooled cake.

Note: All three cakes are suitable for freezing.

CREAM POT TREATS

Mixture

1 pot whipping cream
1 cup sugar
Pinch of salt
3 tsps vanilla sugar
4 eggs
1¾ cups flour
3¾ tsps baking powder
Grated zest of 1 lemon
Margarine for greasing

Topping 1

Makes approximately 8 servings

⅓ cup margarine
½ cup sugar
3 tsps vanilla sugar
2½ tbsps milk
½ cup flaked almonds

Topping 2

Makes approximately 8 servings

1lb apples, peeled
2½ tbsps sugar
1 tsp cinnamon

1 Beat together the cream, sugar, salt, vanilla sugar and eggs. Sift the flour with the baking powder, and fold into the mixture with the grated lemon zest.

2 Pour half the mixture into a greased baking pan and bake in a preheated oven, 400°F for about 15 minutes.

3 Meanwhile, prepare the first topping. Put the margarine, sugar and vanilla sugar, milk and almonds into a saucepan and bring to the boil. Leave to cool. Spread over the cake and bake for a further 15 minutes.

4 Cut the peeled apples into wedges ready for the second cake.

5 Put the second portion of mixture into a shallow 8½-inch cake pan with a removable base. Arrange the apple wedges close together on top, mix the cinnamon with the sugar and sprinkle over the apples. Bake in the preheated oven, 400°F, for about 35 minutes.

MORE VARIETY SPONGES

Basic Sponge Mixture

¼ cup margarine
5 eggs
1 cup sugar
3 tsps vanilla sugar
Pinch of salt
2 cups flour
3¾ tsps baking powder
3¾ tbsps whipping cream
Margarine for greasing
Breadcrumbs

Melt the margarine and leave to cool. Whisk the eggs, sugar, vanilla sugar and salt until light and foamy; gradually whisk in the melted margarine. Sift together the flour and baking powder and fold into the mixture with the cream. Divide the mixture as follows:

For the Fruit Cake, put a scant one-third of the mixture into a 6-inch flan ring with a removable base, which has been greased and sprinkled with breadcrumbs. Baking time will be about 45 minutes. For the Chocolate Coated Sponge, grease an 8-inch loaf pan and sprinkle with breadcrumbs. Turn one-third of the mixture into it. Baking time will be about 45 minutes.

For the Bumble Bee Cake, grease a shallow 6-inch cake pan with a removable base and sprinkle with breadcrumbs. Turn the remaining mixture into it. Part bake for about 15 minutes.

Bake all the cakes together in a preheated oven, 400°-425°F.

BUMBLE BEE CAKE

Makes approximately 4 servings

¼ cup margarine
¼ cup sugar
¼ cup flaked almonds
1¼ tbsp light cream, 1 tbsp flour

Put all the ingredients in a saucepan, bring to the boil, stirring, and spread over the part-baked cake. Return to the oven for a further 15 minutes.

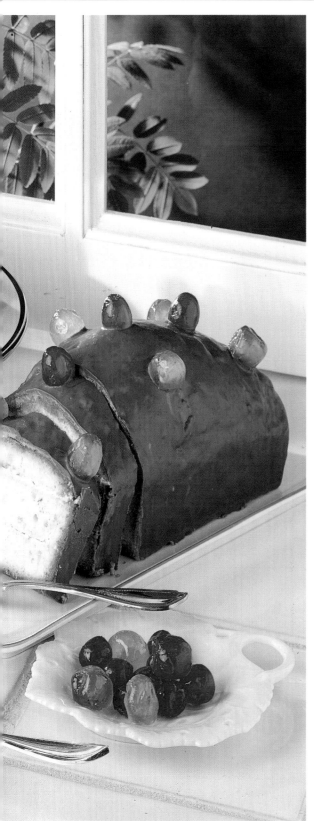

CHOCOLATE COATED SPONGE

Makes 8 servings

2 eggs
1 tbsp sugar
11 tbsps vanilla sugar
Pinch of salt
½ cup margarine

Topping

½ packet chocolate frosting
1¼ tbsp coconut oil
Candied fruit

1 Slice the cooled cake in three, horizontally.

2 Whisk the eggs, sugar, vanilla sugar and salt in a bowl over hot water, until thickened. Leave to cool, stirring occasionally.
3 Meanwhile, beat the margarine until light and fluffy, and beat gradually into the cooled mixture.
4 Sandwich together the three cake layers with the cream.
5 Coat with chocoate frosting. Decorate with candied fruit.

FRUIT CAKE

Makes approximately 4 servings

3¾ tbsps kirsch
1 cup white grapes
2 kiwi fruit
1 small banana
2½ tbsps lemon juice
½ cup white wine
1½ tbsps sugar
Grated zest of ½ lemon
1 packet quick-setting gelatine

1 Sprinkle the kirsch over the cooled cake. Scald the grapes, peel and deseed. Peel and thickly slice the kiwi fruit. Slice the banana, and briefly turn in the lemon juice. Arrange the fruit on top of the cake.
2 Make up a glaze with the white wine, sugar, grated lemon zest and quick-setting gelatine according to the packet instructions. Pour the glaze over

the fruit and leave to set. Serve cold, with whipped cream if desired.

THREE-IN-ONE SHORT PASTRY FLANS

Shortcrust Mixture

3 cups flour
½ cup sugar
Pinch of salt
3 tbsps vanilla sugar
¾ cup margarine
2 small eggs, beaten

Mix the flour, sugar, salt and vanilla sugar together on a pastry board. Dot with small flakes of cold margarine and cut these in with a palette knife. Add the beaten eggs, mix together thoroughly and knead to a smooth dough. Divide into three equal servings and chill.

CHERRY FLAN

Makes approximately 6 servings

1 small jar sour cherries, stoned
1 portion short pastry
Margarine for greasing
1½ tbsps shredded coconut
1 egg
1¼ tbsp sugar
1½ tsps vanilla sugar
½ cup creamed cottage cheese

1 Drain the cherries.
2 Roll out pastry and use to line a greased 7-inch pie pan with a removable base. Sprinkle with the coconut and arrange the cherries on top. Beat the egg, sugar, vanilla sugar and cheese until light and fluffy and spread over the cherries.
3 Bake in a preheated oven, 400°F for about 30 minutes.

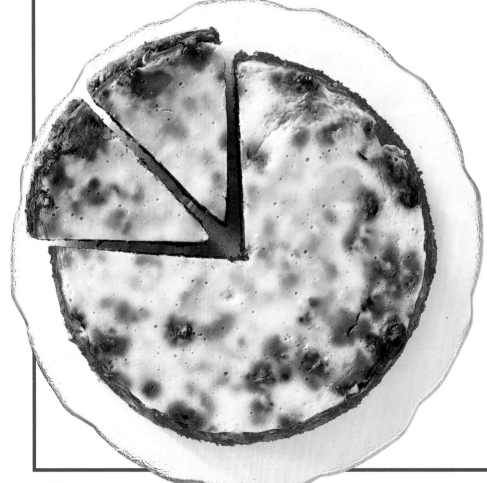

GRANNY'S ALMOND FLAN

Makes approximately 6 servings

1½ tbsps margarine
¼ cup sugar
2 tsps vanilla sugar
1 egg
2½ tbsps whipping cream
⅓ cup ground almonds
1¼ tbsp flour
Good pinch of baking powder
1 portion short pastry
Margarine for greasing
2½ tbsps apricot jam

APPLE FLAN

Makes approximately 6 servings

2 large baking apples
1 tbsp lemon juice
1 egg, separated
¼ cup sugar
1¼ tsps rum
1¼ tbsps flour
Good pinch of baking powder
½ cup ground almonds
1 portion short pastry
Margarine for greasing

1 Peel, core and quarter the apples and sprinkle with lemon juice. Whisk the egg yolk, sugar and rum until light and foamy. Whisk the egg white until stiff and fold into the mixture. Sift together the flour and baking powder, add almonds and fold into the mixture.

2 Roll out the dough and use to line a greased 7-inch pie pan with a removable base. Bake blind for 10 minutes in a preheated oven, 425°F. Reduce the heat to 375°-400°F.

3 Spread the almond mixture into the cooked flan case. Arrange the apples on top, pressing them lightly into the mixture. Return the flan to the oven for about 45 minutes.

1 Beat the margarine, sugar, vanilla sugar, egg and whipping cream until light and fluffy, then fold in the almonds. Sift together the flour and baking powder and fold into the mixture.

2 Roll out the pastry and use to line a greased 7-inch pie pan with a removable base. Bake blind in a preheated oven, 425°F, for 15 minutes. Reduce the heat to 375°-400°F. Spread the apricot jam over the pastry base and pour the almond mixture on top. Return to the oven for a further 45 minutes.

WHOLEFOOD
BAKING

Enjoying your food without feeling guilty is the theme
of this chapter. Whole wheat flour is an important
component of a healthy diet, and it is not only tasty in
bread and rolls but also in a great number of delicious
cakes and cookies as the following recipes
demonstrate.

PICNIC BITES

Makes approximately 24

1½ cups whole wheat flour
1 cup stoneground flour
2½ tsps baking powder
¾ cup oatmeal
¾ cup oatflakes
⅔ cup raisins
¼ cup chopped almonds
1 cup margarine
1 cup sugar
2 tbsps clear honey
2 eggs
1¼ tsps vanilla essence
Margarine for greasing
5 tbsps apricot jam, warmed

1 Mix the flours, baking powder, oatmeal, oatflakes, raisins and almonds together well.
2 Put the margarine, sugar and honey in a saucepan and heat until the sugar has dissolved, stirring continuously. Leave to cool. Add the eggs and vanilla essence and mix into the dry ingredients.
3 Spread the mixture onto a greased baking sheet and bake in a preheated oven, 350°F.
4 Take out of the oven after 5 minutes and spread with the warm apricot jam. Bake for a further 5 minutes. Leave to cool, then cut into small squares.

WHOLE WHEAT COOKIES

Makes approximately 30

2½ cups whole wheat flour
¼ tsp baking powder
½ tsp cinnamon
Pinch of salt
Grated zest of 1 lemon
⅔ cup brown sugar
½ cup ground almonds
¾ cup margarine
2 eggs
1 egg white
1¼ tbsps lemon juice
1 egg yolk for brushing
Brown sugar for sprinkling

1 Sift together the flour, baking powder, cinnamon and salt, and stir in grated lemon zest. Add the remaining ingredients and work to a smooth dough.
2 Roll out the dough, cut out rounds and place on a baking sheet lined with wax paper.
3 Mix the egg yolk with a little water and brush over the cookies. Sprinkle with brown sugar. Bake in a preheated oven, 400°F, for 15-20 minutes.

TIPSY ALMOND COOKIES

Makes 60–70

1 cup margarine
¾ cup sugar
⅓ cup karo syrup
1 tsp cinnamon
1 tsp ground cloves
½ cup almonds, chopped
3-4 tbsps brandy or rum
2 cups oatmeal
2 cups stoneground flour
2½ tsps baking powder
½ cup whole wheat flour
Margarine for greasing

1 Beat the margarine, sugar and syrup until light and fluffy; add the cinnamon, cloves, almonds, brandy or rum, oatmeal and the stoneground flour, sifted together with the baking powder. Knead in the whole wheat flour.
2 Form the dough into two rolls and leave overnight in the refrigerator.
3 Slice the rolls thinly and bake on a greased baking sheet in a preheated oven, 425°F, for about 10 minutes.

SPICY COOKIES

Makes approximately 30

½ cup karo syrup
¼ cup sugar
1 tbsp margarine
Good pinch of ground cloves
Good pinch of cardamom
Good pinch of cinnamon
Good pinch of ground ginger
½ tsp grated orange zest
2 cups stoneground whole wheat flour
½ tsp potash
1¼ tbsps water
Margarine for greasing

1 Heat the syrup with the sugar until the sugar has dissolved. Leave to cool slightly. Stir in the margarine, spices and flour. Dissolve the potash in 1 tbsp water, and mix well into the mixture. Knead the mixture lightly.
2 Roll out the dough to a cookie thickness and cut out shapes as desired.
3 Place the cookies on a greased baking sheet and bake in a preheated oven, 425°F for 10-15 minutes.

into a roll and press firmly round the inside edge of the pan.

2 Bake blind in a preheated oven, 400°F, for 10 minutes. Spread the base with quince jam. Reduce the heat to 350°F.

3 Whisk the eggs and sugar until thick and foamy. Mix the shredded coconut, breadcrumbs, cinnamon, and grated zest with the baking powder and gradually fold into the egg mixture.

4 Spread this topping over the base and return to the oven for a further 40 minutes at the reduced temperature. Dust with powdered sugar before serving.

SOUR CHERRY CRUMBLE

1oz fresh yeast
3/4 cup lukewarm milk
1/3 cup sugar
1 3/4 cups stoneground flour
1 3/4 cups whole wheat flour
3/4 cups buckwheat flour
Pinch of salt
Grated lemon zest
1/4 cup margarine, melted and cooled
2 eggs, beaten
Margarine for greasing

Topping
2lb sour cherries (bottled)

BUCKWHEAT CAKE

Makes approximately 12 servings

4 egg yolks
1 cup sugar
Good pinch of ground cloves
1/2 tsp cinnamon
1/4 cup ground almonds
Grated zest of 1/2 lemon
6 egg whites
1 1/4 cups buckwheat flour
Margarine for greasing
Flour
Whipped cream to decorate, if desired

1 Whisk the egg yolks and sugar until light and foamy; add the spices, almonds and grated lemon zest. Whisk the egg whites until stiff and fold them into the mixture, alternating with the flour.

2 Grease a 9 1/2-inch cake pan with a removable base and sprinkle with flour. Turn the mixture into this. Bake in a preheated oven, 350°F, for about 60 minutes.

3 Decorate the finished caked with whipped cream, if desired.

LIGHT BREAD FLAN

Makes approximately 12 servings

Dough
1 3/4 cups whole wheat and stoneground flour, mixed
1/2 cup buckwheat flour
1/2 cup margarine
1/4 cup sugar
1 egg
Margarine for greasing

Topping
3 1/2 tbsps quince jam
3 eggs
1/2 cup sugar
1 cup shredded coconut
1 cup dry white breadcrumbs
Good pinch of cinnamon
Grated orange or lemon zest
Good pinch of baking powder
Powdered sugar for dusting

1 Mix the flour, margarine, sugar and egg together to make a smooth dough. Chill. Roll out two-thirds and use to line the bottom of a greased 9 1/2-inch cake pan with a removable base. Shape the remaining dough

Crumb Topping

1¾ cups stoneground flour
⅔ cup brown sugar
¼ cup almonds, chopped
Cinnamon
½ cup margarine

1 Crumble the yeast into the milk and stir in a pinch of sugar and flour. Leave, covered, in a warm place for 5-10 minutes until frothy.

2 Put the flour, sugar, salt, lemon zest, the melted and cooled margarine and the beaten eggs into a mixing bowl. Add the frothy yeast, and mix everything together. Knead the dough thoroughly, using an electric mixer if possible.

Cover the dough with foil and leave in a warm place until doubled in size. Knock down the dough and use to line a greased baking sheet.

3 Drain the stoned cherries well. Combine the flour, sugar, almonds, cinnamon and margarine to form a crumb mixture. Arrange the cherries and crumb mixture alternately over the dough.

4 Leave to rise in a warm place for a short time. Bake in a pre-heated oven, 400°-425°F, for about 30 minutes.

Note: Fresh cherries can also be used; they should be sprinkled with sugar after baking.

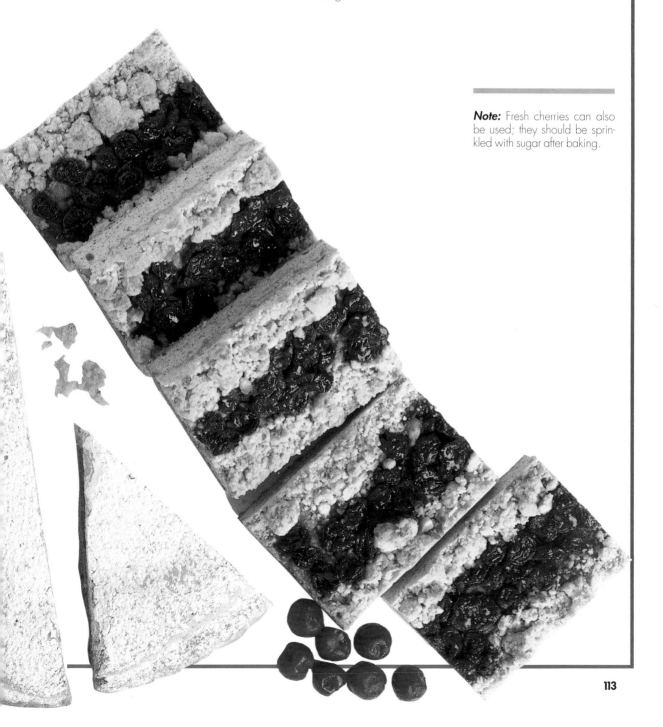

MUESLI CAKE

Makes approximately 16 servings

½ cup margarine
½ cup sugar
3¾ tsps vanilla sugar
3 eggs
Pinch of salt
1¼ tsps cinnamon
Grated zest of 1 lemon
1 cup fruit muesli
1¼ cups whole wheat flour
2½ tsps baking powder
½ cup whipping cream
Margarine for greasing

1 Cream the margarine until fluffy, gradually add the sugar, vanilla sugar and eggs and continue beating until the sugar has dissolved. Add the salt, cinnamon and lemon zest.
2 Mix together the muesli, wholewheat flour and baking powder and stir into the cake mixture alternately with the cream.
3 Pour the mixture into a greased 10-inch loaf pan and bake in a preheated oven, 350°F for 50-60 minutes.

WHOLE WHEAT CAKE WITH PEARS

Makes approximately 12 servings

4 eggs, separated
¾ cup powdered sugar
Grated zest of 1 lemon
1 cup whole wheat flour
1¼ tsps baking powder
13oz pears
Margarine for greasing
Jam or whipped cream, as desired

1 Whisk the egg yolks with the powdered sugar and lemon zest until light and foamy; gradually fold in the flour, sifted together with the baking powder. Whisk the egg whites until stiff and fold them into the mixture. Finally, stir in the peeled, cored and diced pears.
2 Turn the mixture into a greased 9½-inch cake pan with a removable base and bake in a preheated oven, 350°F for abut 60 minutes.
3 Cover with apricot jam, blueberry jam or whipped cream, as desired.

CHOCOLATE AND ALMOND CAKE

Makes approximately 12 servings

1 cup margarine
¾ cup sugar
6 eggs, separated
½ cup chocolate, cut in small pieces
1 cup ground almonds
7½ tbsps orange juice
Grated zest of 1 orange
½ cup graham crackers, crumbled
3 tsps baking powder
Margarine for greasing
2½ tbsps powdered sugar
2½ tbsps cocoa powder

1 Beat the margarine and sugar until light and fluffy. Gradually beat in the egg yolks. Cut the chocolate into small pieces and add to the mixture together with the almonds, orange juice and zest. Mix the cracker crumbs with the baking powder and stir in. Whisk the egg whites until very stiff and fold into the mixture.

2 Turn the mixture into a greased 9½-inch cake pan with a removable base and bake in a preheated oven, 350°F for about 60 minutes.

3 Turn out onto a cooling rack to cool. Sprinkle the cake with sifted powdered sugar and cocoa.

TRADITIONAL CINNAMON CAKE

Makes approximately 20 servings

½ cup margarine
¾ cup sugar
4 eggs
1¾ cups ground almonds
1¾ cups whole wheat and stoneground flour, mixed
½ cup buckwheat flour
3 tsps baking powder
5 tsps cinnamon
½ cup whipping cream
½ tbsp candied ginger
⅓ cup dried figs
¼ cup candied lemon peel

1 Beat the margarine and sugar until light and fluffy. Beat in the eggs and then the almonds. Sift together the flour, baking powder and cinnamon and gradually fold into mixture, alternating with the whipped cream.

2 Finely cut or grate the ginger. Finely slice the figs. Fold both into the mixture together with the lemon peel.

3 Turn into a greased 10-inch loaf pan and bake in a preheated oven, 400°F for 50 minutes. Turn off the heat and leave the cake to stand for a further 5 minutes in the oven.

PEACH LAYER CAKE

Makes approximately 12 servings

4 eggs, separated
5 tbsps warm water
1 cup sugar
Pinch of salt
¼ cup margarine, melted and cooled
1 tbsp cocoa powder
1¼ cups buckwheat flour
3¾ tsps baking powder
Margarine for greasing

Filling

1 14oz can peaches
6 sheets gelatine
1 cup whipping cream

For Decoration

2 cups whipping cream
7½ tsps vanilla sugar

1 Whisk the egg yolks, water, ⅔ cup of the sugar and the salt until light and foamy. Using a balloon whisk, beat the melted and cooled margarine into the egg mixture in a thin trickle. Whisk the egg whites with the remaining sugar until stiff and pile on top of the mixture. Sift the cocoa, flour and baking powder over the egg whites. Fold everything together very carefully.

2 Turn the mixture into a greased 10-inch cake pan with a removable base, and bake in a preheated oven, 350°F, for about 30 minutes. Slice the cooled cake in half horizontally.

3 Drain the peaches, reserving the juice. Cut the fruit into small pieces and mix with ½ cup of the reserved juice. Soak the gelatine, dissolve it over hot water and add to the peach mixture. Spread the half-set mixture over the bottom layer of sponge and place the second layer on top.

4 Whip the cream with the vanilla sugar until stiff and spread all over the cake, reserving some for decoration.

POPPYSEED CAKE WITH VANILLA CREAM

Makes approximately 12 servings

⅓ cup poppy seeds
4 eggs, separated
1¼ cups powdered sugar
3 tsps vanilla sugar
½ cup stoneground flour
½ cup cornstarch
1¼ tsps baking powder
Margarine for greasing

Filling

½ cup cornstarch
1¾ cups milk
¼ cup margarine
1 vanilla pod
⅓ cup sugar
3 tsps vanilla sugar
2 eggs, separated
5 sheets gelatine

For Decoration

¼ cup flaked almonds
Grated chocolate or chocolate
Sprinkles

1 Bring the poppy seeds and water to the boil, leave to soak for 20 minutes, then drain in a sieve. Grind very finely.
2 Whisk the egg yolks with the powdered sugar and vanilla

sugar until light and fluffy. Sift together the flour, cornstarch and baking powder, mix with the ground poppy seeds and fold into the egg mixture. Whisk the egg whites until very stiff, then fold in carefully.

3 Grease a 9½-inch cake pan with a removable base and line with wax paper. Turn the mixture into it and bake immediately in a preheated oven, 400°F, for about 45 minutes. Turn out, and remove the paper. Leave to cool, then slice in half horizontally.
4 Mix the cornstarch with a little milk. Bring the remaining milk to

the boil with the margarine, vanilla, sugar and vanilla sugar and thicken with the cornstarch and the egg yolks. Dissolve the soaked and well-drained gelatine in this. Whisk the egg whites until stiff and fold in.
5 When the cream is half set, use two-thirds to sandwich together the cake layers. Spread the remaining cream all over the cake. Decorate with the flaked almonds and grated chocolate. Chill in the refrigerator for a few hours before serving.

FARMHOUSE APRICOT CAKE

Makes approximately 24 servings

1½oz fresh yeast
¾ cup lukewarm milk
½ cup sugar
Pinch of salt
1¾ cups stoneground flour
1¾ cups whole wheat flour
¾ cup oatmeal
¾ cup ground almonds
2 eggs
½ cup margarine, melted and cooled
Margarine for greasing

Topping

2lb apricots, halved and stoned
¼ cup sugar
¾ cup almonds, chopped

Icing

1½ cups powdered sugar
4 tbsps lemon juice

1 Crumble the yeast into the lukewarm milk, stir in a pinch of sugar and a little flour, cover and leave in a warm place for 5-10 minutes until frothy. Mix together the salt, flours, oatmeal and almonds, add the frothy yeast, eggs and margarine and knead to a smooth dough. Cover and leave in a warm place until doubled in size.
2 Knead the dough again. Roll out and use to line a greased baking sheet. Arrange the halved and stoned apricots on top. Sprinkle with the sugar and chopped almonds. Bake in a preheated oven, 375°-400°F, for approximately 25 minutes.
3 Mix the powdered sugar and lemon juice and spread over the cake. Leave to harden.

CARROT CAKE

Makes approximately 12 servings

5 eggs, separated
1 cup sugar
Grated zest of 1 lemon
5 tbsps lemon juice
1 cup hazelnuts or filberts, ground
1 cup carrots, grated
¾ cup buckwheat flour
3¾ tsps baking powder
Pinch of salt

Icing

1¼ cups powdered sugar
2½ tbsps rum
1-2 tbsps lemon juice
Marzipan carrots, to decorate

1 Whisk the egg yolks with the sugar until light and fluffy. Add, one by one, the lemon zest and juice, nuts and carrots. Sift the buckwheat flour with the baking powder and fold in. Whisk the egg whites with the salt until stiff and fold into the mixture.
2 Grease a 10-inch cake pan with a removable base and dust it with flour. Turn mixture into this and bake in a preheated oven, 375°-400°F for 50-60 minutes.
3 Combine the powdered sugar, rum and lemon juice and spread over the cooled cake. Decorate with marzipan carrots.

PEAR CAKE

Makes approximately 12 servings

3/4 cup stoneground flour
1 1/4 cups whole wheat flour
2 1/2 tsps baking powder
1/4 cup sugar
4 tsps vanilla sugar
Pinch of salt
1/4 cup margarine
Margarine for greasing
1/2 cup low fat creamed cottage cheese, well drained
1 egg
2 1/2 tbsps milk

Topping
1 14oz can pear halves
1 7oz bottle cranberries

Crumb Topping
3/4 cup whole wheat flour
3/4 cup stoneground flour
1/3 cup sugar
Pinch of salt
4 tsps vanilla sugar
1/2 cup margarine

1 Mix together the flour, baking powder, sugar, vanilla sugar and salt on a pastry board. Dot with the well-chilled margarine and the cheese and mix every-thing together with a palette knife. Work in the egg, beaten with the milk, and knead to a smooth dough. Chill.
2 Drain the pear halves and the cranberries. Make up a crumb mixture using the flour, sugar, salt, vanilla sugar and margarine.
3 Roll out the pastry dough and use to line a greased 10-inch pie pan with a removable base. Arrange the pear halves on top, spread the cranberries over and cover with the crumb mixture. Bake in a preheated oven, 425°F, for approximately 60 minutes.

APPLE AND ALMOND CAKE

Makes approximately 12 servings

Mixture
1 3/4 cups stoneground flour
1/2 cup finely ground wholewheat flour
1/4 cup sugar
Pinch of salt
1/2 cup margarine
1 egg, beaten
Margarine for greasing

Topping
3 eggs, separated
2/3 cup sugar
1 1/4 tbsps lemon juice
1 1/4 tbsps rum
1 large and 6 small apples, peeled
1/2 cup buckwheat flour

Good pinch of baking powder
1 3/4 cups ground almonds
Melted margarine
Powdered sugar for dusting

1 Mix together the flours and sugar on a pastry board, dot generously with cold margarine and cut in with a palette knife. Make a well in the center and put in the beaten egg. Mix well and knead quickly to a

2 Peel and slice the apples and arrange on top. Sprinkle over the raisins together with the sesame seeds.
3 Bake in a preheated oven, 400°F, for about 60 minutes. Cut into slices to serve.

CRUMB SLICES

Makes approximately 12 slices

2/3 cup margarine
2/3 cup sugar
Pinch of salt
1 egg
Grated zest of 1 lemon
1 3/4 cups whole wheat flour
1 1/4 cups stoneground flour
1/4 cup buckwheat flour
3 3/4 tsps baking powder
Margarine for greasing
1 1/2 lb apples
1 1/2 tbsps sesame seeds
1/3 cup raisins
1/2 cup almonds, chopped
1/2 cup ground almonds

1 Beat the margarine with the sugar, salt, egg and lemon juice until light and fluffy. Sift together the flour and baking powder, and stir a few spoonfuls into the cake mixture. Sprinkle the remainder over the top and rub in with your fingertips to a crumb consistency. Divide into two servings. Turn one portion into a greased 10-inch cake pan with a removable base.

smooth dough. Chill for 30 minutes.

2 Line a deep 10-inch pie pan with a removable base. Bake the pastry case blind in a preheated oven, 400°-425°F, for 15 minutes.

3 Meanwhile, whisk the egg yolks with the sugar until light and fluffy. Add the lemon juice and rum and grate in the large apple.

Whisk the egg whites until stiff, and pile on top of the mixture. Sift over the buckwheat flour, add the almonds and carefully fold everything together. Pile into the cooked pastry case.

4 Halve and core the small apples, and score them in a fan shape. Arrange the apple halves on the almond mixture, cut side down, and brush with melted margarine.

5 Bake at 350°-400°F for a further 50 minutes. Dust immediately with powdered sugar.

CRANBERRY CAKE WITH MERINGUE

Makes approximately 24 servings

1 tbsp fresh yeast
½ cup lukewarm milk
¼ cup sugar
1¾ cups stone-ground and whole wheat flours, mixed
½ cup buckwheat flour
Pinch of salt
¼ cup ground almonds
¼ cup margarine, melted
Margarine for greasing

Topping
1lb cranberries

Meringue
3 egg whites
¾ cup powdered sugar
½ cup ground almonds

1 Crumble the yeast into the lukewarm milk, stir in a pinch of sugar, cover and leave in a warm place for about 10 minutes until frothy. Mix together the sugar, flour, salt, almonds and melted margarine, add the frothy yeast and knead to a smooth dough. Cover and leave in a warm place until doubled in size. Knead well and use to line a greased baking sheet.

2 Meanwhile, wash and pick over the cranberries. Spread over the dough and leave in warm place to rise again. Bake in a preheated oven, 425°F, for about 30 minutes.

3 Whisk the egg whites until stiff, then whisk in the powdered sugar and almonds. Spread this meringue on the cooked cake and either place under the broiler to brown or put into the oven at 475°F for 6 minutes.

APRICOT AND WALNUT CAKE

Makes approximately 12 servings

1 cup margarine
1 cup sugar
3 tsps vanilla sugar
4 eggs
3-4 tsps cinnamon
½ tsp ground cloves
½ tsp ground ginger
¾ cup whole wheat flour
1¼ cups stone-ground flour
1¼ tbsps clear honey
¾ cup walnut halves
½ cup fresh apricots, stoned and cut into chunks
Margarine for greasing
Milk chocolate couverture

1 Beat the margarine, sugar, vanilla sugar and eggs until light and fluffy. Sift together the flour, baking powder, cinnamon, cloves and ginger and fold into the mixture, together with the honey. Reserve six walnut halves for decoration and roughly chop remainder. Cut the apricots into large chunks and stir them into the mixture with the chopped walnut.
2 Turn the mixture into a greased 12-inch loaf pan and bake in a preheated oven, 350°F, for about 75 minutes.
3 Leave to cool, then coat with the melted chocolate couverture and decorate with the reserved walnut halves.

RED BERRY SAVARIN

Makes approximately 12 servings

½oz fresh yeast
7½ tbsps lukewarm milk
¼ cup sugar
¾ cup stone-ground flour
½ cup whole wheat flour
½ cup buckwheat flour
½ cup rye flour
Pinch of salt
⅓ cup margarine, melted
5 eggs, beaten
Margarine for greasing

Filling

4 cups red berries (raspberries, strawberries etc), frozen
⅔ cup sugar
Grated zest of ½ lemon
1¼ tbsps lemon juice
7½ tbsps rum

1 Crumble the yeast into the lukewarm milk, and stir in 1 tbsp sugar and 1 tbsp flour. Cover and leave in a warm place for about 15 minutes until frothy. Put the flour, salt, sugar, margarine and beaten eggs into a bowl, and add the frothy yeast. Mix to a dough and knead thoroughly. Cover and leave to rise in a warm place. Knock down and press into a greased 10-inch tube or ring pan. The dough should only come half way up the sides of the pan.
2 Leave to rise again in a warm place. Bake in a preheated oven, 350°-400°F, for about 30 minutes.
3 Meanwhile, sprinkle half the sugar over the berries. Leave to soften. Drain, reserving the juice. Mix the juice with the remaining sugar, the lemon peel and juice and boil until the mixture is reduced to about ½ cup. Add the rum. Turn the savarin out while still hot, slice in half horizontally and soak with the juice mixture, reserving a little.

4 Turn the berries in the reserved juice, then use to sandwich together the two savarin layers.

ALMOND AND HAZELNUT CAKE

Makes approximately 16 servings

½ cup margarine
½ cup sugar
1 tsp cinnamon
3 tsps vanilla sugar
2 eggs
½ cup hazelnuts or filberts, chopped
½ cup almond kernels, chopped
½ cup whole wheat flour
¾ cup stone-ground flour
2½ tsps baking powder
⅓ cup whipped cream
2½ tbsps rum
Margarine for greasing

1 Beat the margarine, sugar, cinnamon, vanilla sugar and eggs until light and fluffy. Fold in the nuts. Sift the flour with the baking powder and gradually fold into the mixture, together with the cream. Stir in the rum.
2 Turn the mixture into a greased 10-inch loaf pan and bake in a preheated oven, 350°F, for about 45 minutes.

HAZELNUT LAYER CAKE

Makes approximately 12 servings

8 eggs, separated
2½ cups sugar
Pinch of salt
2 cups hazelnuts or filberts, ground
2½ tsps baking powder
¾ cup stone-ground flour
Margarine for greasing

Filling

2 cups whipping cream
3¾ tbsps sugar
Hazelnut or filbert kernels for decoration

1 Whisk the egg yolks with the sugar until very light and foamy. Whisk the egg whites with the salt until stiff, and pile onto the beaten yolks. Sprinkle with the ground nuts and sift over the flour and the baking powder. Carefully fold everything together.
2 Grease the base of a 10½-inch cake pan with a removable base. Turn the mixture into it and bake in a preheated oven, 350°-400°F, for 30-35 minutes. Turn off the heat and leave to stand in the oven 5-10 minutes.
3 Carefully remove the cake from the oven and leave to cool in the pan, to avoid the risk of collapse.
4 Whip the cream with the sugar. Slice the cake horizontally into three layers and sandwich together using most of the cream. Decorate with the remaining cream and nut kernels.

DRIED FRUIT CAKE

Makes approximately 16 servings

½ cup prunes, stoned and diced
½ cup dried apricots, diced
½ cup dried pears, diced
1¼ cups margarine
1¼ cups sugar
Pinch of salt
6 eggs
Grated zest of 1 lemon
3 tsps vanilla sugar
1¾ cups stone-ground flour
½ cup whole wheat flour
¾ cup oatmeal
3 tsps baking powder
¾ cup walnuts, chopped
Margarine for greasing

1 Dice the prunes, apricots and pears.
2 Beat the margarine, sugar, salt, eggs. lemon peel and vanilla sugar until light and fluffy.
3 Mix the flours with the oatmeal, and sprinkle a little over the fruit. Mix the remainder with the baking powder and stir into the cake mixture. Fold in the dried fruit and the nuts.
4 Turn into a greased 8½-inch gugelhupf or tube pan and bake in a preheated oven, 350°F for 60-70 minutes.

CHERRY CAKE

Makes approximately 16 servings

4 eggs, separated
½ cup sugar
1 tsp cinnamon
Grated zest of 1 lemon
¾ cup whole wheat zwieback, grated
1lb jar sour cherries, stoned
Margarine for greasing

1 Whisk the egg yolks, sugar, cinnamon and lemon peel until light and fluffy. Whisk the egg whites until stiff and fold into the mixture. Grate the zwieback and fold in, together with the drained cherries.
2 Grease and line a 10-inch loaf pan, turn the mixture into it and bake in a preheated oven, 350°F, for 50-60 minutes.

MIXED NUT LOAF

Makes approximately 16 servings

1 cup margarine
1 cup sugar
4 eggs
Pinch of salt
¾ cup mixed nuts, ground
3¾ tbsps milk
Grated zest of ½ lemon
2 tsps baking powder
2 cups stone-ground flour

1 Beat the margarine and sugar until light and fluffy, then gradually beat in the eggs. Stir in the salt, nuts, milk and lemon peel. Sift together the flour and baking powder and fold in.
2 Turn the mixture into a greased 10-inch loaf pan and bake in a preheated oven, 350°F, for 50-60 minutes.

BANANA AND WALNUT CAKE

Makes approximately 12 servings

¾ cup stone-ground flour
½ cup buckwheat flour
2½ tsps baking powder
½ cup oatmeal
1 cup walnuts, chopped
½ cup oat flakes
2 small bananas
2 eggs
⅓ cup margarine
¾ cup sugar
2½ tbsps clear honey
Margarine for greasing
Powdered sugar for dusting

1 Sift the flour with the baking powder and cinnamon. Mix with the oatmeal, chopped walnuts and oat flakes.
2 Mash the bananas with a fork and mix with the eggs. Heat the margarine, sugar and honey, stirring continuously, until the sugar has dissolved. Leave to cool, then stir into the banana mixture. Beat into the flour mixture.
3 Turn into a greased 8½-inch tube or ring pan and bake in a preheated oven, 350°F, for about 50 minutes.
4 Dust the cooled cake with powdered sugar.

BROWN BREAD CAKE

Makes approximately 12 servings

3 eggs, separated
½ cup powdered sugar
¼ cup chocolate, grated
½ cup ground almonds
½ tsp cinnamon
Good pinch of ground cloves
Aniseed

Grated zest of 1 lemon
¾ cup wheat bread, dried and crumbled
½ cup red wine
Margarine for greasing
5 tbsps cranberries
⅔ cup cream, whipped

1 Whisk the egg yolks with the powdered sugar until light and fluffy. Stir in the chocolate, almonds, cinnamon, cloves, aniseed and lemon peel. Whisk the egg whites until stiff and fold in carefully. Dry the bread out in the oven and crumble finely. Mix with the red wine and stir into the mixture.
2 Turn the mixture into a greased 10½-inch cake pan with a removable base and bake in a preheated oven, 350°F, for about 60 minutes.
3 Fold the cranberries into the whipped cream and spread over the cake.

COFFEE IN THE AFTERNOON

For a change, serve coffee and freshly baked, delicious-smelling cakes and cookies in the afternoon, Continental style. Here are a variety of sweet temptations.

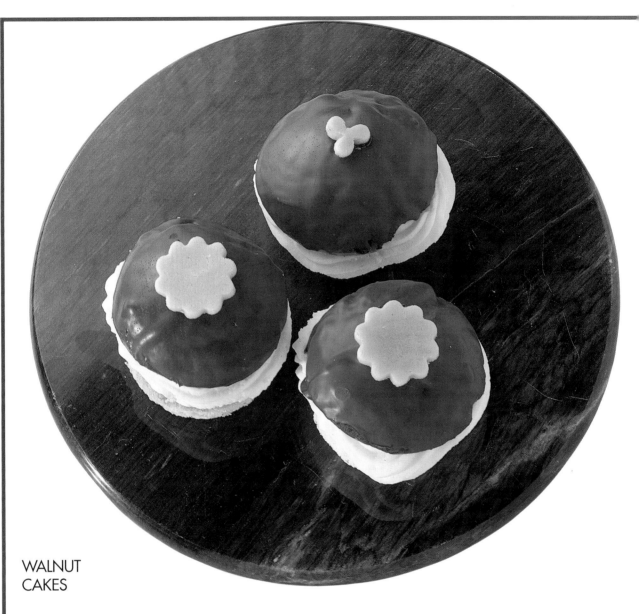

WALNUT CAKES

Makes 12

5 eggs, separated
3¾ tbsps warm water
1⅓ cups powdered sugar
Pinch of salt
½ cup walnuts, ground
½ cup flour
⅓ cup cornstarch
1¼ tsps baking powder
Coconut oil
Sugar for dusting

Filling
¾ cup whipping cream
1 tbsp sugar
3 tsps vanilla sugar

½ cup walnuts, ground

Icing
⅔ cup powdered sugar
1¼ tbsps cocoa
2½ tbsps rum
1¼ tbsps water
1 tbsp coconut oil

For Decoration
½ cup marzipan paste

1 Whisk the egg yolks with the lukewarm water, sugar and a pinch of salt until light and fluffy. Whisk the egg whites until stiff, and pile on top of the mixture. Fold in the walnuts. Sift over the flour, cornstarch and baking powder. Using a balloon whisk, carefully fold everything together.
2 Grease and line a baking sheet. Spread the mixture onto it and bake in a preheated oven, 400°-425°F, for approximately 15 minutes.

3 Sprinkle sugar over the cooked cake. With the aid of a dish towel, turn it over, remove the paper and leave to cool. Cut into 2½-in rounds.
4 Whip the cream with the sugar and vanilla sugar until stiff. Fold in the walnuts. Use the walnut cream to sandwich together the cake rounds in pairs.
5 Mix together the powdered sugar, cocoa, rum, water and coconut oil and frost the cakes.
6 Roll out the marzipan paste, cut out shapes, and use to decorate the cakes.

ECLAIRS WITH VANILLA CREAM

Makes 10 éclairs

¾ cup water
Pinch of salt
3 tsps vanilla sugar
¼ cup margarine
1 cup flour
4 eggs
Margarine for greasing
Flour

Icing

¾ cup powdered sugar
2½ tsps cocoa powder
2½ tbsps water

Filling

¾ cup milk
1 vanilla pod
Pinch of salt
3 eggs, separated
⅓ cup sugar
6 sheets gelatine
½ cup cream, whipped

1 Bring the water, salt, vanilla sugar and margarine to the boil, remove from the heat, and add the flour. Using a wooden spoon, beat the mixture until smooth, return to the heat and continue beating until the mixture comes away from the sides of the saucepan in a ball. Beat in one egg immediately, then gradually beat in the remaining eggs.
2 Use an icing bag to pipe double finger-length strips onto a greased and floured baking sheet. Bake in a preheated oven, 425°F for about 30 minutes.
3 Mix the icing ingredients. Split the éclairs immediately and ice the tops while still warm. Leave to cool.
4 Bring the milk, vanilla pod and salt to the boil and let it cool. Remove the pod. Whisk the egg yolks and sugar until light and fluffy, then add the vanilla milk. Soak the gelatine, dissolve it over a low heat, stir into the mixture and leave until half set.
5 Whisk the egg whites until stiff, and fold into the half-set mixture, together with the whipped cream. When filling has set to a firm consistency, pipe into the bottom half of each éclair. Replace the tops.

POPPY SEED CAKE

Makes approximately 24 servings

5 cups flour
2 packets dried yeast
²⁄₃ cup sugar
²⁄₃ cup margarine, melted
²⁄₃ cup lukewarm milk

Filling

2¹⁄₂ cups milk
1 cup margarine
2 cups poppy seeds
1 cup raisins
²⁄₃ cup semolina
1 tsp lemon juice
4 egg whites

1 Put the flour in a bowl, make a well in the center and add the yeast, melted margarine and lukewarm milk. Mix well. Knead to a smooth dough, cover and leave in a warm place until dough has doubled in size.
2 Knead again. Roll out thinly and use to line a well greased 12-inch x 16-inch baking sheet.
3 Meanwhile, bring the filling milk to the boil. Stir in the sugar, margarine, poppy seeds, raisins and semolina. Allow to boil for a moment. Set aside to cool. Stir in the lemon juice; whisk the egg whites until stiff and fold in.
4 Spread the filling over the dough and bake in a preheated oven, 400°-425°F, for about 35-40 minutes.

CRUNCHY CREAM WAFFLES

Makes approximately 12 servings

1¹⁄₃ cups whipping cream
1¹⁄₄ cups flour
Pinch of salt
¹⁄₂ cup water
¹⁄₄ cup margarine
3³⁄₄ tsps vanilla sugar
Margarine for greasing
Powdered sugar for dusting

1 Whip the cream until stiff Mix together the flour, salt and water. Quickly fold in the whipped cream. Chill in the refrigerator for 1 hour.
2 Melt the margarine and leave to cool. Stir into the mixture together with the vanilla sugar.
3 Brush the waffle iron with margarine. Cook the waffle mixture 2-3 tbsps at a time for about 2-3 minutes.
4 Dust the waffles with powdered sugar before serving.

DECORATIVE APPLE CAKES

Makes approximately 8 servings

Mixture

⅔ cup margarine
1 cup sugar
3 tsps vanilla sugar
6 eggs
2 packets chocolate pudding mix
¾ cup flour
¾ cup ground almonds
2 small apples, peeled and grated
Margarine for greasing
Breadcrumbs

For Decoration

½ cup marzipan paste
Food coloring
Chocolate leaves and sugar flowers

1 Cream the margarine until fluffy, beat in the sugar, vanilla sugar, eggs, chocolate pudding mix, flour and almonds. Finally, add the grated apple.

2 Grease two apple-shaped molds or deep muffin pans, and sprinkle with breadcrumbs. Turn mixture in and bake in a preheated oven, 350°-400°F, for about 45 minutes. Leave to cool in the moulds for abut 5 minutes, then turn out.

3 Color the marzipan paste, roll out between two sheets of foil and wrap round the cakes. Decorate with leaves and flowers.

ICED HAZELNUT TRIANGLES

Makes approximately 30 triangles

1 cup margarine
1 cup sugar
3 tbsps vanilla sugar
Pinch of salt
3 eggs
5 tbsps whipping cream
1¾ cups hazelnuts or filberts, ground
2 cups flour
3¾ tsps baking powder
Margarine for greasing

Icing

1½ cups powdered sugar
2½ tsps instant coffee powder
2-3 tbsps water
30 hazelnut or filbert kernels for decoration

1 Mix together the margarine, sugar, vanilla sugar, salt, eggs, whipping cream, nuts, flour and baking powder.

2 Spread the mixture onto a greased baking sheet and bake in a preheated oven, 400°F, for 15-20 minutes.

3 Meanwhile, mix together the powdered sugar, coffee powder and water. Cut the cake into 30 small triangular pieces, while it is still warm. Ice each triangle and decorate with a hazelnut kernel.

FRANKFURT RING LAYER CAKE

Makes approximately 20 servings

1 cup margarine	
1 cup sugar	
2 cups flour	
Pinch of salt	
4 eggs	
1½ tsps baking powder	
Margarine for greasing	

Filling

1¾ cups milk	
¼ cup sugar	
1 packet cake filling, vanilla flavor	
1 cup margarine	

For Decoration

1¼ cups almonds, chopped	
¼ cup sugar	
1 tbsp margarine	
Whipped cream	
10 cocktail cherries	

1 Beat the margarine, sugar, salt and eggs until light and fluffy. Sift together the flour and baking powder and fold in gradually.

2 Turn into a greased 10½-inch ring or tube pan and bake in a preheated oven, 350°F, for about 60 minutes. Turn out onto a wire rack and leave to cool. Slice the ring horizontally into three.

3 Make up the vanilla filling with the milk and sugar according to the packet instructions. Sandwich together the layers with half this cream. Cover the top and sides of the finished cake with the remaining cream.

4 Cook the almonds in sugar and margarine until a golden brown; remove from pan immediately. Leave to cool, then sprinkle over the cake. Decorate with piped whipped cream and cocktail cherries.

ALMOND AND CINNAMON PASTRIES

Makes approximately 20 pastries

1 cup well-chilled margarine
½ cup flour
1½oz fresh yeast
⅔ cup lukewarm milk
¼ cup sugar
4 cups flour
Pinch of salt
¼ cup cinnamon sugar
¼ cup almonds, chopped
Egg yolk

1 Cut the margarine into the flour using a palette knife. Knead quickly to a smooth dough and chill in the refrigerator.
2 Make a yeast dough from the yeast, milk, sugar, flour, salt, margarine and egg. Leave to rise in a warm place until doubled in size. Knead again, and roll out to a rectangle about 8 inches x 12 inches.
3 Roll out the first dough between two sheets of wax paper to a rectangle 8 inches x 6 inches. Lay this over one half of the yeast dough rectangle. Fold the empty half over and roll out again to form a rectangle as above. Fold the dough inhalf, short sides together. Cover

and chill for about 10 minutes.
4 Turn the dough so the fold is on the right-hand side. Roll out into a rectangle and fold in half as above. Chill. Repeat the process once more. FInally, roll out the dough to a rectangle about

16 inches x 20 inches, brush with milk and sprinkle with a mixture of the cinnamon sugar and almonds.
5 Roll up the dough lengthwise and cut into ¾-inch-thick slices. Line a baking sheet with wax paper, arrange the pastries on it and leave in a warm place to rise again. Bake in a preheated oven, 400°F, for 10-15 minutes. Mix the egg yolk with a little water and brush over the pastries shortly before the end of cooking time.

Variation:
Cut the final dough rectangle into squares of about 4½in. Place a piece of marzipan in the center of each square, and fold up like an envelope. Leave to rise, then bake.

over. Sprinkle with salt, and knead well to a smooth dough. Leave to stand in a bowl of cold water for 2-3 hours.

2 Drain the dough well and roll out on a floured pastry board to about ⅛ inch thick. Cut out 2½-inch rounds. Place on a greased baking sheet. Preheat the oven for just the time it takes to reach 400°-425°F and bake for 15-20 minutes.

3 Mix the powdered sugar and vanilla sugar and sprinkle over the thaler while they are still warm.

Variation:
The thaler can also be coated with lemon icing, or sandwiched together with jam.

YEAST THALER

Makes 30-40 cakes

3¼ cups flour
1 cup coconut butter
½oz fresh yeast
½ cup lukewarm milk
Salt
Coconut butter
¾ cup powdered sugar
7½ tsps vanilla sugar

1 Sift the flour into a bowl. Using a kitchen knife, flake the coconut butter very finely into the flour. Crumble the yeast into the lukewarm milk and pour

BRANDY CUP-CAKES

Makes 16 cakes

1 packet yellow cake mix with nuts

Filling

½ cup dried apricots
½ cup water
10 tbsps apricot brandy
1 cup marzipan paste
⅓ cup powdered sugar

Icing

7oz chocolate couverture
Hazelnut or filbert kernels for decoration

1 Make up the cake mix according to the packet instructions and turn into 3-inch cup cake liners. Bake in a preheated oven, 350°F, for about 20 minutes.

2 Boil the apricots with the water and 6 tbsps of the apricot brandy for about 10 minutes, then leave them to cool in the liquid. Drain and dice. Knead together the marzipan paste, powdered sugar, remaining brandy and the apricots. Stir in about 4 tbsps of the apricot liquid to make a mixture of spreading consistency.

3 Slice the cup-cakes horizontally, then sandwich them together again with the marzipan mixture.

4 Melt the chocolate couverture over hot water. Ice the cup-cakes and decorate with nut kernels.

LEMON CREAM CAKES

Makes approximately 10 cakes

4 eggs, separated
2½ tbsps lukewarm water
⅔ cup sugar
3 tsps vanilla sugar
Pinch of salt
¾ cup flour
½ cup cornstarch
Good pinch of baking powder
Margarine for greasing
Sugar for dusting

Filling
¼ cup cornstarch
¾ cup milk
¼ cup sugar
Grated zest of 1 lemon
Pinch of salt
3¾ tbsps lemon juice
⅓ cup margarine

Icing
¾ cup powdered sugar
3¾ tbsps lemon juice
2½ tbsps coconut oil
Glacé cherries for decoration

1 Whisk the egg yolks with the lukewarm water, sugar, vanilla sugar and salt until light and fluffy. Whisk the egg whites until stiff, and pile onto the yolk mixture. Sift over the flour, cornstarch and baking powder. Using a balloon whisk, carefully fold everything together.

2 Grease a baking sheet and line it with wax paper. Spread in the mixture and bake in a preheated oven, 400°-425°F for 10-15 minutes. Dust with sugar, turn out onto a wire cooling rack, remove the paper and leave the sponge to cool. Cut into 2½-inch rounds.

3 Mix the cornstarch with a little milk. Bring the rest of the milk, the sugar, lemon zest and salt to the boil, and thicken with the cornstarch. Remove from the heat, stir in the lemon juice and leave to cool. Cream the margarine until light and fluffy, then gradually stir the cornstarch mixture into it. Use to sandwich the sponge rounds together in pairs.

4 Mix together the powdered sugar, lemon juice and coconut oil. Use to ice the cakes, then decorate with the glacé cherries.

STRAWBERRY CREAM ROLL

Makes 16 servings

4 eggs, separated
3¾ tbsps warm water
½ cup sugar
3-4 tsps vanilla sugar
¼ cup margarine, melted and cooled
½ cup cornstarch
1¼ tsps baking powder
1½ tbsps ground almonds
Margarine for greasing
Sugar for dusting

Filling

1 cup strawberries
3 tsps vanilla sugar
1¼ cups whipping cream
¼ cup powdered sugar
5 sheets gelatine

1 Beat the egg yolks, water, sugar and vanilla sugar to a thick, creamy consistency, then stir in the melted and cooled margarine. Whisk the egg whites until very stiff. Pile onto the yolk mixture. Sift the flour, cornstarch, baking powder and almonds, over the egg whites. Carefully fold everything together.
2 Grease a baking sheet and line with wax paper. Spread in the sponge mixture, and bake in a preheated oven, 425°F, for 10-12 minutes.
3 Turn the cooked sponge out onto a dish towel sprinkled with sugar, remove the paper, roll the cake up with the towel and leave to cool.

4 Wash, clean and halve the strawberries, sprinkle with vanilla sugar and leave to soften.
5 Whip the cream with the sugar. Soak the gelatine, dissolve it over a low heat and leave to cool. Carefully fold into the whipped cream. As soon as the mixture starts to set, fold in the strawberries.
6 Unroll the sponge, spread it with the strawberry cream and roll up again. Chill until set.

FESTIVE MERINGUES

Makes 24

2 egg whites
Pinch of salt
½ cup sugar
2 cups whipping cream
3 tsps vanilla sugar
¼ cup cashew nuts, chopped
1 tbsp candied cherries, finely chopped

1 Whisk the egg whites with the salt until stiff, working quickly so they do not dry out. Gradually whisk in half the sugar, then carefully fold in the remainder.
2 Line a baking sheet with wax paper. Using two teaspoons spoon 48 little mounds of meringue onto the sheet, or pipe out rosettes of the mixture. Put in a very low oven, 250°F, for 1 hour, or until quite dry but still light in color.

400°-425°F, for 15 minutes. Reduce the heat to 350°F.

3 Meanwhile, purée the drained apricots with the jam and ¼ cup of the almonds.

4 Stone and finely chop the dates. Whisk the egg whites until very stiff. Mix the sugar, the remaining almonds and the dates together, and fold into the egg whites. Spoon the mixture into an icing bag fitted with a plain nozzle. Pipe a strip along each long edge of the cooked cake base. Pipe a series of parallel lines every 2 inches. Fill the gaps with the apricot mixture.

5 Return to the oven for a further 15-20 minutes. When cold, cut between the parallel lines and then into 2-inch-wide slices.

3 Shortly before serving, whip the cream with the vanilla sugar, and use to sandwich the meringues together in pairs. Decorate the cream filling with the nuts and cherries.

APRICOT AND DATE SLICES

Makes 35 slices

2½ cups flour
¾ cup powdered sugar
Pith of 2 vanilla pods
Pinch of salt
1 cup margarine
1 egg yolk
9 tbsps whipping cream
Margarine for greasing

Topping

1 7oz can tinned apricots
5 tbsps apricot jam
1¼ cups ground almonds
1 cup dates
4 egg whites
⅔ cup powdered sugar

1 Mix together the flour, powdered sugar, vanilla, salt, margarine, egg yolk and cream to a smooth dough. Chill.

2 Roll the dough out and use to line a greased baking sheet. Bake in a preheated oven,

RASPBERRY SPONGE ROLL

Makes approximately 16 servings

4 eggs, separated
3¾ tbsps warm water
½ cup sugar
½ cup flour
¾ cup cornstarch
Margarine for greasing
Sugar for dusting

Filling
¾ cup whipping cream
1 tbsp sugar
2 cups raspberries
¼ cup sugar

1 Whisk the egg yolks, warm water and sugar until light and fluffy. Whisk the egg whites until stiff, and pile onto the yolk mixture. Sift over the flour and cornstarch, then carefully fold everything together.
2 Line a greased baking sheet with wax paper, grease the paper and spread the mixture over it. Bake in a preheated oven, 425°F, for 10-12 minutes.
3 Sprinkle sugar onto a dish towel, quickly turn the hot sponge base out onto it, remove the wax paper and roll up the sponge in the dish towel.
4 Whip the cream with the sugar. Mash the raspberries with a fork, sweeten with the sugar and fold into the whipped cream. Unroll the sponge roll, spread with the raspberry cream, roll up again and chill.

NOUGAT ROLL

Makes approximately 16 servings

4 eggs, separated
3¾ tbsps warm water
½ cup sugar
Salt
½ cup cornstarch
¾ cup flour

Good pinch baking powder
Sugar for dusting

Filling
⅓ cup coconut oil
3½oz chocolate nougat
2 eggs
¾ cup powdered sugar
Salt
Cinnamon
¼ cup candied lemon peel

¼ cup candied orange peel
½ cup hazelnuts or filberts, chopped
3-4 tbsps rum

1 Whisk the egg yolks with the water, sugar and salt until light and fluffy. Whisk the egg whites until stiff, then pile onto the yolk mixture. Sift over the flour, cornstarch and baking powder.

CAKE ROLL WITH KIRSCH

Makes approximately 20 servings

4 eggs, separated
3¾ tbsps warm water
½ cup sugar
3 tsps vanilla sugar
Pinch of salt
¾ cup flour
½ cup cornstarch
Good pinch baking powder
Margarine for greasing
Sugar for dusting

Filling
1 sheet red gelatine
5 sheets gelatine
¾ cup kirsch
¾ cup whipping cream
1 tbsp sugar

1 Whisk the egg yolks, water, sugar, vanilla sugar and salt until light and fluffy. Whisk the egg whites until stiff and pile onto the yolk mixture. Sift over the flour, cornstarch and baking powder and carefully fold everything together.

2 Line a greased baking sheet with wax paper and spread the mixture into it. Bake in a preheated oven, 400°-425°F, for 10-12 minutes.
3 Sprinkle a dish towel with sugar and quickly turn the cooked sponge out onto it. Remove the wax paper, and roll up the sponge in the dish towel. Leave to cool.
4 Soak and then dissolve the gelatine over hot water, and stir it into the kirsch. Leave to set. Whip the cream with the sugar

Using a balloon whisk, carefully fold everything together.

2 Line a baking sheet with wax paper, spread the mixture over it, and bake in a preheated oven, 400°F, for about 12 minutes.

3 Sprinkle sugar onto a dish towel, and turn the sponge out onto it. Remove the paper and quickly roll up the sponge in the towel. Leave to cool.

4 Melt the nougat over a pan of warm water, and stir in the coconut oil. Whisk the eggs with the powdered sugar, salt and cinnamon until light and foamy. Chop the candied peel and the nuts, and stir into the slightly cooled nougat mixture together with the rum. Leave in the refrigerator until it is firm enough to spread.

5 Unroll the sponge roll carefully, spread with the nougat mixture, roll up again and chill.

until thick, then carefully fold into the half-set kirsch mixture.

5 Unroll the sponge carefully, spread with the filling and roll up again. Cover and leave in the refrigerator until the filling has set.

CHOCOLATE SADDLE

Makes 16 servings

4 eggs
⅔ cup sugar
3 tsps vanilla sugar
Pinch of salt
2½ tbsps rum
Grated zest of ½ lemon
½ cup margarine, melted
¾ cup flour
¾ cup wheat semolina
¾ cornstarch
½ cup cocoa powder

2½ tsps baking powder
Margarine for greasing
Flour

Icing

1 cup powdered sugar
2½ tbsps cocoa powder
½ tsp cinnamon
1-2 tbsps rum

1 Whisk the eggs, sugar, vanilla sugar and salt until light and fluffy. Whisk in the rum, lemon peel and margarine. Sift together the flour and baking powder, mix with the semolina, cornstarch and cocoa powder and gradually fold into the cake mixture. If the mixture is too stiff, add a little milk.

2 Grease a loaf pan and sprinkle with flour. Turn the mixture into this and bake in a preheated oven, 350°F, for abut 60 minutes. Turn out onto a wire cooling rack and leave to cool.

3 Mix together the powdered sugar, coco powder, cinnamon and rum until smooth and use to ice the cake.

MARZIPAN CAKE

Makes approximately 24 servings

½oz fresh yeast
⅔ cup lukewarm milk
½ cup sugar
4 cups flour
Pinch of salt
½ cup margarine, melted and cooled
1 egg, beaten
Margarine for greasing

Filling

1 cup marzipan paste
1 egg white, stiffly beaten
1 tbsp sugar
1 tbsp margarine, melted
1 tbsp cinnamon sugar

Glaze

1 egg yolk
1¼ tbsps water

1 Crumble the yeast into the milk, and stir in a pinch of sugar and flour. Cover and leave in a warm place for 5-10 minutes until frothy. Put the flour, sugar, salt, margarine and beaten egg into a bowl. Mix in the frothy yeast to make a dough, knead thoroughly and leave in a warm place to rise.
2 Mix the marzipan paste, stiffly-beaten egg white and sugar to a smooth paste.
3 Knead the yeast dough again, and divide it into three

portions. Roll out one portion and use to line a greased baking pan. Spread with the marzipan mixture.

4 Roll out the second portion of dough to fit the pan, lay it on top of the marzipan, pressing

the edges together lightly.
5 Brush with the melted margarine and sprinkle with cinnamon sugar. Roll out the third portion to fit, and place it on top, pressing down lightly. Leave in a warm place to rise again. Carefully score a diamond pattern on the top. Mix the egg yolk with the water and brush over the dough, to glaze.

6 Brush lightly with the egg and water a second time, then bake in a preheated oven, 350°F, for about 30 minutes. Cut the cold cake into slices.

STRAWBERRY CREAM PUFFS

Makes approximately 10 puffs

¾ cup water
Pinch of salt
3 tsps vanilla sugar
¼ cup margarine
½ cup flour
4 eggs
Margarine for greasing
Flour

Filling

1lb strawberries
1½ cups whipping cream
¼ cup sugar
Powdered sugar for dusting

1 Bring the water, salt, vanilla sugar and margarine to the boil. Remove from heat, pour in all the flour, and beat with a wooden spoon until smooth. Return to the heat and continue beating until the mixture shrinks away from the sides of the pot in a ball. Beat in the eggs one by one.
2 Grease a baking sheet, dust with flour and spoon about ten small dollops of mixture onto it. Bake in a preheated oven, 425°F, for about 30 minutes.
3 Cut the puffs in half immediately, then leave to cool.
4 Mash the strawberries. Whip the cream with the sugar until thick and fold in the strawberries. Fill

the bottom half of each puff with cream and replace the tops. Dust with powdered sugar.

MINCE PIES

Makes approximately 20 pies

Filling

¾ cup apples, chopped
¾ cup raisins
⅓ cup currants
1 tbsp margarine
⅓ cup brown sugar
1 tsp cinnamon
½ tsp ground cloves
½ tsp nutmeg, grated
⅓ cup brandy
Juice and grated zest of 1 lemon

Pastry

4 cups flour
⅔ cup sugar
Pinch of salt
1¼ cups margarine
2 eggs
Margarine for greasing
Egg white
Powdered sugar for dusting

1 Simmer all the filling ingredients together for about 30 minutes, uncovered, over a low heat, stirring occasionally, then leave to cool.
2 Make a dough from the pastry ingredients. Chill.
3 Roll out the dough and cut out 3-inch rounds. Put half of these on a greased baking sheet and heap a little of the filling on each one. Cut small star shapes out of the centers of the remaining rounds. Brush the outer rings with egg white and press them onto the mince pie bases. Top with the star-shaped 'lids'. Brush with egg white and bake at 400°-425°F, for about 25 minutes until golden brown. When cool, dust with powdered sugar.

ANTOINETTE SLICES

Makes approximately 48 slices

1/4 cup candied lemon peel
1/4 cup candied orange peel
1/2 cup raisins
3-4 tbsps cognac, lightly heated
1/2 cup walnut kernels, chopped
1/2 cup pistachio nuts, chopped
1/2 cup margarine
1/2 cup brown sugar
Pinch of salt
3 eggs
2 tsps ground cardamom
2 tsps ground red pepper
2 tsps ground cinnamon
1/2 cup clear honey
1 3/4 cups flour

Icing
3/4 cup powdered sugar
5 tbsps brandy
Walnut kernels, to decorate

1 Roughly chop the lemon and orange peel and the raisins. Turn them in the brandy, cover and leave to soak. Roughly chop the walnuts and pistachios.
2 Cream the margarine, sugar and salt until light and fluffy. Beat in the eggs one at a time, then the spices, honey and flour. Fold in the brandy-soaked fruit and the nuts with a spoon.
3 Line an 8-inch x 6-inch baking sheet with wax paper. Turn the mixture into this and smooth the top. Bake in a preheated oven, 350°-400°F for 15-20 minutes.
4 Mix together the powdered sugar and brandy and use to ice the warm cake. Decorate with walnut kernels. When cold, cut into small pieces.

VICARAGE TEA PARTY STOLLEN

Makes approximately 20 servings

1oz fresh yeast
2/3 cup lukewarm milk
1/3 cup sugar
4 cups flour
1/2 tsp salt
1/2 cup margarine, melted and cooled
Grated zest of 1 lemon
2 eggs, beaten
Margarine for greasing

Filling
1/2 cup marzipan paste
1/2 cup brown sugar
1 cup hazelnuts or filberts, ground
2 egg whites
2 1/2 tbsps rum
1/2 tsp cinnamon
1 egg yolk
1 1/4 tbsp water

Icing
3/4 cup powdered sugar
1-2 tbsps lemon juice
1/4 cup crushed glazed nuts

1 Crumble the yeast into the milk and stir in a pinch of sugar and flour. Leave covered in a warm place for 10-15 minutes until frothy. Mix together the flour, sugar, salt, margarine, lemon zest, eggs and frothy yeast and knead well, preferably using an electric mixer with pastry hook. Cover with foil and leave in a warm place until doubled in size.

For Soaking

½ cup rum

¼ cup ground almonds

⅓ cup milk

Filling

¾ cup whipping cream

1 tbsp sugar

Chopped pistachio nuts, to decorate

1 Crumble the yeast into milk, and stir in a pinch of sugar and flour. Cover and leave in a warm place for 5-10 minutes until frothy. Put the sugar, flour, salt, lemon zest, cooled margarine and the beaten eggs into a bowl, and add the frothy yeast. Mix well together and knead the dough thoroughly. Cover with foil and leave in a warm place until doubled in size.

2 Knead the risen dough again. Grease eight small ring moulds and divide the mixture between them. Bake in a preheated oven, 400°F, for 30-35 minutes.

3 Leaving the hot babas in their moulds, moisten them generously with the rum and leave to cool. Meanwhile, bring the almonds to the boil in the milk. When cold, use to moisten the babas.

4 Whip the cream with the sugar until thick. Unmould the babas, split and fill with the cream, then sprinkle with the pistachio.

---

2 Meanwhile, mix together the marzipan paste, sugar, nuts, egg whites, rum and cinnamon. Roll out the risen yeast dough to an 18-inch square, and spread with the filling, leaving the edges clear. Brush the edges with egg yolk mixed with water. Roll up the stollen, pressing the edges together.

3 Place on a greased baking sheet and score the top of the stollen at 1-inch intervals. Leave to rise in a warm place for 15 minutes, then bake in a preheated oven, 400°-425°F, for 30 minutes. Brush with beaten egg yolk 10 minutes before the end of baking time.

4 Mix together the powdered sugar and lemon juice and spread over cooked stollen. Sprinkle with crushed glazed nuts.

RUSSIAN BABAS

Makes 8 babas

¾oz fresh yeast

⅔ cup lukewarm milk

⅓ cup sugar

2 cups flour

Pinch of salt

Grated zest of 1 lemon

½ cup margarine, melted

4 eggs, beaten

Margarine for greasing

TREAT YOURSELF

A variety of cakes for different occasions: little cakes for two, fun cakes for children's parties, and quick treats for the unexpected guest.

MANDARIN CAKE

Makes approximately 6 servings

½ cup margarine

½ cup sugar

Pinch of salt

2 eggs

1 cup flour

1¼ tsps baking powder

Grated zest of 1 lemon

2½ tbsps lemon juice

14oz can mandarins

2½ tbsps flour

Margarine for greasing

Breadcrumbs

Icing

½ cup powdered sugar

3¾ tbsps orange liqueur or orange juice

1 Cream the margarine, sugar, salt and eggs until light and fluffy. Sift together the flour and baking powder, and fold into the mixture. Add the lemon zest and juice. Drain the mandarins, dip the segments in flour and fold them into the mixture.
2 Grease a 6-inch loaf pan. Sprinkle with breadcrumbs and turn the mixture into it. Bake in a preheated oven, 350°F for 45-50 minutes.
3 Mix the powdered sugar with the orange liqueur and spread over the finished cake.

CREAM PUFFS

Makes 4 puffs

1lb flakey pastry, frozen

Sugar

Filling

¾ cup cream, whipped

Sugar

1-2 sheets gelatine

1 Thaw the pastry, and roll it out on a pastry board dusted with sugar. Cut out eight ovals measuring 3 in long.
2 Rinse a baking sheet with cold water, and place the pastry puffs on it, sugared side up. Prick each puff several times with a tooth pick and leave to stand for 15 minutes. Bake in a preheated oven, 450°-475°F, for 8-10 minutes.
3 Sweeten the cream to taste. Dissolve the gelatine and fold it into the whipped cream. Use this to sandwich together the pastry ovals in pairs.

MARBLE CAKE

Makes 6 servings

⅔ cup margarine
⅔ cup sugar
1½ tsps vanilla sugar
Pinch of salt
3 eggs
1½ cups flour
1¼ tsps baking powder
Margarine for greasing
Breadcrumbs
¼ cup cocoa
2½ tbsps rum

1 Cream the margarine, sugar, vanilla sugar, salt and eggs until light and fluffy. Sift together the flour and baking powder, and fold into the mixture.

2 Grease a 6-inch ring or tube pan, sprinkle with breadcrumbs and turn half the mixture into it. Stir the cocoa and rum into the remaining mixture and turn into the pan. Swirl a fork through both mixtures to create a marble effect. Bake the cake in a pre-heated oven, 350°F, for 45-50 minutes.

LITTLE CHOCOLATE CAKES

Makes 10 cakes

Sponge Mixture

½ cup margarine
½ cup sugar
Pinch of salt
4 eggs
7oz milk chocolate
1¼ tsps baking powder
1 cup flour
Margarine for greasing

Icing

1 cup powdered sugar
3¾ tbsps lemon juice
2½ tbsps rum

1 Cream the margarine, sugar salt and eggs until light and fluffy. Break up the chocolate, pour hot water over and leave to stand for a few minutes. Drain and stir the chocolate into the cake mixture. Sift together the flour and baking powder and fold into the mixture.

2 Turn the mixture into greased muffin or cup cake pans. Bake in a preheated oven, 350°F, for about 20 minutes.

3 Meanwhile, mix together the powdered sugar, lemon juice and rum until smooth. Spread this over the warm cakes.

GRAPE CAKE

Makes approximately 6 servings

Pastry Base
⅔ cup flour
¾ tbsp sugar
1 tbsp shredded coconut
1½ tbsps margarine
Margarine for greasing
2½ tbsps apricot jam

Sponge Mixture
2 eggs, separated
2½ tbsps warm water
⅓ cup sugar
⅓ cup flour
⅓ cup cornstarch
Good pinch of baking powder

Topping
1lb black grapes
½ cup white wine
2 tbsps water
2½ tbsps sugar
1¼ heaped tbsps cornstarch
¾ cup whipping cream
1 tbsp sugar

1 Make a pastry dough from the flour, sugar, coconut and margarine. Knead and chill for about 30 minutes. Roll out and use to line a greased 7-inch flan or pie pan with a removable base. Bake in a preheated oven, 425°F, for 10 minutes. Reduce the heat to 400°F.

2 Whisk the egg yolks with the water and sugar until light and fluffy. Whisk the egg whites until stiff, and fold them into the mixture. Sift over the flour, cornstarch and baking powder. Using a balloon whisk, carefully fold everything together.

3 Spread the apricot jam over the cooked pastry base, pour the sponge mixture on top and return to the oven for 25 minutes. Leave to cool, then slice through the sponge top horizontally.

4 Halve and deseed grapes and arrange them on the bottom layer of the sponge, reserving about fifteen for decoration. Put the wine, water, sugar and cornstarch into a saucepan, mix well, and bring slowly to the boil, stirring continuously. Pour carefully over the grapes. Replace the second sponge layer.

5 Whip the cream with the sugar, spread it over the cake and decorate with the reserved grapes.

SNAIL RING

Makes approximately 8 servings

1 oz fresh yeast

½ cup lukewarm milk

1 tbsp sugar

2 cups flour

Pinch of salt

⅓ cup margarine, melted and cooled

Filling

½ cup raisins

2½ tbsps rum

⅓ cup margarine

⅓ cup sugar

1¼ tsps cinnamon

¼ cup ground almonds

1 tbsp chopped candied orange peel

1 tbsp chopped candied lemon peel

Margarine, melted

1¼ tbsps apricot jam

1 Crumble the yeast into the milk, adding a pinch of flour and sugar. Leave in a warm place until frothy. Put the flour, sugar, salt and margarine into a bowl, mix in the frothy yeast and knead thoroughly to a smooth dough. Set aside in a warm place to rise.
2 Soak the raisins in the rum.

3 Roll out the risen dough to a thickness of ¼ inch. Spread with the margarine. Mix together the sugar, cinnamon, almonds, orange and lemon peel and soaked raisins and spread over the dough, pressing in lightly.
4 Cut the dough into 3-inch-wide strips and fold each one in half lengthwise. Roll up one strip and place it in the center of a greased 6-inch cake pan with a removable base, open edge downwards. Curl the re-maining strips around this center, brushing the outer edge of each one with a little melted margarine, and working until the tin is full.
5 Leave to rise in a warm place for 15 minutes, then bake in a preheated oven, 400°F, for 30-35 minutes.
6 While the cake is still warm, spread with the apricot jam, to glaze.

QUEEN CAKE

Makes approximately 6 servings

Sponge Mixture
½ cup margarine
½ cup sugar
1½ tsps vanilla sugar
Pinch of salt
2 eggs
1 cup flour
¼ cup cornstarch
1¼ tsps baking powder
¼ cup candied lemon peel
¼ cup chopped almonds
1¼ tbsps rum
Margarine for greasing

Icing
½ cup powdered sugar
1¼ tbsps lemon juice
1 tbsp mixed candied peel
6 glacé cherries

1 Cream together the margarine, sugar, vanilla sugar, salt and eggs until light and fluffy. Sift together the flour, cornstarch and baking powder, then fold into the mixture. Stir in the finely-chopped lemon peel, the almonds and rum.
2 Turn the mixture into a greased 6-inch cake pan with a removable base and bake in a preheated oven, 350°F, for about 40 minutes.
3 Mix together the powdered sugar, lemon juice and water and spread over the warm cake. Decorate the cake with the chopped mixed peel and the glacé cherries.

JELLIED FRUIT ROUND

Makes approximately 6 servings

Pastry
¾ cup flour
Pinch of salt
¼ cup powdered sugar
2 tsps vanilla sugar
1½ tbsps margarine
Margarine for greasing

Topping
¼ cup marzipan paste
2½ tbsps rum
1 12oz bottle sour cherries
1 large banana
2½ tbsps lemon juice
2 packets quick-setting gelatine
¼ cup flaked almonds, toasted

1 Make the pastry dough and chill.
2 Roll the pastry out thinly and use to line a greased 6-inch flan or pie pan with a removable base. Bake in a preheated oven, 400°F, for about 15 minutes.
3 Mix the marzipan paste with the rum and spread over the pastry base.
4 Drain the sour cherries thoroughly, reserving the juice. Peel and slice the banana, sprinkling the slices with lemon juice. Arrange the fruit on the marzipan.
5 Make up the quick-setting gelatine according to the

packet instructions, using the reserved cherry juice and additional water as required. Pour over the fruit. Sprinkle with the toasted flaked almonds.

FRENCH WAFFLES

Makes 12 waffles

1 packet frozen flakey pastry, thawed
Sugar
¾ cup whipping cream
Sugar to taste
1-2 sheets gelatine
2¼ tbsps raspberry jam

1 Roll the pastry out to a rectangle about 7 inches x 19 inches.
2 Cut out 2½-inch rounds. Sprinkle the pastry board with sugar and roll out each round to an oblong shape about 4 in long. Rinse a baking sheet in cold water, and place the pastries on it, sugary side up. Prick each pastry several times with a tooth pick and leave to stand for 15 minutes. Bake in a preheated oven, 450°-475°F, for about 8 minutes. Leave until completely cold.
3 Whip the cream and sweeten to taste. Stir in the dissolved gelatine.
4 Spread jam on the unsugared side of each waffle and sandwich together in pairs

with the whipped cream.

BUTTERFLY CAKES

Makes approximately 6 cakes

⅓ cup margarine
½ cup sugar
3 tsps vanilla sugar
Pinch of salt
2 eggs
1¾ cups flour
1 tsp baking powder
½ tsp cinnamon
Grated zest of 1 lemon

Filling
¾ cup whipping cream
1 tbsp sugar
½ cup hazelnuts or filberts, ground
Powdered sugar for dusting

1 Cream together the margarine, sugar, vanilla sugar and salt until light and fluffy. Beat in the eggs, one by one. Sift together the flour, baking powder and cinnamon. Stir in the lemon zest and fold into the cake mixture.
2 Divide between six cup cake or muffin pans or wax paper cases and bake in a preheated oven, 350°F, for about 25 minutes. Leave to cool.
3 Whip the cream with the sugar until thick, then carefully fold in the nuts. Slice the top off each cake and cut each top in half.
4 Pipe the cream onto each cake, then press the halved tops into the cream to form 'wings'. Dust with powdered sugar.

RASPBERRY ECLAIRS

Makes 5 éclairs

½ cup water
Pinch of salt
1½ tsps vanilla sugar
3 tbsps margarine
¾ cup flour
2 eggs
Margarine for greasing
Flour

Filling

1 cup raspberries
1½ tsps vanilla sugar
1½ tbsps sugar
1 cup whipping cream
Powdered sugar for dusting

1 Bring the water, salt, vanilla sugar and margarine to the boil. Remove from heat, add the flour and beat until smooth. Return the pan to the heat and continue beating until the mixture comes away from the sides of the saucepan in a ball. Remove from the heat and beat in one egg. Beat in the remaining eggs one by one.

2 Sprinkle a greased baking sheet with flour. Put the mixture into an icing bag fitted with a large nozzle and pipe five strips about 4 in long onto the sheet.

3 Bake in a preheated oven, 425°F, for about 30 minutes. Using scissors, cut the tops off the éclairs as soon as they come out of the oven. Leave to go quite cold.

4 Wash, clean and halve the raspberries, sprinkle with the vanilla sugar and 2 tsps of the sugar and leave to soften. Whip the cream with the remaining sugar and spoon into an icing bag.

5 Spread the drained raspberries over the bottom half of each éclair, pipe the cream over and replace the tops.

LEMON PIE

Makes approximately 6 servings

Pastry
¾ cup flour	
Pinch of salt	
¼ cup margarine	
1-2 tbsps water	
Margarine for greasing	

Filling
2 eggs, separated	
⅓ cup sugar	
Grated zest of ½ lemon	
6 tsps lemon juice	
Powdered sugar for dusting	

1 Use the flour, salt, margarine and water to make a basic short pastry.

2 Roll the pastry out and use to line a 7-inch greased pie pan. Prick the base several times with a fork and bake blind in a preheated oven, 400°F, for 25-30 minutes. Reduce the heat to 350°F.

3 Whisk the egg yolks, 1 tbsp of the sugar, the lemon zest and juice together in a bowl over hot water until thick and creamy. Remove from the heat.

4 Whisk the egg whites with the remaining sugar until very stiff, then carefully fold them into the hot filling mixture.

5 Turn the filling into the hot pie base and return to the oven for a further 10 minutes. Dust with powdered sugar.

NUTTY CHOCOLATE CAKE

Makes approximately 8 servings

Sponge Mixture
½ cup baking chocolate	
⅓ cup margarine	
⅓ cup sugar	
2 eggs, separated	
½ tbsp hazelnuts or filberts, ground	
1½ heaped tbsps flour	
Good pinch of baking powder	
Margarine for greasing	

Filling
2 tbsps apricot jam	
1 cup whipping cream	
1 tsp vanilla sugar	
10 small macaroons, to decorate	

1 Melt the chocolate in a bowl over a pan of hot water. Cream the margarine with the sugar, reserving 1 tbsp, until light and fluffy. Add the cooled chocolate, the egg yolks and nuts.

2 Whisk the egg whites with the remaining sugar until stiff and fold carefully into the chocolate mixture. Gently fold in the flour, sifted together with the baking powder.

3 Turn the mixture into a greased 7-inch cake pan with a removable base and bake in a preheated oven, 350°F, for about 30 minutes.

4 Slice the cake in half horizontally and spread each layer with apricot jam. Whip the cream with the vanilla sugar and use to sandwich together the cake layers. Decorate with the macaroons.

MOTHER'S DAY BUTTERFLY

Makes approximately 8 servings

3 cups flour
3 tsps baking powder
½ cup sugar
3 tsps vanilla sugar
Pinch of salt
Grated zest of 1 orange
½ cup margarine
4 eggs
2½ tbsps lemon juice
4 tbsps orange juice
Margarine for greasing

Icing

¼ cup powdered sugar
About 5 tbsps orange juice
Food coloring
Sugar letters
2 tbsps apricot jam

1 Sift together the flour and baking powder, add the rest of the cake ingredients and mix to a creamy consistency, using an electric mixer. Begin mixing at a low speed, then mix at the highest speed for not more than 1 minute.
2 Turn the mixture into an ovenproof butterfly mould and bake in a preheated oven, 400°F, for about 45 minutes.
3 Turn the cooked butterfly out of the mould and leave to cool.
4 Mix together the powdered sugar and orange juice and color as desired. Spread over the cake and leave to harden. Decorate the butterfly as desired with more icing and the jam.

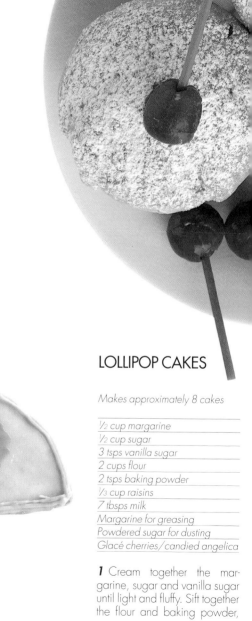

LOLLIPOP CAKES

Makes approximately 8 cakes

½ cup margarine
½ cup sugar
3 tsps vanilla sugar
2 cups flour
2 tsps baking powder
⅓ cup raisins
7 tbsps milk
Margarine for greasing
Powdered sugar for dusting
Glacé cherries/candied angelica

1 Cream together the margarine, sugar and vanilla sugar until light and fluffy. Sift together the flour and baking powder,

MOTHER'S DAY HEART

Makes approximately 8 servings

1 cup margarine
1 cup sugar
3 tsps vanilla sugar
Pinch of salt
Grated zest of 1 orange
4 eggs
3 cups flour
3 tsps baking powder
2½ tbsps lemon juice
⅔ cup orange juice
Margarine for greasing

Icing

1 egg white
⅔ cup powdered sugar
Sugar flowers and leaves

1 Cream together the margarine, sugar, vanilla sugar, salt, orange zest and eggs until light and fluffy. Sift together the flour and baking powder and gradually fold into the mixture, alternating with the lemon and orange juice.

2 Turn the mixture into a heart-shaped cake pan and bake in a preheated oven, 350°F, for about 45 minutes.

3 Whisk the egg whites until stiff, then whisk in sufficient powdered sugar to achieve a piping consistency. Using an icing bag, decorate the cake with the icing as desired, finishing it off with the sugar flowers and leaves.

reserving a little flour for the raisins. Fold into the cake mixture. Add the milk. Turn the raisins in the reserved flour and fold into the mixture.

2 Grease an 8 cup muffin pan and divide the mixture evenly. Bake in a preheated oven, 350°F for about 45 minutes.

3 Once the cakes have cooled, dust them with powdered sugar and decorate with a lollipop, made from a glacé cherry and a stick of candied angelica.

Variation:
These cakes can also be iced with glacé icing.

CHILDREN'S FROGGY CAKES

Makes approximately 16

3 eggs, separated
2½ tbsps water
½ cup sugar
Pinch of salt
⅔ cup flour
½ cup cornstarch
3 tsps baking powder

Filling and Topping
1 packet vanilla pudding mix
Green food coloring
1 cup powdered sugar
1 tbsp cocoa powder
3-4 tbsps water
2½ tbsps coconut oil
M+M's to decorate

1 Whisk the egg yolks with the water, sugar and salt until light and foamy. Whisk the egg whites until stiff and pile them onto the yolk mixture. Sift over the flour, cornstarch and baking powder. Using a balloon whisk, carefully fold everything together.

2 Spoon the mixture into an icing bag fitted with a large, round nozzle and pipe into cupcake liners about 2½ inches in diameter. Bake in a preheated oven, 350°F for 15-20 minutes. Once cooled, slice each cake in half horizontally.

3 Make up the pudding according to the instructions and color with green food coloring. When almost set, spoon onto the cake bases.

4 Mix together the powdered sugar, cocoa powder, water and coconut oil until smooth and use to ice the tops. Add M+M's for eyes, pressing them into the soft icing. Replace the tops at an angle on top of the filling.

CARNIVAL MASKS

Makes approximately 15 cookies

Pastry

2½ cups flour
1 cup ground almonds
½ cup sugar
6 tsps vanilla sugar
1 level tsp cinnamon
1 egg
1 egg yolk
1 cup margarine, chilled

Icing

1 egg white
¾ cup powdered sugar
Food coloring
Chocolate couverture

1 Sift the flour onto a pastry board and add the almonds, sugar, vanilla sugar and cinnamon. Make a well in the center and put in the egg and egg yolk. Dot with the chilled margarine and mix quickly to a dough. Knead, wrap in foil and chill in the refrigerator for at least 1 hour.

2 Cut out cardboard patterns for the mask. Roll out the dough on a floured board to a thickness of about ¼ inch. Place the cardboard patterns on top, and cut out the masks.

3 Arrange the masks on a baking sheet lined with wax paper and bake in a preheated oven, 400°F, for 10-15 minutes. Leave to cool on a cooling rack.

4 Whisk the egg whites until stiff, then stir in the powdered sugar. Color the frosting as desired. Melt the chocolate couverture in a bowl over a pan of hot water. Draw fun faces on the masks with the icing and melted chocolate.

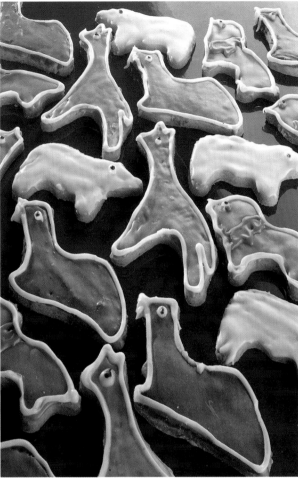

LEMON COCONUT ICE CAKE

Makes approximately 20 servings

1 cup coconut butter
1 cup powdered sugar
2 eggs
2½ tbsps lemon juice
Grated zest of 1 lemon
1 cup shredded coconut
8oz store bought chocolate cake, cut into about 30 squares
Gum drops, to decorate

1 Cream the coconut butter with the powdered sugar, eggs, lemon juice, lemon zest and coconut.

2 Line an 8-inch loaf pan with wax paper and fill with alternate layers of the coconut mixture and chocolate cake, ending with a layer of

the coconut mixture.
3 Chill in the refrigerator. Decorate with gum drops before serving.

ANIMAL SHAPES

Makes approximately 30 cookies

2 cups flour
Good pinch baking powder
¼ cup sugar
Pinch of salt
½ cup margarine
1 egg
Margarine for greasing

Icing

1 egg white
1½ cups powdered sugar
Food coloring

1 Mix together the flour, baking powder, sugar and salt on a pastry board. Dot with flakes of cold margarine and cut in with a palette knife. Add the egg and mix quickly to a smooth dough. Set aside in a cool place.

2 Roll out the pastry, cut out animal shapes and bake on a greased baking sheet at 425°F for about 5 minutes. Leave to cool.

3 Beat the egg white until stiff, and stir in the powdered sugar. Divide into servings, color and use to decorate the baked animal shapes.

CARAMEL CREAMS

Makes approximately 30 creams

½ cup sugar
¾ cup whipping cream
2 tbsps margarine
1 tsp clear honey
3 tsps vanilla sugar
1 tbsp cocoa powder
Vegetable oil for greasing

1 Melt the sugar in saucepan, stirring continuously, until the sugar has dissolved, but not colored. Add the whipping cream, bring to the boil, stirring continuously, and continue boiling for about 10 minutes until the mixture starts to thicken.

2 Add the margarine, honey, vanilla sugar and cocoa and continue boiling for a further 8-10 minutes until the mixture starts to shrink away from the bottom of the saucepan. Quickly pour into an oiled 8-inch loaf pan.
3 When the mixture is half set, cut it into small squares using a knife dipped in cold water.

PARTY CAKES

Makes approximately 16 cakes

1 cup margarine
1 cup sugar
4 eggs
3 cups flour
3 tsps baking powder
12 tbsps milk
7oz semi-sweet chocolate morsels
Margarine for greasing

Icing
10oz tub of choc frosting
M+M's, to decorate

1 Cream together the margarine, sugar and eggs until light and fluffy. Sift together the flour and baking powder and fold it in alternately with the milk. Fold in the chocolate morsels.
2 Grease 2, 8 cup muffin or cup cake pans, fill them with the mixture and bake in a pre-heated oven, 350°F, for 30-40 minutes. Turn out and leave to cool.
3 Cover with frosting. Decorate with M+M's, and more frosting, if desired.

FLOWERPOTS

Makes 4 pots

2½ cups flour
1 packet dried yeast
¼ cup sugar
½ tsp salt
⅓ cup softened margarine
1 egg
½ cup lukewarm milk
Jam
½ cup marzipan
¾ cup powdered sugar
Food coloring
Cake decorations, e.g. sugar flowers, leaves and letters

1 Mix together the flour and dried yeast in a bowl, add the remaining ingredients and mix everything together thoroughly until you have a soft smooth dough. Knead and leave to prove in a warm place for about 1 hour.

2 Grease four clean 3-inch earthenware flowerpots and line with wax paper, or substitute similar-sized ramekins. Fill each pot three-quarters full with the yeast mixture. Leave to rise in a warm place for a short while, brush with milk if desired, and bake in a preheated oven, 400°F, for about 20 minutes. Turn out and leave to cool.

3 Spread the jam all around the sides of each cake. Knead together the marzipan and powdered sugar and color as desired. Roll it out and cut into four wide strips. Press the strips around the outsides of the flowerpot cakes to form a decorative cover. Fold the upper edge of the paste slightly over the top of each cake and press down. Decorate with sugar flowers and leaves or sugar letters.

Note: If you find the marzipan pot covers too much work, use crêpe or tissue paper instead.

BACK-TO-SCHOOL GOODIES

Makes approximately 15 cookies

4 cups flour	
2 cups margarine	
2 small eggs	
2 egg yolks	
2 cups sugar	
6 tsps vanilla sugar	

Decoration

2 egg whites	
2½ cups powdered sugar	
Food coloring	

1 Make a firm dough from the first six ingredients and chill for about 30 minutes.

2 Cut out cardboard patterns of various school items, e.g. copy book, pencils, fountain pen, ruler, etc.

3 Roll out the dough to a thickness of ¼ inch-½ inch. Cut shapes out of the dough using the cardboard patterns. Line a baking sheet with wax paper, put the shapes on this and bake in a preheated oven, 400°F, for about 15 minutes. Place on a cooling rack to cool.

4 Whisk the egg whites until stiff, mix with the powdered sugar and divide into servings, coloring each portion differently as desired. Using an icing bag decorate the shapes as imaginatively as possible.

POPCORN LOLLIPOPS

Makes 8 lollipops

¼ cup popcorn (unsalted)	
½ cup sugar	
½ cup water	
2½ tbsps whipping cream	
⅓ cup chocolate	
2½ tbsps coconut oil	

1 Put the popcorn in a bowl. Heat the sugar in a saucepan until it has lightly caramelized. Carefully stir the water into the caramel. Add the cream and stir until the mixture drops thickly off a spoon. Pour this over the popcorn, stir in well, then leave for a short while.

2 Shape the mixture into balls with damp hands, spearing a few at a time onto long wooden kebab sticks. Leave to harden for a few hours in a tall container, such as a spaghetti jar.

3 Melt the chocolate, add the coconut oil and dip the lollipops in this to cover. Leave to harden.

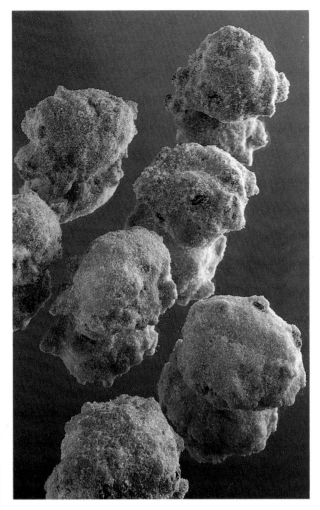

QUICK DOUGHNUTS

Makes approximately 18 doughnuts

1 cup margarine
¼ cup sugar
3 eggs
Pinch of salt
2 tsps baking powder
3 cups flour
½ cup water
½ cup raisins
Vegetable oil for deep-frying
Cinnamon sugar for dredging

1 Cream together the margarine, sugar, eggs and salt until light and fluffy. Sift together the flour and baking powder and fold in alternately with the water. Fold in the raisins.
2 Use a tablespoon to cut out doughnuts and deep-fry in small batches in the hot vegetable oil, 350°F, for 5-6 minutes. Drain and dredge with the cinnamon sugar.

DAMSON PARCELS

Makes approximately 10 parcels

8oz package frozen puff pastry, thawed
3 tbsps damson or plum jam
⅓ cup powdered sugar
1-2 tbsps lemon juice

1 Roll out the pastry and cut into about ten rectangles. Put 1 tsp damson or plum jam in the middle of each. Dampen the edges, fold two sides inwards, overlapping them slightly, and press the ends together tightly to seal.
2 Rinse a baking sheet in cold water and arrange the parcels

on it. Prick each one several times with a tooth pick and leave to stand for 15 minutes. Bake in a preheated oven, 450°-475°F, for 20-25 minutes.
3 Mix the powdered sugar with the lemon juice and use to frost the damson parcels.

WALNUT BALLS

Makes approximately 35 pieces

1 cup white chocolate
¾ cup powdered sugar
7½ tbsps kirsch, lightly warmed
1 cup walnut halves

1 Melt the chocolate in a bowl over a pan of hot water. Use a hand-held electric mixer to work in the sifted powdered sugar and the lightly-warmed kirsch.
2 Leave the mixture to cool, then shape into nut-sized balls.

3 Sandwich mixture together with walnut halves. Put into paper candy cups before serving.

CREAM CHEESE FRITTERS

Makes 12 fritters

2 tbsps margarine
2 tbsps sugar
3 tsps vanilla sugar
1 egg
Grated zest of 1 lemon
½ tsp salt
1 cup low fat cream cheese
2 level tsps baking powder
1 cup flour
Vegetable oil for deep-frying
Cinnamon sugar for dusting

1 Cream together the margarine, sugar, vanilla sugar and egg until light and fluffy. Add the lemon zest, salt and low fat cream cheese. Sift together the flour and baking powder and fold in.
2 Using two tablespoons, scoop 12 servings out of the mixture and deep-fry in the hot vegetable oil, 350°F, for about 5 minutes.
3 Sprinkle with cinnamon sugar and serve immediately.

JAM ROSETTES

Makes approximately 12 servings

⅔ cup margarine

½ cup sugar

2 eggs

1 egg yolk

¼ cup ground almonds

1 tsp cinnamon

½ cup whipping cream

4 cups flour

Finishing

1 egg white

Vegetable oil for deep-frying

Various jams

Powdered sugar for dusting

1 Cream the margarine and sugar until light and fluffy. Beat in the eggs and egg yolk, the almonds, cinnamon, cream and a little of the flour. Fold in the remaining flour and chill for 1 hour.

2 Roll the dough out to a thickness of ⅛ inch. Cut out rounds with a fluted 2½-inch cookie cutter. Brush the pastry rounds with egg white and stick together in threes, to form rosette shapes. Press down in the middle to make a hollow.

3 Deep-fry the rosettes in hot fat, 350°F, for 2-3 minutes on each side.

4 When cold, dust with powdered sugar and fill the centers with different kinds of jam.

APPLE PASTRIES

Makes 10

8oz package frozen puff pastry, thawed
4 apples, peeled and cored
Sugar
1½ tbsps almonds, chopped
1 tbsp raisins
2½ tbsps rum
Water
1 egg yolk
Sugar for dusting

1 Stew the peeled and cored apples with sugar to taste, the raisins, rum and a little water, if necessary. When just cooked but not disintegrated, set aside to cool.

2 Roll out the pastry and cut out ten squares. Spread a little of the apple mixture onto the center of each square. Dampen the pastry edges with water, fold them over, and press the ends to seal. Place the parcels, seam side up, on a baking sheet which has been rinsed in cold water. Score each pastry three times with a sharp knife.

3 Prick each pastry several times, brush with beaten egg yolk and leave to stand for 15

minutes. Sprinkle with sugar and bake in a preheated oven, 450°-475°F, for about 20 minutes.

ORANGE DUMPLINGS

Makes 4 dumplings

8oz package frozen puff pastry, thawed
4 small oranges
⅓ cup raisins
2 tbsps pistachios, peeled
2 tbsps flaked almonds
4 tbsps honey
2½ tbsps Grand Marnier
2 egg yolks
2 tbsps ground almonds

1 Peel the oranges carefully.

2 Mix the raisins with the coarsely-chopped pistachios, flaked almonds, honey and Grand Marnier.

3 Roll out the puff pastry into four 7-inch squares. Beat the egg yolk with 1 tbsp water, roll the oranges in it and then in the ground almonds and place one in the center of each pastry square. Spread the raisin mixture over the oranges.

4 Fold up the corners of the pastry squares over the oranges and press together to seal. Cut out decorative shapes from the pastry trimmings and stick onto the dumplings.

5 Brush the pastry with egg yolk and arrange on a foil-lined baking sheet; the foil is important as a lot of fruit juice escapes during cooking. Bake in a preheated oven, 450°-475°F, for about 20 minutes. Serve hot or cold.

LIGHTNING CRANBERRY CAKE

Makes 12 servings

1 cup powdered sugar
4 eggs, separated
2 cups ground almonds
Margarine for greasing

Topping
4 cups whipping cream
7oz can of cranberries
Flaked chocolate, to decorate

1 Whisk the powdered sugar and egg yolks until light and fluffy, stir in the almonds. Whisk the egg whites until stiff and fold in.
2 Grease the base of a 10-inch cake pan with a removable base. Turn the mixture into this and bake in a preheated oven, 350°F, for about 30 minutes. Turn out and leave to cool.
3 Whip the cream with the vanilla sugar. Reserve a little of the cream, and fold the drained cranberries into the remainder. Spread the cranberry cream over the cooled base. Decorate with the reserved cream and the flaked chocolate. Serve cold.

ICED JAM PUFFS

Makes 5 puffs

8oz package frozen puff pastry, thawed
2 tbsps jam
2 tbsps powdered sugar
1 tbsp water

1 Roll out the pastry and cut into five rectangles. Put 2 tsps of jam in the center of each. Dampen the edges and fold them over lengthwise. Press edges to-gether to seal and make five cuts on the closed side of each puff.
2 Prick each puff several times with a tooth pick. Rinse a baking sheet in cold water and place the jam puffs on it. Leave to stand for 15 minutes. Bake in a preheated oven, 450°-475°F, for 20-25 minutes.
3 Mix the powdered sugar with the water and frost the jam puffs while they are still warm.

Note: If you would prefer to have ten small jam puffs, simply halve the pastry rectangles and fill each with 1 tsp jam.

MARZIPAN POCKETS

Makes 15 servings

1lb package frozen puff pastry, thawed
1 cup marzipan or almond paste
2 tbsps powdered sugar
5 tbsps kirsch
1 egg, separated
1 tbsp water

1 Blend the marzipan or almond paste with the kirsch and the powdered sugar.
2 Roll out the pastry and cut out fifteen 4½-inch rounds. Heap a little of the marzipan filling onto one half of each pastry round, brush the pastry edges with egg white, fold the empty half over and press the edges together firmly to seal.
3 Mix the egg yolk with the water and brush over the pastries to glaze. Decorate with pastry shapes made from the trimmings and glaze with egg and water. Rinse a baking sheet in cold water, arrange the pastries on it and bake in a preheated oven, 400°-425°F, for 20-25 minutes until golden brown.

Note: The pastry pockets may be filled with a variety of sweet or savory fillings.

CHEESY CUSHIONS

Makes 10

1lb package frozen puff pastry, thawed
1 cup low fat creamed cottage cheese
Grated zest of 1 lemon
1 tbsp lemon juice
2 tbsps sugar
1 tbsp hazelnut or filbert kernels, ground
¼ cup raisins
Egg white
Vegetable oil for deep-frying
Powdered sugar

1 Mix together the cheese, lemon zest, lemon juice, sugar, nuts and raisins.
2 Roll out the pastry and cut out ten rectangles 4½ inches x 6 inches. Heap a little cheese mixture onto one half of each rectangle, brush the edges of the pastry with egg white, fold the empty pastry half over and press the edges together well to seal.
3 Deep-fry in hot vegetable oil, 350°F, for 10-15 minutes. Drain and dust with powdered sugar.

Note: These pastries should be eaten the day they are made.

TIRAMISU

Makes approximately 6 servings

2 tsps espresso coffee powder
½ cup water, boiling
6 egg yolks
⅔ cup sugar
1½ cups full fat cream cheese
½ cup low fat creamed cottage cheese
5 tbsps coffee liqueur
5oz lady's fingers
Cocoa powder

1 Dissolve the espresso coffee in the boiling water and leave to cool. Whisk the egg yolks with the sugar over a pan of hot water until thick and creamy. Add the cheeses, stirring in alternate tablespoonfuls of cream cheese and cottage cheese. Mix the espresso with the coffee liqueur.

2 Line a rectangular dish with lady's fingers, sprinkle with the coffee and cover with a layer of the cream cheese mixture, followed by another layer of lady's fingers sprinkled with coffee. Repeat the layers until all the sponge fingers and cheese mixture have been used up. Finish with a layer of the cheese mixture. Leave overnight to set.

3 Before serving, dust the Tiramisu with cocoa powder.

COTTAGE CHEESE CAKE

Makes approximately 12 servings

1 cup margarine
1½ cups sugar
6 egg yolks
4 cups low fat creamed cottage cheese
Juice and grated zest of 1 lemon
2 packets vanilla pudding mix
¼ cup chopped pistachios
5 egg whites
Margarine for greasing
5-6 tbsps grated zwieback
1 egg yolk
1-2 tbsps evaporated milk

1 Beat the margarine, sugar and egg yolks until thick and creamy. Stir in the cheese, lemon juice and zest, pudding mix and pistachios. Whisk the egg whites until stiff and fold into the mixture.

2 Grease the base of a 10-inch cake pan with a removable base and sprinkle thickly with the grated zwieback. Turn the cheese mixture into this.

3 Mix the egg yolk with the evaporated milk and brush over the top. Bake in a preheated oven, 300°F, for 75-80 minutes.

NUTTY CHEESECAKE

Makes approximately 20 servings

2/3 cup margarine
1/2 cup sugar
Pinch of salt
5 eggs
1 cup creamed cottage cheese
1 cup nougat
1 cup hazelnuts or filberts, ground
1/2 cup hazelnuts or filberts, chopped
1 3/4 cups flour
2 tsps baking powder
Margarine for greasing
Fine breadcrumbs
Powdered sugar for dusting

1 Beat the margarine, sugar and salt until light and fluffy, then beat in the eggs one by one. Melt the nougat, drain the cheese, mix them together, then fold into the cheesecake mixture. Fold in the nuts and the flour, sifted together with the baking powder.

2 Grease a 9-inch cake pan with a removable base and sprinkle with breadcrumbs. Turn the mixture into this. Bake in a preheated oven, 350°F, for 60-70 minutes.

3 Leave to cool, then dust with powdered sugar.

CREAMY LEMON CHEESECAKE

Makes approximately 12 servings

1 cup Graham crackers
2/3 cup margarine
1 packet (4 1/2 oz) lemon jello
3/4 cup boiling water
1 1/2 cups cream cheese
2 cups low fat creamed cottage cheese
1 cup sugar
6 tsps vanilla sugar
2 tbsps orange liqueur
1 1/2 cups whipping cream
Grated chocolate

1 Crumble the Graham crackers finely. Slightly warm the margarine and mix it well with the cracker crumbs. Turn two-thirds of this mixture into a flan or pie pan with a removable base, pressing it down well to line the bottom of the pan.

2 Melt the jello in the boiling water and leave until it is beginning to set. Mix the cream cheese, cottage cheese, sugar, vanilla sugar and liqueur and stir into the jello. Whip the cream until stiff and fold it in.

3 Sprinkle the top of the cheesecake with the remaining Graham crackers and finish with grated chocolate.

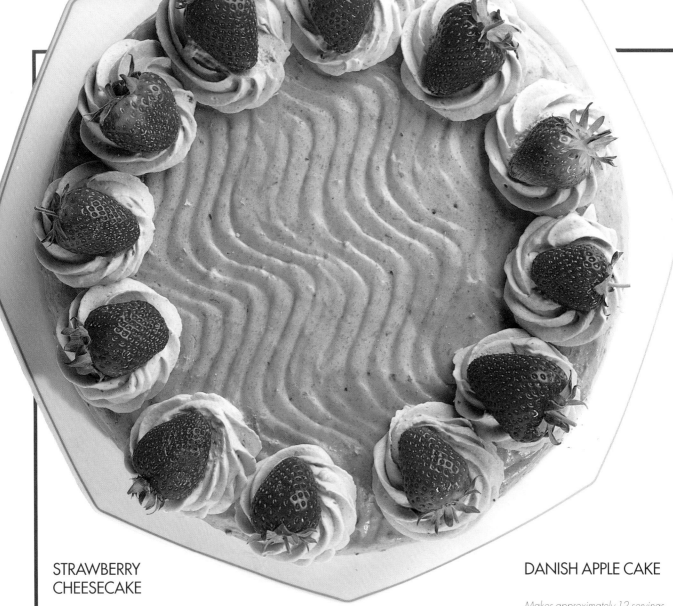

STRAWBERRY CHEESECAKE

Makes approximately 12 servings

½ cup margarine
½ cup sugar
3 tsps vanilla sugar
Grated zest of ½ lemon
3 eggs
1 cup flour
½ tsp baking powder
Margarine for greasing

Topping

2½ cups frozen strawberries, thawed
3 cups low fat creamed cottage cheese
1 cup sugar
3 tsps vanilla sugar
Grated zest of 1 lemon
½ cup lemon juice

12 sheets gelatine
2 sheets red gelatine
1 cup cream, whipped
7 tbsps kirsch

1 Cream together the margarine, sugar, vanilla sugar, salt, lemon zest and eggs until light and fluffy. Sift together the flour and baking powder and fold it gradually into the mixture.
2 Turn the mixture into a greased 9½-inch flan or pie pan with a removable base and bake in a preheated oven, 350°F for about 45 minutes. Turn the cake out and leave to cool.

3 Mash the strawberries and mix them into the cheese, with the sugar, vanilla sugar, lemon juice and zest.
4 Soak the gelatine, dissolve it over a low heat, then stir it into the strawberry mixture. Set aside to cool. When half set, fold it into the whipped cream.
5 Slice the cooled cake in half horizontally and sprinkle kirsch over each layer. Sandwich the layers together with half of the strawberry cheese mixture. Spread the rest over the top and sides of the cake. Decorate as desired.

DANISH APPLE CAKE

Makes approximately 12 servings

3lb cooking apples
½ cup white wine
2 tbsps lemon juice
Grated zest of ½ lemon
1 cup sugar
½ cup raisins
9oz zwieback
6 tsps vanilla sugar
½ cup margarine
Margarine for greasing
½ cup cream, whipped

1 Peel and core the apples and cut them into medium-sized wedges. Bring the wine to the boil with the lemon juice and zest and ½ cup of the sugar. Stew the apples in this over a low heat until they are soft but retain their shape. Carefully fold in the raisins and leave to cool.

2 Crush the zwieback with a rolling pin. Mix them with the vanilla sugar, the remaining sugar and the margarine. In two batches, spread the mixture onto a baking sheet and toast lightly. Leave to cool.

3 Grease a 9½-inch flan or pie pan with a removable base. Fill with alternate layers of toasted zwieback and apple, starting and finishing with a layer of zwieback. Press each layer down with a spatula. Leave to soften for several hours.

4 Turn out the apple cake and decorate with whipped cream.

APRICOT CHEESECAKE

Makes approximately 12 servings

2 cups flour
Good pinch of baking powder
½ cup margarine
2½ tbsps sugar
1 egg
Margarine for greasing

Topping

1½ tbsps ground almonds
14oz can apricots
½ cup margarine
1 cup sugar
3 eggs
3 cups low fat creamed cottage cheese

1 packet vanilla pudding mix
1 tsp lemon juice
1 egg yolk
Water

1 Mix the flour, baking powder, margarine, sugar and egg to a smooth dough.

2 Roll out a generous half of the dough and use to line a greased 9½-inch flan or pie pan with a removable base. Sprinkle over the ground almonds.

3 Drain the apricots. Beat together the margarine, sugar, eggs, cheese, pudding mix and lemon juice.

4 Spread the apricots over the pastry base and pile the cheese mixture on top, smoothing it over evenly.

5 Roll out the remaining dough and use a pastry wheel to cut it into ½-inch-wide strips. Weave the strips into a lattice over the top of the cheesecake. Bake the cheesecake in a preheated, oven 350°-400°F for 60-70 minutes. Beat the egg yolk with the water and brush this over the cheesecake after 50 minutes. Finish baking.

6 Leave the cheesecake to cool in the tin and turn out when cold.

SUMMER CHEESECAKE

Makes approximately 12 servings

1¼ cups flour
¼ cup margarine
1 tbsp sugar
Pinch of salt
1 egg yolk
1¼ tbsps milk
Margarine for greasing

Topping

3 egg yolks
⅔ cup sugar
3 tsps vanilla sugar
2 cups creamed cottage cheese
Juice from 1 lemon
8 sheets gelatine
4 egg whites
¾ cup whipping cream
1½lbs fresh strawberries, washed
and picked over

1 Make a short pastry dough using the flour, margarine, sugar, salt, egg yolk and milk. Mix well, then knead and chill for several hours. Roll out the pastry and use to line a greased 9½-inch flan or pie pan with a removable base. Bake in a pre-heated oven, 400°-425°F, for about 20 minutes. Leave to cool.
2 Turn the cooled pastry base out onto a cake dish and re-place the ring part of the tin over.
3 Whisk the egg yolks, sugar and vanilla sugar until light and fluffy, then add the cheese and lemon juice. Soak the gelatine, dissolve it over low heat and mix it into the cheese mixture.
4 Whisk the egg whites until stiff and whip the cream until thick. Fold them into the half-set cheese mixture. Spread the base of the cake with the straw-berries, reserving some for dec-oration. Pour the cheese mixture over and leave overnight in the refrigerator to set. Decorate with the reserved strawberries.

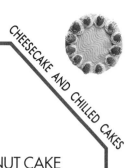

COOKIE LAYER CAKE

Makes approximately 20 servings

| ¾ cup coconut butter |
| 2 eggs |
| ½ cup powdered sugar |
| Pinch of salt |
| 2 tbsps cocoa powder |
| 1¼ tsps instant coffee |
| 1¼ tsps hot water |
| 3 tbsps ground almonds |
| 25 plain firm cookies |
| Gum drops, almonds, etc., to decorate |

1 Melt the coconut butter and leave to cool. Whisk the eggs, powdered sugar, salt and cocoa powder until light and fluffy. Mix the coffee with the hot water and add to the mixture together with the almonds. Mix in the coconut butter.
2 Line an 8-inch loaf pan with wax paper. Fill with alternate layers of chocolate mixture and cookies, beginning and ending with a chocolate layer.
3 Before the top layer of chocolate mixture has hardened, dec-

orate as desired, then chill before serving.

COCONUT CAKE

Makes approximately 12 servings

| 2 cups coconut butter |
| 4 eggs |
| 2 cups powdered sugar |
| 5 tbsps lemon juice |
| 2½ cups shredded coconut |
| 2 packets lady's fingers |
| Gum drops, to decorate |

1 Melt the coconut butter and leave to cool. Whisk the eggs and powdered sugar until light and fluffy, add the lemon juice and coconut and slowly stir in the coconut butter.
2 Line a greased 8½-inch cake pan with wax paper and fill with alternate layers of coconut mixture and lady's fingers arranged in a star pattern. Finish with a layer of coconut mixture.
3 Decorate the cake with lady's fingers and gum drops. Chill for at least half a day before serving.

BAKING FOR FESTIVE OCCASIONS

Here are some original ideas and some old favorites for Christmas, Easter and many other festive occasions.

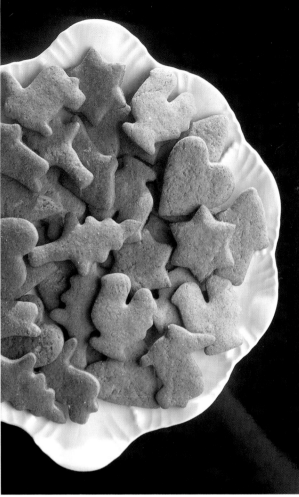

ADVENT ROSES

Makes 20 cookies

2 cups flour
Pinch of salt
½ cup powdered sugar
7 tbsps margarine
Margarine for greasing

Topping
1 egg yolk
3 tbsps flaked almonds
3½ tbsps orange jam

1 Mix the flour, salt, powdered sugar and margarine to a dough. Chill.
2 Roll the dough out and cut out round flower shapes.
3 Mix the egg yolk with a little water and brush over half the pastry flowers. Press the egged surface onto the flaked almonds. Turn right side up and arrange the flowers on a greased baking sheet, setting aside the plain pastry flowers. Bake in a preheated oven, 400°F, for about 10 minutes.
4 Bake the plain pastry flowers in the same way. Leave to cool.
5 Sandwich the plain and almond-decorated flowers together with a little jam.

GOLDEN SYRUP COOKIES

Makes approximately 80 cookies

¼ cup karo syrup
½ cup sugar
½ cup margarine
3 cups flour
1 level tsp baking powder
Good pinch ground cloves
2½ tsps cardamom
2½ tsps cinnamon
Grated zest of ½ lemon
2-3 tbsps water
Margarine for greasing

1 Heat the syrup, sugar and margarine until the sugar has dissolved.
2 Sift together the flour, baking powder, cloves, cardamom and cinnamon. Add the lemon zest and the cooled syrup mixture and mix together well, adding a little water if necessary. Leave until cold.
3 Roll the dough out. Cut out into hearts, stars, animal shapes, etc. Arrange on a greased baking sheet and bake in a preheated oven, 425°F for 10 minutes.

PEANUT COOKIES

Makes approximately 70 cookies

½ cup margarine
¾ cup sugar
3¾ tsps vanilla sugar
1 egg
¾ cup unsalted peanuts, ground
1¼ tsps baking powder
1½ cups flour
Peanuts, to decorate
Margarine for greasing

1 Cream the margarine until light, then gradually beat in the sugar, vanilla sugar and egg, followed by the ground peanuts and the flour, sifted with baking powder.
2 Chill for about 60 minutes in the refrigerator. Shape into hazelnut-sized balls. Decorate with halved peanuts and place on a greased baking sheet, leaving space between.
3 Bake in a preheated oven, 400°F, for about 30 minutes.

SPECULOOS

Makes approximately 100 cookies

4 cups flour
2½ tsps cinnamon
1¼ tsps ground cloves
1¼ tsps cardamom
Good pinch of ground ginger
Good pinch of grated zest of orange
⅔ cup margarine, cut into small pieces
1 cup sugar
6 tsps vanilla sugar
1 egg
8¾ tbsps whipping cream
1¼ tsps bicarbonate of soda
Margarine for greasing

1 Sift the flour and spices onto a pastry board. Make a well in the middle and put in the margarine, sugar, vanilla sugar and egg. Add the cream with the bicarbonate of soda dissolved in it. Mix everything together to a smooth dough and chill.
2 Roll the dough out and cut into character shapes, e.g. Santa Claus, gnomes, fairies, nursery-rhyme characters, etc.
3 Place on a greased baking sheet and bake in a preheated oven, 400°-425°F, for 8-10 minutes.

BROWN AND WHITE COOKIES

Makes approximately 80 cookies

1 cup margarine
½ cup sugar
Pinch of salt
Pith of 1 vanilla pod
Good pinch of bicarbonate of soda
1¼ tsps water
3 cups flour
1 heaped tbsp flour
Margarine for greasing
2 tbsps hazelnut or filbert kernels
1 tbsp cocoa powder

1 Cream together the margarine, sugar, salt and vanilla until light and fluffy. Dissolve the bicarbonate of soda in the water and stir it into the mixture together with the flour.

2 Divide the dough into two portions. Knead the additional heaped tbsp of flour into one portion, shape into a roll and cut into about 40 slices. Roll these into balls and place on a greased baking sheet. Make a slight hollow in the center of each with your thumb and put a nut kernel in each hollow.

3 Mix the cocoa powder into the remaining dough, then proceed as before.

4 Bake the cookies in a preheated oven, 350°-400°F for 12-15 minutes. Make sure the light-colored cookies do not brown.

CONTINENTAL CHRISTMAS CAKE

Makes approximately 12 servings

1 cup flour
1½ tbsps sugar
1½ tbsps shredded coconut
⅓ cup margarine
2 tbsps apricot jam

Sponge Mixture

2 eggs, separated
2½ tbsps water
2½ tbsps sugar
½ cup flour
1 heaped tbsp cornstarch

Topping

1lb apples
¾ cup white wine
1½ tbsps sugar
Grated zest of 1 lemon
2 cups seedless white grapes
1 14oz can mandarins
2½ tbsps lemon juice
½ cup white wine
¼ cup sugar
3 packets quick-setting gelatine
¾ cup cream, whipped

1 Make a pastry dough from the flour, sugar, coconut and margarine. Knead, roll out and use to line a 9½-inch cake pan with a removable base. Prick the pastry base in several places with a fork and bake in a preheated oven, 425°F, for about 15 minutes.

2 Meanwhile, whisk the egg yolks, water and sugar until thick and creamy. Whisk the egg whites until stiff, and pile on top of the mixture. Sift the flour and cornstarch over the egg whites and carefully fold everything together.

3 If the apricot jam is quite firm, mix it with a little water, then spread it over the hot pastry base. Turn the sponge mixture into the pan. Bake for a further 12-15 minutes. Leave to cool.

4 Peel and core the apples and cut each one into eight pieces. Put them into a saucepan with the white wine, sugar and lemon zest and simmer gently for about 5 minutes. Leave to drain in a colander.

5 Wash and peel the grapes and leave them to drain. Drain the mandarins and reserve the juice.

6 Make up the juice from the apples, grapes and mandarins to 1¾ cups with the lemon juice and white wine and sweeten to taste with sugar. Using this liquid, make up the quick-setting gelatine, according to the packet instructions.

7 Place the ring part of the cake pan over the cake. Fold the fruit carefully into the gelatine and spread over the cake. When partly set, decorate with the whipped cream.

179

TREE TOPS

Makes approximately 70 servings

1 cup margarine
1 cup sugar
7½ tsps vanilla sugar
5 eggs
1¾ cups flour and cornstarch, mixed
⅓ cup ground almonds
Good pinch of cardamon
Good pinch of cinnamon
1 cup chocolate couverture, melted

1 Cream together the margarine, sugar, vanilla sugar and eggs until light and fluffy. Mix together the flour, cornstarch, almonds and spices and fold into the mixture.
2 Line a large rectangular baking pan with wax paper. Spread one-sixth of the mixture into the pan and either put under a preheated broiler or into the oven, 450°-475°F, for about 2 minutes.
3 Spread a second layer of mixture on top and cook in the same way. Repeat for the remaining four layers.
4 Turn out the cake and cut into triangles while still warm. To cut triangles, first cut the cake into pieces 1½-inch square, then halve these diagonally. Leave to cool.
5 Melt the chocolate couverture. Use a fork to dip each tree top into the chocolate. Leave on a cooling rack to harden.

Note: Don't put the baking sheet too close to the direct heat of the broiler.

DATE COOKIES

Makes approximately 75 cookies

½ cup margarine
½ cup sugar
1 egg
2½ tbsps lemon juice
Grated zest of ½ lemon
2 cups flour

Good pinch of baking powder
1 cup dates
¾ cup almonds, chopped
Margarine for greasing

1 Cream the margarine until light. Beat in, one by one, the sugar, egg, lemon juice and zest. Gradually fold in the flour, sifting the baking powder in with the last portion of flour.
2 Stone and chop dates. Add the chopped almonds and dates to the cookie mixture and drop in teaspoonfuls onto a greased baking sheet.
3 Bake the cookies in a preheated oven, 425°F for about 15 minutes until they are golden brown.

FRUIT AND SPICE COOKIES

Makes approximately 24 cookies

4 eggs
1 cup sugar
Pinch of salt
3 tsps mixed spice
⅓ cup candied lemon and orange peel
2 cups flour
1 tsp baking powder
¾ cup flaked almonds

Rice papers, 2½-3 in in diameter
¼ cup powdered sugar
Grated zest of 1 orange
1¼ tbsps orange juice

1 Whisk the eggs, sugar, salt and spices until thick and foamy. Finely chop the lemon and orange peel. Sift together the flour and baking powder, mix with the peel and fold into the egg mixture, together with the flaked almonds. Leave to stand for 1 hour.
2 Put a heaped tablespoonful of the mixture on each round of rice paper and leave to dry overnight. The following day, bake the cookies in a preheated oven, 350°F for about 25 minutes.
3 Mix together the powdered sugar, orange zest and juice. Ice half the cookies while they are still warm and leave the remainder plain.

PEAR TREATS

Makes approximately 15 servings

1/3 cup dried pears, diced
5 tbsps water
7 1/2 tbsps pear liqueur
7 1/2 tbsps vanilla sugar
2 1/2 tbsps light cream
1/2 cup white chocolate, diced
1 tbsp coconut butter

1 Dice the pears, and simmer them in the water for 5 minutes. Add half the pear liqueur and the vanilla sugar and stir to a paste.

2 Bring the cream to the boil and melt the chocolate and coconut butter in it. Remove from the heat and beat in the remaining pear liqueur. Leave to cool, stirring occasionally, until the mixture has thickened enough for piping.

3 Using an icing bag, pipe a little of the chocolate mixture into small paper candy cups, spoon a little pear paste on top and finish with a little more of the chocolate mixture.

CHOCOLATE MARZIPAN PIES

Makes approximately 30 pies

1 3/4 cups flour
1/2 cup powdered sugar
1/3 cup margarine
3 egg yolks
Margarine for greasing

Filling

1/2 oz crystallized ginger
1 1/4 tbsps ginger syrup
1/2 cup marzipan

Icing and Decoration

Egg white
1/4 cup chocolate couverture, melted
Strips of crystallized ginger, or crystallized violets

1 Sift the flour and powdered sugar onto a board, cut in the margarine with a palette knife. Make a well in the center, add the egg yolks and work the ingredients quickly to a dough, kneading lightly. Chill for about 2 hours in the refrigerator.

2 Grate the ginger and blend into the marzipan with the ginger syrup.

3 Roll out the pastry dough and cut out 2-inch rounds. Place half the rounds on a greased baking sheet and top with a little marzipan filling, leaving the edges clear. Brush these with egg white. Cover with the remaining rounds, pressing the edges together firmly to seal. Bake in a preheated oven, 425°F, for about 10 minutes.

4 Coat the finished cakes with the melted chocolate couverture and decorate with strips of crystallized ginger or crystallized violets.

RICH FRUIT CAKE

Makes approximately 12 servings

1½ cups margarine	½ cup glacé cherries, halved and dipped in flour
1½ cups sugar	2 cups almonds, chopped
6 eggs	¼ cup crystallized ginger, chopped
3¾ cups flour	
5 tbsps milk or brandy	Margarine for greasing
1¼ tsps cinnamon	Fruit and nuts, to decorate
½ tsp ground cloves	5 tbsps apricot jam
½ tsp ground ginger	
2 cups raisins	
Grated zest of 1 orange	
Grated zest of 1 lemon	
⅓ cup mixed candied peel	

1 Cream together the margarine, sugar and eggs until light and fluffy. Add the flour, brandy and spices in that order. Fold in the raisins, grated orange and lemon zest, chopped candied peel, cherries, almonds and ginger.

2 Grease a 10½-inch cake pan with a removable base and line with wax paper. The strip around the sides should be at least 3 inches high. Turn the mixture into this and arrange the fruit and nut decoration on top, without pressing in.

3 Bake the cake in a preheated oven, 275°F for about 3 hours. After 1 ½ hours, cover the cake with wax paper. Leave to cool in the pan.

4 Warm the jam, strain through a strainer and spread over the cake, while this is still warm.

Note: This cake tastes best when it is at least one week old. Ideally it should be baked a few weeks in advance and stored either in a cake safe or wrapped in foil.

CHOCOLATE FRUIT BOMBS

Makes 24 small cakes

1¼ cups clear honey
1 cup sugar
½ cup margarine
1½ tbsp cocoa powder
3 eggs
Grated zest of 1 orange
2½ tbsps orange juice
2½ tsps cinnamon
2½ tsps ground cloves
1 tsp cardamom
3¼ cups flour
3¾ tsps baking powder
⅓ cup candied lemon peel
¾ cup almonds, chopped
Margarine for greasing

Filling

1 cup marzipan
⅓ cup candied cherries, halved
⅓ cup candied orange peel
1 tsp rosewater

Icing

7 tbsps apricot jam
2½ tbsps water
¾ cup chocolate couverture, melted

1 Put the honey, sugar and margarine in a saucepan and heat, stirring continuously, until the sugar has dissolved. Leave to cool. Stir in the cocoa, eggs, orange zest and juice and spices. Mix together the flour, baking powder, candied lemon peel and almonds, then mix into the honey mixture to make a smooth dough.

2 Make 2-inch-round molds from extra-strong tin foil doubled and pinched together with paper clips. The moulds should also be 2 inches deep. Place them on a greased and lined baking sheet and put in a layer of the cake mixture.

3 Mix together the marzipan, halved cherries, diced orange peel and rosewater and put a little into each ring.

4 Add a second layer of the cake mixture and bake in a preheated oven, 350°F, for about 20 minutes. Remove the foil and leave to cool.

5 Strain the jam through a strainer and heat in a saucepan with the water. Brush this over the cakes. Melt the chocolate couverture and use to coat the cooled cakes.

ALMOND LOG

Makes approximately 30 servings

2½oz fresh yeast
½ cup lukewarm milk
1¾ cups flour
1 tsp salt
1 cup soft margarine

Filling

¼ cup each of candied
orange and lemon peel
⅓ cup glacé cherries, halved
2½ tbsps rum
3 cups almonds, chopped
1 cup marzipan
Margarine for greasing

To Finish

⅓ cup margarine, melted
3 tsps vanilla sugar
3 tbsps powdered sugar

1 Crumble the yeast into the lukewarm milk. Add a pinch of sugar and leave in a warm place for about 10 minutes, until frothy. Mix together the flour, sugar and salt, dot with the margarine cut in pieces, add the frothy yeast, and knead to a smooth dough.

2 Soak the lemon and orange peel and the halved cherries in the rum for about 30 minutes. Knead into the dough, together with the almonds. Cover and leave to rise in a warm place, until doubled in size. Knead again and roll out into a 12-inch circle. Make a hollow down the center of the dough and brush with a little water.

3 Shape the marzipan into a long roll, place it in the hollow, fold the dough over and press the edges lightly together.

4 Place the log on a greased baking sheet and leave to rise in a warm place for about 20 minutes. Brush the log with water and bake in a preheated oven, 350°F, for about 60 minutes.

5 Brush the finished almond log with the melted margarine and sprinkle with the vanilla sugar. Leave to cool. Dust with the powdered sugar.

SPICY CHRISTMAS RING CAKE

Makes approximately 20 servings

1 cup margarine
1 cup sugar
Salt
6 eggs
2½ tsps cinnamon
1¼ tsps ground cloves
½ tsp ground cardamom
1¼ tsps ground ginger
1¼ tsps grated zest of orange
¾ cup almonds, chopped
3½oz semi-sweet plain chocolate
2½ cups flour
¾ cup cornstarch
3¾ tsps baking powder
2½ tbsps rum
Margarine for greasing
Powdered sugar for dusting

| Grated zest of ½ lemon |
| Pinch of salt |
| 2½ tbsps rum flavoring |
| 1¼ tbsps bitter almond flavoring |
| 1¼ tbsp lemon flavoring |
| 1 egg |
| 1 packet vanilla pudding mix |
| ⅔ cup margarine |
| 1 cup creamed cottage cheese |
| ⅔ cup raisins |
| 1 cup almonds, chopped |
| ⅓ cup candied orange peel |

To Finish

| Flour for dusting |
| Melted margarine |
| Flaked chocolate |
| Powdered sugar |

1 Gradually work all the ingredients to a dough. Roll the dough into a log shape. Dust well with flour and sprinkle a baking sheet generously with flour to prevent the dough spreading.

2 Bake in the center of a preheated oven, 350°-400°F for about 60 minutes.

3 While still hot, brush the fruit log with melted margarine. Leave to go cold. Decorate with flaked chocolate and dust with powdered sugar.

1 Beat the margarine until smooth. Gradually beat in the sugar, salt and eggs and continue beating until the sugar has dissolved. Stir in the spices, orange zest and almonds.

2 Break chocolate into small pieces, put into a small bowl and cover with hot water. Leave to melt, then drain and add the chocolate to the mixture.

3 Sift together the flour, cornstarch and baking powder and fold into the mixture, together with the rum.

4 Turn the mixture into a greased 8½-inch ring or tube pan. Bake in a preheated oven, 350°F, for 50-60 minutes. Dust with powdered sugar before serving.

LIGHT FRUIT LOG

Makes approximately 20 servings

Mixture

| 4 cups flour |
| 3¾ tsps baking powder |
| ⅔ cup sugar |
| 3 tsps vanilla sugar |

VANILLA PAISLEYS

Makes approximately 50 cookies

1¾ cups flour
Pith of 1 vanilla pod
Pinch of salt
½ cup ground almonds
⅔ cup margarine
1 egg yolk
⅓ cup sugar
Margarine for greasing
1½ tbsps powdered sugar
3 tsps vanilla sugar

1 Make a smooth dough with the flour, vanilla, salt, almonds, margarine, egg yolk and sugar and chill it in the refrigerator for about 1 hour.
2 Shape the dough into rolls the thickness of a finger, then cut into strips 2 inches long. Bend and flatten each strip slightly to make paisley shapes.
3 Arrange on a greased baking sheet and bake in a preheated oven, 350°-400°F for about 13 minutes.
4 Mix the powdered sugar with the vanilla sugar and press the warm paisleys in this to coat.

MACAROON HATS

Makes approximately 40 servings

2 cups flour
⅔ cup powdered sugar
½ cup margarine
Pith of 1 vanilla pod
3 egg yolks
Margarine for greasing

Macaroon Mixture

3 egg whites
⅔ cup sugar
1½ cups ground almonds
1 heaped tsp cinnamon

1 Make a short pastry dough using the flour, powdered sugar, margarine, vanilla and egg yolks. Chill.
2 Whisk the egg whites until stiff. Whisk in the sugar, then fold in the almonds and cinnamon.
3 Roll out the pastry to a rectangle the thickness of the back of a knife. Cut this into strips 1½ inches wide, then cut these into elongated diamond shapes. Arrange on a greased baking sheet and pipe a blob of the macaroon mixture on top of each diamond.
4 Bake in a preheated oven, 350°-400°F for about 20 minutes.

HAZELNUT FINGERS

Makes approximately 60 cookies

1 cup margarine
1 cup sugar
3 tsps vanilla sugar
2 egg yolks
1¼ cups flour
½ level tsp baking powder
1¾ cups ground hazelnuts or almonds
Margarine for greasing
½ cup chocolate couverture, melted

1 Cream the margarine until light, then beat in the sugar, vanilla sugar and egg yolks and continue beating until the sugar has dissolved. Sift together the flour and baking powder and fold into the mixture, together with the nuts.

2 Spoon the mixture into an icing bag fitted with a medium nozzle and pipe out 2-inch-long strips onto a greased baking sheet. Bake at 400°F for 10-15 minutes. Leave to cool.

3 Melt the chocolate couverture over a pan of hot water and use to decorate the hazelnut fingers.

GINGER SNAPS

Makes approximately 30 cookies

⅓ cup margarine
½ cup sugar
¼ cup karo syrup
3 tsps vanilla sugar
1 tbsp crystallized ginger, finely chopped
2½ tbsps ginger syrup
1 cup flour
Margarine for greasing

Icing
⅔ cup powdered sugar
1¼ tbsps cocoa powder
1¼ tbsps ginger syrup
1-2 tbsps water
2½ tbsps coconut oil

1 Cream together the margarine, sugar, syrup and vanilla sugar until light and fluffy. Fold in the ginger, ginger syrup and flour. Drop teaspoonfuls of the mixture onto a greased baking sheet, leaving large gaps between. Dip a knife in cold water and flatten the uncooked snaps.

2 Bake in a preheated oven, 400°-425°F, for 3-5 minutes.

3 Leave to cool slightly, then, while still warm, carefully remove each snap and bend round a roll of foil or a rolling pin.

4 Mix together the icing ingredients and use to coat half of each snap.

EASTER BUNS

Makes 16 buns

1oz fresh yeast
¾ cup lukewarm milk
Pinch of salt
4 cups flour
⅓ cup sugar
Pinch of salt
⅓ cup margarine, melted and cooled
1 egg
Margarine for greasing

Filling

½ cup whipping cream
⅓ cup sugar
¾ cup flaked almonds
½ cup raisins

To Finish

¼ cup margarine
Powdered sugar

1 Crumble the yeast into the lukewarm milk, stir in a little sugar and leave in a warm place for about 15 minutes, until frothy. Mix together the flour, sugar and salt in a bowl, then stir in the melted and cooled margarine, the egg and the frothy yeast. Knead continuously until the dough shrinks away from the sides of the bowl and is no longer sticky. Leave to rise in a warm place for another 30 minutes.

2 Meanwhile, mix together the cream, sugar, flaked almonds and raisins and set aside until the liquid has been almost absorbed.

3 Knead the dough again, roll into a rectangle about ½ inch thick. Spread with the filling mixture and roll up.

4 Cut into sixteen equal slices and place on a greased baking sheet. Leave to rise in a warm place, then bake in a preheated oven, 400°F, for about 20 minutes. During the last ten minutes of baking time, brush the buns several times with melted margarine. When cold, dust the buns with powdered sugar.

EASTER BUNNIES

Makes 2 large, or about 10 small, rabbits

1½oz fresh yeast
¾ cup light cream, lukewarm
¾ cup sugar
3 cups flour
Grated zest of 1 lemon
Pith of 1 vanilla pod
⅔ cup melted margarine
3 eggs, beaten
½ cup almonds, chopped
Margarine for greasing

1 Crumble the yeast into the lukewarm cream and stir in a pinch of sugar and flour. Cover and leave in a warm place for 5-10 minutes until frothy.
2 Mix together the flour, sugar, salt, lemon zest, vanilla, cooled margarine and beaten eggs in a bowl. Add the frothy yeast and the almonds, mix to a dough and knead thoroughly. Cover with foil and leave in a warm place until doubled in volume.
3 Knock down, put into greased rabbit-shaped moulds as desired, cover and leave in a warm place to rise again. Bake in a preheated oven, 350°F, for about 30 minutes.

EASTER NESTS

Makes approximately 12 nests

¾ cup water
Pinch of salt
1¼ tsps sugar
3¾ tsps vanilla sugar
⅓ cup margarine
1 cup flour
4 eggs
Margarine for greasing
Flour

Filling

¾ cup milk
Pith from 1½ vanilla pods
Pinch of salt
4 egg yolks
⅓ cup sugar
6 sheets gelatine
¾ cup cream, whipped
4 egg whites
Powdered sugar
Easter chicks and eggs for decoration

1 Bring the water, salt, sugar, vanilla sugar and margarine to the boil. Pour all the flour in and beat the mixture over a low heat until it comes away from the sides of the saucepan in a ball. Remove from the heat and beat in one of the eggs. Leave to cool slightly, then beat in the remaining eggs one at a time.
2 Spoon the mixture into an icing bag with a large, serrated nozzle and pipe out rings about 2½ inches in diameter onto a greased and floured baking sheet. Bake in a preheated oven, 350°-400°F, for about 30 minutes. Use scissors to cut the rings in half as soon as they are removed from the oven, then leave to cool.

3 Bring the milk to the boil with the vanilla and salt. Leave to cool. Whisk the egg yolks with the sugar until light and foamy. Soak the gelatine, dissolve it over a low heat, and stir it into the yolk mixture, together with the cooled milk. Set aside to cool.
4 When the mixture is half set, fold in the whipped cream. Whisk the egg whites until stiff and fold in. When almost set, spoon the cream mixture into an icing bag and use to sandwich the nest rings together. Dust the nests with powdered sugar and fill with little sugar Easter eggs and chicks.

EASTER ALMOND RING

Makes approximately 16 servings

1 cup margarine
1 cup sugar
Pinch of salt
6 eggs
1¼ cups flour
2½ tsps baking powder
2 cups ground almonds
3½oz semi-sweet, flaked chocolate
2½ tbsps brandy
Margarine for greasing
Fine breadcrumbs

1 Beat the margarine, sugar and salt until light and fluffy. Beat in the eggs one at a time. Sift together the flour and baking powder, and fold into the mixture together with the almonds, flaked chocolate and brandy.
2 Grease a fluted 10½-inch ring or tube pan and sprinkle with breadcrumbs. Turn the mixture into this and bake in a preheated oven, 350°F, for 60-70 minutes.

PLAITED EASTER RINGS

Makes 8 rings

1oz fresh yeast
¾ cup lukewarm milk
4 cups flour
Pinch of salt
⅓ cup sugar
⅓ cup margarine, melted and cooled
1 egg
⅓ cup raisins
3¾ tbsps rum
⅓ cup candied orange and lemon peel
Margarine for greasing

To Finish

8 hard boiled eggs, shelled
1 egg white
Colored sugar beads

1 Crumble the yeast into the lukewarm milk, add a pinch of sugar and flour and leave in a warm place for about 15 minutes until frothy. Mix together the flour, salt and sugar, then stir in the melted and cooled margarine, the egg and the frothy yeast. Mix to a dough and knead until smooth. Leave to rise for about 30 minutes in a warm place.
2 Soak the raisins in the rum before kneading them into the risen dough, together with the orange and lemon peel.
3 Divide the dough into eight equal servings. Make three rolls of equal length from each portion and plait them together. Bend each plait into a ring.
4 Arrange the rings on a greased baking sheet and place a hard boiled egg in the center of each ring, pointed end up.
5 Leave the rings in a warm place to rise, then bake in a preheated oven, 400°F, for about 20 minutes. While still hot, brush the rings with lightly-beaten egg white and sprinkle with sugar beads.

PANNETONE

Makes approximately 12 servings

2oz fresh yeast
¾ cup lukewarm milk
⅔ cups sugar
5 cups flour
1 cup margarine, melted and cooled
1 egg
4 egg yolks
1 tsp salt
Grated zest of 1 lemon
½ cup almonds, chopped
1 cup candied orange and lemon peel
⅔ cup raisins
Margarine for greasing
Egg yolk

1 Crumble the yeast into the lukewarm milk, add a pinch of sugar and leave in a warm place for 10 minutes, until frothy. Mix together the flour, sugar, margarine, egg, egg yolk, salt, lemon zest and frothy yeast to a dough. Knead until smooth, using the pastry hook on an electric mixer, if possible. Knead in the almonds, candied peel and raisins. Cover and leave in a warm place until doubled in volume.
2 Meanwhile, grease a soufflé dish 4½ inches deep, and line with wax paper. Knead the dough again, put it into the soufflé dish and leave to rise in a warm place for another 20 minutes.
3 Brush the dough with egg yolk and make two criss-cross slashes in the top. Bake in a preheated oven, 350°F, for about 90 minutes.

EASTER PLAIT

Makes approximately 20 servings

1½oz fresh yeast
¾ cup lukewarm milk
⅔ cup margarine
6 cups flour
Pinch of salt
⅓ cup sugar
1 egg
Margarine for greasing
Milk for brushing
1 egg yolk
1 tbsp milk
1 tbsp coarse sugar
¼ cup flaked almonds

1 Crumble the yeast into the lukewarm milk, add a pinch of sugar, cover and leave in a warm place, until frothy. Meanwhile, melt the margarine. Put the flour into a bowl, and add the salt, sugar, egg, egg yolk, cooled margarine and frothy yeast. Mix to a dough and knead until smooth. Cover and leave to rise in a warm place.

2 With floured hands, use three-quarters of the dough to form three equal rolls. Plait the rolls together and place the plait on a greased baking sheet. Make a thinner plait with the remaining dough. Brush the surface of the larger plait with milk. Lay the smaller plait on top, pressing it down lightly and leave to rise in a warm place for 10 minutes.

3 Bake in a preheated oven, 400°-425°F for 30-35 min-

utes. Beat the egg yolk with the milk, brush over the plait 10 minutes before the end of

baking time and sprinkle with the coarse sugar and flaked almonds.

EASTER BUNNIES

Makes 3 bunnies

½ cup margarine
½ cup sugar
Pinch of salt
1 egg
1 cup low fat creamed cottage cheese
3 cups flour
3¾ tsps baking powder
Egg yolk
Jelly beans
Powdered sugar

1 Cream together the margarine, sugar, salt and egg until light and fluffy. Beat in the cheese. Sift together the flour and baking powder, and fold half into the mixture. Knead in the remainder. Cover and chill for about 30 minutes.

2 Meanwhile, cut out a cardboard pattern for an Easter bunny.

3 Roll out the dough to a thickness of ½ inch and, using the pattern, cut out three Easter bunnies. Beat the egg yolk with water and brush over the bunnies. Roll out the remaining

has melted, then drain. Mix the melted nougat into the egg mixture. Whisk the egg whites stiffly and pile onto the mixture. Sift over the flour, cornstarch and baking powder. Carefully fold everything together.

2 Line a baking sheet about 12 inches x 16 inches with wax paper, grease it and spread the mixture over. Bake in a preheated oven, 350°F, for about 15 minutes.

3 Turn out onto a cooling rack, and quickly remove the wax paper. Leave to cool. Cut out twenty equal-sized ovals to make the eggs. Whip the cream with the sugar and vanilla sugar until stiff. Soak the gelatine, dissolve it over a low heat, then fold it thoroughly into the cream.

4 Pipe the mixture onto ten of the ovals and top with the remaining ten, to make filled eggs.

5 Melt the chocolate nougat with the coconut butter and use to ice eggs. Decorate with the chopped pistachios.

dough to a thickness of ¼ inch, cut out ears, paws, and an eye for each of the bunnies and attach them. To make the basket, make thin rolls of dough, plait them, make them into a basket shape and attach to the bunnies.

4 Brush the bunnies again with egg yolk and bake in a preheated oven 350°-400°F for 10-12 minutes. Mix a little powdered sugar with a little water and use to stick jelly beans onto the basket.

NOUGAT EGGS

Makes 10 eggs

4 eggs, separated
5 tbsps warm water
½ cup sugar
Pinch of salt
¼ cup margarine, melted and cooled
4oz nougat
¾ cup flour
½ cup cornstarch
1¼ tsps baking powder

Filling

¾ cup whipping cream
1 tbsp sugar
3 tsps vanilla sugar
2 sheets gelatine

Topping

3oz chocolate nougat
1 tbsp coconut butter
¼ cup pistachios, chopped

1 Whisk the egg yolks, water, sugar and salt until thick and foamy, then whisk in the melted and cooled margarine and cocoa. Pour hot water over the nougat, leave until the nougat

CRUSTY HOME-MADE BREAD

Home-made breads made with whole wheat flour or with savory fillings are simply the best.
This section's delicious recipes are for interesting breakfast and brunch breads: tasty croissants, brioches or crusty loaves of bread, which get the day off to a good start.

NUT AND MUSHROOM LOAF

Makes approximately 10 slices

1oz fresh yeast
½ tsp sugar
½ cup lukewarm milk
1 tbsp flat mushrooms, dried
2 cups hard wheat flour
½ tsp salt
Pinch of cinnamon
1 tbsp soft margarine
1 cup hazelnut or filbert kernels
Milk to glaze

1 Crumble the yeast into the lukewarm milk. Cover and leave in a warm place for about 10 minutes until frothy. Soak the mushrooms in water, then allow to drain. Put the flour, salt, cinnamon, margarine, nuts and mushrooms into a bowl. Add the frothy yeast mixture, mix it all together well, then knead until you have a smooth, elastic dough. Cover and leave in a warm place to rise, until doubled in volume.

2 Knead again, form into a long loaf shape and set aside on a sheet of wax paper in a warm place to prove. Brush with milk and score a pattern of diamond shapes on top of the loaf with a sharp knife.

3 Bake in a preheated oven, 400°F for 45 minutes.

POPPYSEED BREAD

Makes approximately 15 slices

1oz fresh yeast
¾ cup lukewarm water
½ tsp sugar
3 cups hard wheat flour
1¼ tsps vinegar
1¼ tsps salt
1½ tbsps margarine, melted
Poppy seeds

1 Crumble the yeast into the lukewarm water, stir in the sugar and set aside in a warm place for 10 minutes, until frothy. Mix together the flour, vinegar, margarine and frothy yeast. Work into a smooth dough, knead, cover and leave to rise until doubled in volume.

2 Knock the dough down, form into a long loaf shape and leave to prove on a sheet of wax paper in a warm place. Brush with water and sprinkle generously with poppy seeds. Using a sharp knife, make two or three diagonal cuts across the top of the loaf.

3 Bake for about 60 minutes in a preheated oven, 400°F.

COUNTRY BREAD

Makes approximately 25 slices

6 cups rye flour
2 cups hard wheat flour
2oz sourdough
1¼ cups lukewarm buttermilk
Salt
Caraway seeds
Margarine for greasing

1 Mix the flours together. Mix the sourdough with half the buttermilk and ¾ cup of the flours. Cover and leave to work for 4 hours in a warm place. Knead in the remaining buttermilk and a further 3¼ cups of the flours. Cover and leave to stand overnight.

2 Next day, knead the dough until firm, adding remaining flour, salt and caraway seeds.
3 Place the dough in a greased loaf pan and allow to prove for 45-50 minutes. Bake at 475°F for ten minutes. Lower the heat to 425°F and bake for further 60 minutes.

PROVENCAL BREAD

Makes approximately 14 slices

1 small onion, chopped
1 tbsp margarine
½oz fresh yeast
½ tsp sugar
½ cup buttermilk
1¾ cups hard wheat flour
½ cup whole wheat oat flakes
1 tsp salt
1 cup cottage cheese
2½ tbsps fresh mixed herbs, finely chopped
Milk to glaze

1 Lightly fry the onion in the margarine. Leave to cool. Mix the yeast, buttermilk and sugar together. Put flour, oat flakes, salt and cottage cheese into a bowl. Pour over the yeast and milk mixture and work the ingredients together until you have a smooth dough. Add the onion and herbs and knead them well in. Cover and leave to stand in a warm place to rise. Knead again.
2 Grease and line an 8-inch loaf pan. Put in the dough and leave in a warm place to prove. Brush the dough with milk.
3 Bake in a preheated oven 400°F for about 45 minutes.

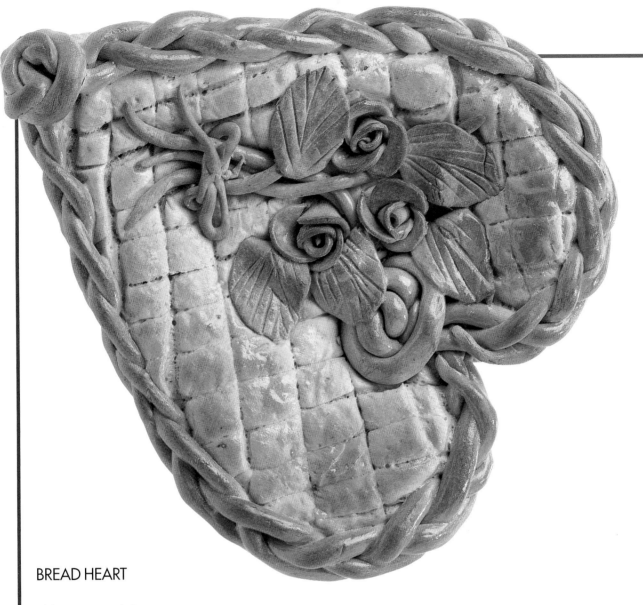

BREAD HEART

Makes approximately 8 servings

| 2 cups hard wheat flour |
| 2 cups rye flour |
| 1 1/2 oz fresh yeast |
| 3/4 cup lukewarm water |
| 1 1/2 tbsps melted margarine |
| 1 egg |
| Salt |
| Margarine for greasing |
| Lentils, rice or beans for baking blind |

Filling

| 1 large onion |
| 1 small red pepper |
| 1 small leek |
| 1 small fresh chilli |
| 1 carrot |
| 2 small pickles |
| 2 eggs |

| 2 cups mixed beef and pork, ground |
| Seasoning |
| Paprika |
| Egg white to glaze |

1 Mix together the flours and sift them into a bowl. Make a well in the center and crumble the yeast into it. Add a little of the water and flour and mix to a thickish paste. Leave to work for 15 minutes in a warm place. Add the remaining water, the margarine, egg and salt. Mix the ingredients to a dough and knead thoroughly. Cover and leave in a warm place to rise until doubled in volume, about 30 minutes.

2 Meanwhile, peel the onions, and wash and trim the pepper, leek and chilli; peel and blanch the carrots. Dice the onions, pepper and pickles and finely chop the chilli. Slice the leek into thin rings and dice the carrot. Mix the vegetables with the eggs and meat. Season to taste with salt, pepper and paprika.

3 Roll out two-thirds of the dough to a thickness of 3/4 inch and use to line a large, well-greased heart-shaped baking pan. Cover the dough with wax paper, spread lentils, rice or beans over and bake blind at 400°F for 10 minutes.

4 Remove the lentils, rice or beans and the wax paper and spread the meat mixture over the dough. Return to the oven for about 40 minutes.

5 Roll out the remaining third of the dough to a thickness of about 1/2 inch. Cut out a heart shape to fit the pan. Lay over the cooked meat mixture and press firmly down. Use any dough trimmings to make decorations and stick on the heart with egg white. Return to the oven for about 15-20 minutes. Can be served hot or cold.

SUNFLOWER

Makes 8 rolls

2 cups whole wheat flour
2 cups hard wheat flour
1oz fresh yeast
2½ tsps sugar
1 cup lukewarm water
¼ cup margarine
1¼ tsps salt
2½ tsps white vinegar
Margarine for greasing
Poppy seeds, sesame seeds or
sunflower seeds for sprinkling

1 Put the flours in a bowl, make a hollow in the center and crumble the yeast into it. Stir in the sugar and some of the lukewarm water. Allow this to work for about 15 minutes in a warm place. Add the margarine, vinegar, salt and the rest of the water. Work to a smooth dough and leave to rise in a warm place for another 30 minutes.

2 Shape the dough into a roll and cut this into eight equal pieces. Form each piece into a ball and arrange them on a greased baking sheet in a circle, with one roll in the center, all touching each other. Leave in a warm place to prove. Brush with water and sprinkle with poppy, sesame or sunflower seeds.

3 Bake in a preheated oven, 400°-425°F for 25-30 minutes.

CRUSTY HERB STICKS

Makes 6 medium French bread loaves

⅓ cup margarine
¾ cup lukewarm water
1½oz fresh yeast
2½ cups rye flour
2½ cups stone-ground flour
1¼ tsps salt
1 pinch sugar
1¼ tbsps fresh, mixed herbs, chopped
5 tbsps parsley, chopped
Margarine for greasing

1 Melt the margarine in the water, crumble in the yeast and mix well. Mix the rye flour with half of the stone-ground flour and stir into the yeast mixture. Beat the mixture thoroughly. Cover and set aside in a warm place for 30 minutes. Knead the remaining flour, the salt, sugar, parsley and mixed herbs into the dough.

2 Divide into six portions and shape them into French bread shapes. Grease two long loaf pans, patterned if possible, and press three loaves into each. Leave in a warm place to prove.

3 Bake in a preheated oven, 425°F for 20-30 minutes. Shortly before the end of baking time turn out, brush the patterned

side with a little water and put back in oven, patterned side up, to finish baking the crust.

ONION BREAD

Makes approximately 16 slices

1 cup rye flour
2 cups stone-ground flour
1oz fresh yeast
½ tsp sugar
¾ cup lukewarm water
3oz sourdough
1-2 tsps salt
2 tbsps packaged dry fried onions
Black pepper, ground coriander and cardamom
Margarine for greasing

1 Put the flour into a large bowl, and make a well in the center. Into this put the yeast, mixed with the sugar and 2-4 tbsps of the lukewarm water. Cover the bowl with a towel and leave to work in a warm place for 15 minutes. Add the remaining flour, the sourdough, salt and spices and mix together well.
2 Knead the dough thoroughly until smooth and no longer sticky. Set aside in a warm place to rise until doubled in volume.
3 Knead the onions into the dough. Shape into an oblong loaf. Place on wax paper and leave in a warm place to prove. Brush the bread with warm water and score the top several times with a sharp knife.
4 Bake on a greased baking sheet in a preheated oven, 425°F for about 50 minutes.

FRIESLAND BLACK BREAD

Makes approximately 18 slices

6 cups finely-milled rye flour
2 cups hard wheat flour
2oz sourdough
2½ cups lukewarm water
1¼ tsps salt
Margarine for greasing

1 Put half the quantity of each flour into a bowl and warm it. Make a well in the center. In a second bowl, mix the sourdough with 1¾ cups of the lukewarm water and pour into the well. Stir in slowly to make a thickish paste. Cover the bowl and leave overnight in a warm place.
2 Add the remaining water and the salt. Slowly stir in the remaining flours. Knead the dough lightly until just firm. Shape into a ball, place in a warm, floured bowl, cover and leave to stand for 3 hours.
3 Shape the dough into a round, flattish loaf. Place on a greased baking sheet and leave to prove for 1½ to 2 hours.
4 Bake in a preheated oven, 475°F for 10 minutes. Reduce the heat to 400°F and bake for further 60-70 minutes.

1 Mix the yeast with 2½ tbsps of the lukewarm water, stir in the remaining water, the salt and spices. Knead to a smooth dough with the flour, cover and leave to rise in a warm place for about 45 minutes.

2 Thoroughly knead again. Divide the dough into five servings and roll out each one very thinly. Cut into rectangles 4 inches x 2 inches, put on a greased and floured baking sheet and prick each one several times with a fork.

3 Bake in a preheated oven, 475°F for 5-7 minutes.

SWEDISH CRISPBREADS

Makes 40-50 crispbreads

½oz fresh yeast
⅔ cup lukewarm water
1¼ tsps salt
1¼ tsps caraway seeds, ground
1¼ tsps fennel seeds, ground
2 cups rye flour
Margarine for greasing
Flour

FLAT LOAF

Makes approximately 24 slices

8 cups hard wheat flour
3oz fresh yeast
1¼ tbsps sugar
1-2 tsps salt
⅔ cup vegetable oil
1¾ cups lukewarm water
¾ cup sesame seeds for sprinkling
Margarine for greasing

1 Sift the flour into a bowl, and crumble in the yeast. Add the sugar, salt and oil. Stir in the lukewarm water, working from the center out. Mix well and knead thoroughly. Cover and leave in a warm place to rise for 25-30 minutes.

2 Thoroughly knead the dough again. Divide into four equal servings and roll each one into a flattish round loaf. Brush with water, sprinkle with sesame seeds and leave to rise in a warm place for another 5-10 minutes.

3 Place the loaves on a greased baking sheet and bake in a preheated oven, 425°F for 20-25 minutes.

SESAME BREAD

Makes approximately 15 slices

2½oz fresh yeast
1¾ cups lukewarm milk
2½ tbsps sugar
2½ cups hard wheat flour
2 cups rye flour
1¾ cups whole wheat flour
Pinch of salt
⅓ cup margarine, melted and cooled
¾ cup sesame seeds
Margarine
1 egg, separated
Sesame seeds

1 Crumble the yeast into the lukewarm milk, reserving 3¾ tbsps of the milk. Mix in a little sugar and flour and leave in a warm place for about 15 minutes until frothy. Put sugar, flour, salt, margarine and sesame seeds into a bowl. Add the frothy yeast and knead all the ingredients to a smooth, elastic dough. Cover and leave to rise in a warm place, until doubled in volume.

2 Thoroughly knead a second time and divide the dough into three servings, each one smaller than the last. Roll each portion with three equal lengths and plait them together. Place the largest plait on a greased baking sheet; brush the bottom of the second-largest with egg white and stick onto the first. Using the same method, top with the smallest dough plait.

3 Leave to prove in a warm place, brush with melted margarine and bake in a preheated oven, 400°F for about 45 minutes.

4 Mix egg yolk with milk. After 20 minutes baking time brush over the loaf and sprinkle with sesame seeds.

SUNFLOWER SEED BREAD

Makes approximately 25 slices

½ cup wheat grains
6 cups coarse rye flour
1¾ cups strong whole wheat flour
1¼ tbsps salt
2½oz fresh yeast
2 cups lukewarm water
¼ cup margarine, melted and cooled
½ cup sunflower seeds
Margarine for greasing
Milk
Sunflower seeds

1 Pour hot water over the wheat grains and leave overnight to swell. Drain well in a colander. Knead the flour, salt, crumbled yeast, lukewarm water and margarine to a smooth dough. Cover and leave to rise in a warm place, until doubled in volume. Mix together the sunflower seeds and wheat grains and knead into the dough.

2 Reserving a little dough for decoration, shape the rest into a loaf. Place on a greased baking sheet and brush with milk. Roll the reserved dough into three lengths, plait them together and press onto the top of the loaf. Cover and leave to prove in a warm place.

3 Brush the loaf with milk and bake in a preheated oven, 350°-400°F for about 50 minutes. Ten minutes before the end of baking time, sprinkle the loaf with sunflower seeds.

SWEDISH RINGS

Makes approximately 20 rings

2½oz fresh yeast
1¾ cups lukewarm milk
1¼ tbsps sugar
6 cups rye flour
1¼ cups hard wheat flour
1 tbsp margarine, melted and cooled
2½ tsps salt
3 tbsps karo syrup
Grated zest of orange, grated fennel and/or powdered aniseed

1 Crumble the yeast into the lukewarm milk and add the sugar and a little flour. Cover and leave for 5-10 minutes in a warm place, until frothy. Put the flours into a bowl and add the margarine, salt, syrup and frothy yeast. Mix in the orange zest, fennel and/or aniseed according to taste. Mix together thoroughly. Knead, cover and leave to rise in a warm place, until doubled in volume.

2 Knock back and knead again. If necessary, add a little milk, as the dough must not be too firm. Roll out five circles, 8 inches in diameter and cut a hole in the center.

3 Prick the dough several times with a fork. Place on a greased baking sheet, brush with water, leave to prove in a warm place for a short while and bake in a preheated oven, 400°-425°F for 10-15 minutes.

Note: This dough also makes good rolls. Bake them for 20-25 minutes.

STUFFED BREAD

Makes approximately 10 slices

2 cups hard wheat flour
2 cups rye flour
1oz fresh yeast
Pinch of sugar
¾ cup lukewarm water
1¼ tbsps margarine, melted and cooled
1 egg yolk
Salt

Stuffing

7oz mushrooms
1 small leek
¼ cup margarine
2 cups ham, cooked and cut into julienne strips
Seasoning
Egg yolk

1 Sift the flours together into a bowl. Make a well in the center and crumble in the yeast. Mix this to a thickish paste with the sugar, and a little of the water and flour. Leave to work in a warm place for 15 minutes. Add the remaining water, the margarine, egg yolk and salt. Mix everything together well and knead the dough thoroughly. Cover and leave in a warm place until doubled in volume.
2 Wash and dice the mushrooms. Wash the leek and cut it into thin rings. Sauté the mushrooms and leek in the margarine and leave to cool. Mix with the ham and season to taste.
3 On a floured board, roll out the dough to a rectangle about ¾ inch thick. Spread the stuffing mixture over the dough and roll the dough up in the shape of a loaf. Prick several holes in the top of the bread. Make a few decorative rounds from dough trimmings and fix to the bread with egg yolk.
4 Bake in a preheated oven, 400°-425°F, for 40-50 minutes.

TURKISH SESAME RINGS

Makes about 20 rings

1oz fresh yeast
1¼ tsps sugar
¾ cup lukewarm milk
1¾ cups hard wheat flour
1¾ cup stone-ground flour
1¼ cups oatmeal
¼ cup sesame seeds
1-2 tsps salt
Milk
Sesame seeds
Margarine for greasing

1 Crumble the yeast into the lukewarm milk with the sugar. Sift the flours together and stir 1¾ cups of this into the yeast mixture. Leave to work in a warm place for 15 minutes. Sift the remaining flour over, add the oatmeal, sesame seeds and salt and mix everything together. Knead to a smooth dough. Cover and leave to rise in a warm place for 30 minutes.
2 On a floured board, roll out the dough to a rectangle. Use a pastry wheel to cut the rectangle into strips ¾ inch wide. Twist the strips, and join the ends to make a circle. Brush with milk and sprinkle with sesame seeds.
3 Place on a greased baking sheet, cover with a dish towel and leave to prove in a warm place for 20 minutes. Bake in a preheated oven, 425°F, for 20-25 minutes.

ROLLS WITH BACON

Makes 10 rolls

1 cup smoked ham, diced
2 cups whole wheat flour
1 cups hard wheat flour
1oz fresh yeast
Pinch of sugar
½ cup lukewarm water
⅓ cup lukewarm buttermilk
2-3 tsps salt

1 Sauté the ham, drain in a colander and leave to cool.
2 Sift the flours into a bowl, make a well in the center and crumble in the yeast. Stir in a little of the water, the sugar and a little of the flour and leave in a warm place for about 15 minutes, until frothy. Gradually work in the remaining water, the buttermilk and salt. Thoroughly knead the dough.
3 Mix the ham into the dough. Cover and leave for about 30 minutes in a warm place, until doubled in volume.
4 Thoroughly knead the dough a second time. Shape into small oval rolls. Place on a greased and lined baking sheet and leave in a warm place to prove. Brush with water and bake in a preheated oven, 400°F, for 25-30 minutes.

SPICED BREAD

Makes approximately 18 slices

2½ cups coarse rye flour
2½ cups whole wheat flour
1 tsp salt
1¼ cups water
1oz fresh yeast
¼ cup margarine, melted and cooled
2½ tbsps sesame seeds
3¾ tbsps mixed spicy herbs
Good pinch of black pepper
Margarine for greasing
Milk

1 Mix the flours, salt, lukewarm water, crumbled yeast, and margarine together and knead to a smooth dough. Cover and leave in a warm place until doubled in volume. Knead in the remaining ingredients.
2 Put a good three-quarters of the dough into a greased 10-inch loaf pan. Brush the dough with milk. Roll the remaining dough into two equal strips, twist them round each other and press the twist lightly onto the top of the loaf.
3 Leave the bread in a warm place to prove, brush with milk

and bake in a preheated oven, 400°F, for about 40 minutes.

Note: A small, ovenproof container filled with water should also be placed in the oven during baking.

HERB LOAF

Makes approximately 16 slices

2 cups hard wheat flour
2 cups rye flour
1oz fresh yeast
Pinch of sugar
¾ cup lukewarm water
1¼ tbsps margarine, melted and cooled
1 egg yolk
Salt
1 bunch parsley
1 bunch dill
1 sprig basil
1 sprig marjoram
½ tsp caraway seeds
Seasoning
Margarine for greasing

1 Sift the flours into a bowl, make a well in the center and crumble in the yeast. Mix to a thickish paste with the sugar, and a little of the water and flour. Leave to work in a warm place for about 15 minutes. Mix in the remaining water, margarine, egg yolk and salt to make a dough. Thoroughly knead the dough. Cover and leave in a warm place for about 30 minutes, until doubled in volume.

2 Finely chop the parsley, dill, basil and marjoram and mix with the caraway seeds. Add a little seasoning and knead them well into the dough.
3 Shape the dough into a loaf, put on a greased baking sheet and bake in a preheated oven, 400°-425°F, for 30-40 minutes.

FRUIT AND NUT LOAF

Makes approximately 20 slices

2 cups dried pears
2 tbsps dried bananas
2 tbsps prunes
1½ tbsps candied lemon peel
¼ cup dried apricots
1¼ cups stone-ground whole wheat flour
2 cups hard wheat flour
¾ cup oatmeal
¾ cup lukewarm milk
1oz fresh yeast
Pinch of sugar
1 tsp salt

1 cup whipping cream, warmed
1 tbsp margarine, melted
¼ cup raisins
¼ cup sugar
Grated zest of half a lemon
Good pinch of ground cloves
Good pinch each of ground
ginger, cinnamon and cardamom
1¼ tbsps kirsch
¾ cup hazelnut or filbert kernels,
chopped
Margarine for greasing
1 egg yolk

1 Finely dice the pears, bananas, prunes, lemon peel and apricots. Put the flours and oatmeal into a bowl, make a well in the center and pour in the lukewarm water. Crumble in the yeast with the sugar and a little flour. Leave in a warm place for about 10 minutes, until frothy. Add the salt, lukewarm whipping cream and margarine. Mix all the ingredients to a smooth dough and knead thoroughly.

2 Mix together the raisins, sugar, lemon zest, cloves, ginger, cinnamon, cardamom, kirsch, diced fruit and chopped nuts.

3 Roll out the dough, place the fruit mixture on top and wrap the dough around this, to form a loaf. Place the loaf on a greased baking sheet, prick the dough several times with a tooth pick and leave to prove in a warm place for 20 minutes.

4 Bake in a preheated oven, 350°F, for about 60 minutes. After 45 minutes, mix the egg yolk with a little water and brush over the loaf.

209

CROISSANTS

Makes 15 croissants

1oz fresh yeast
¾ cup whipping cream, warmed
¼ cup sugar
1¾ cups flour
Pinch of salt
1 cup margarine, melted and cooled
2 eggs
Margarine for greasing

1 Crumble the yeast into the whipping cream and blend with a pinch of sugar and flour. Cover and leave in a warm place for 5-10 minutes, until frothy. Put the sugar, flour, salt, margarine and egg yolks into a bowl, then add the frothy yeast. Mix to a smooth dough, and knead thoroughly.

2 Cover with foil and leave in a warm place for about 20 minutes, until doubled in volume. Knead thoroughly for a second time. Divide the dough into three servings. Roll out each portion into a circle about ¼ inch thick.

3 Using a pastry wheel or knife, cut each circle into five triangles. Starting at the broad edge, roll the dough loosely up towards the point. Bend into a crescent shape and place on a greased baking sheet. Leave to prove in a warm place for a short while, then bake in a preheated oven, 400°F, for about 30 minutes.

PIROZHKI

Makes approximately 10 servings

1½oz fresh yeast
¾ cup lukewarm milk
Pinch of sugar
4 cups flour
½ tsp salt
⅓ cup margarine, melted and cooled
1 egg, beaten
Margarine for greasing

Stuffing

1 cup bacon, diced
2 leeks
1 large clove of garlic
Salt
1 cup mushrooms, sliced
3 hard-boiled eggs
2 tbsps pickles, diced
1 bunch dill
2 small onions
3 cups ground pork
Salt and pepper
1 egg yolk
2½ tbsps milk

1 Crumble the yeast into the lukewarm milk, add a pinch of sugar and flour, cover and leave in a warm place for 5-10 minutes, until frothy. Put the flour, salt, margarine and egg into a bowl, then add the frothy yeast. Mix everything to a smooth dough and knead thoroughly. Cover with foil and leave to rise in a warm place until doubled in volume. Knead again and set aside to prove.

2 Dice the bacon and soften in a frying pan. Wash and halve the leeks, cut them into thin strips and sauté in the bacon fat. Crush the garlic with a little salt. Wash and thinly slice the mushrooms, then add them to the leeks together with the garlic. Using an egg slicer, slice the eggs first lengthwise and then diagonally. Dice the pickles, finely chop the dill and dice the onions. Mix all the foregoing ingredients together with the ground pork and season with salt and pepper. Knead the dough again and roll it out into a rectangle 12 inches x 16 inches.

Spread the meat and vegetable mixture over the dough, leaving a 1¼-inch edge clear all round. Mix the egg yolk with the milk, and brush around the edges. Carefully roll up the dough and press the edges together to seal.

3 Shape the roll into a semicircle. Place on a greased baking sheet. Score the top of the roll with the back of a knife. Leave to prove in a warm place. Brush the remaining egg yolk mixture over the pirozhki. Bake in a preheated oven, 400°F, for about 45-50 minutes. If necessary, cover the loaf with foil to prevent the crust burning.

SCONE TRIANGLES

Makes 6 triangles

2 cups flour
Pinch of salt
2½ tsps baking powder
⅓ cup margarine
1 egg
7½ tbsps milk
Margarine for greasing

1 Make a smooth dough with the flour, salt, baking powder, margarine, egg and milk. Roll out into a circle about 9½ inches in diameter. Cut into six triangular wedges.

2 Place on a greased baking sheet and bake in a preheated oven, 400°F, for about 15 minutes. Serve warm.

Note: The scones are delicious spread with butter, jam and stiffly whipped heavy cream.

SESAME SEED PRETZELS

Makes 6 pretzels

½oz fresh yeast
5 tbsps lukewarm milk
2 cups flour
1½ tbsps margarine
1 egg
½ tsp salt
1 tsp sugar
1 egg yolk
Sesame seeds

1 Crumble the yeast into the lukewarm milk. Put the flour, margarine, egg, salt and sugar into a bowl, add the yeasted milk and knead all the ingredients to a smooth dough.

2 Cover with foil and leave the dough to rise in a warm place. Knead the dough a second time, shape it into a long roll and cut it into six servings. Roll each portion out to a long length and twist this into traditional pretzel forms.

3 Place the pretzels on greased and lined baking sheet, and leave them in a warm place to prove. Brush with egg yolk and sprinkle with sesame seeds. Bake in a preheated oven, 425°F, for about 15 minutes.

SUNDAY LOAF

Makes approximately 15 slices

1½oz fresh yeast
2½ tbsps sugar
1¾ cups milk
8 cups flour
1 cup margarine, melted and cooled
Grated zest of 1 lemon
1 egg
Margarine for greasing

1 Stir the yeast and sugar into the lukewarm milk and leave covered for about 10 minutes, until frothy. Sift the flour into a bowl. Mix in the margarine, lemon zest and egg. Add the frothy yeast and mix well. Knead to a smooth dough.
2 Leave to rise in a warm place, until doubled in volume. Put into a greased 14-inch loaf pan and bake in a preheated oven, 350°F, for about 25 minutes.

RAISIN BUNS

Makes 10 buns

2 cups flour
1oz fresh yeast
1 tbsp sugar
½ cup lukewarm milk
2½ tbsps margarine
1 cup raisins

1 Make a smooth dough mixture with the flour, yeast, sugar, salt, milk and margarine. Add the raisins. Knead the dough thoroughly, then leave to rise in a warm place.
2 Shape the dough into ten rolls and place on a greased and lined baking sheet. Leave in a warm place to prove. Bake in a preheated oven, 400°F, for 15-20 minutes.

HERB ROLL

Makes approximately 8 slices

Stuffing
1 bunch each chives, parsley, dill
1 small onion
2 cloves garlic

Dough
½ cup creamed cottage cheese
1¼ tsps salt
2 small eggs
2½ tbsps margarine, melted
1¾ cups flour
2 tsps baking powder
Margarine

1 Wash and finely chop the herbs. Finely dice the onions and crush the garlic. Mix these ingredients together.
2 Make a smooth dough from the dough ingredients and roll out into a rectangle 6 inches x 16 inches. Spread the dough very thinly with the melted margarine and sprinkle generously with the stuffing.
3 Roll the dough up from the short side and put into a well greased loaf pan. Score the surface of the roll, decorate with shapes made from the dough trimmings and bake in the center of a preheated oven, 350°F, for about 40 minutes.

HAM LOAVES

Makes 2 loaves

1½oz fresh yeast
¾ cup lukewarm milk
Pinch of sugar
10oz smoked ham, in one piece
1 large bunch parsley, chopped
4 cups flour
1¼ tsps salt
¼ cup margarine, melted
Margarine for greasing
Egg yolk

1 Crumble the yeast into the lukewarm milk, and stir in a pinch of sugar and a little flour. Cover and leave in a warm place for 10 minutes, until frothy.
2 Meanwhile, dice the ham and sauté until transparent. Stir in the chopped parsley and leave to cool.
3 Put the flour, salt and margarine into a bowl, and add the frothy yeast. Mix and knead to a smooth dough. Cover the dough and leave in a warm place, until doubled in volume. Knead in the ham mixture and shape the dough into two elongated loaves.
4 Place on a greased baking sheet and leave to prove in a warm place for 20 minutes.

Score the top of each loaf diagonally two or three times, brush with egg yolk and bake in a preheated oven, 400°F, for 30-35 minutes.

BRIOCHE RING

Makes approximately 8 servings

4 cups flour
1oz fresh yeast
⅓ cup lukewarm milk
⅔ cup margarine
¼ cup sugar
1 heaped tsp salt
1 egg
5 egg yolks
Grated zest of half a lemon
Margarine for greasing

1 Make a dough from the flour, yeast, lukewarm milk, margarine, sugar, salt, egg, 4 of the egg yolks and the lemon zest. Knead everything thoroughly to a smooth dough. Leave in a warm place until doubled in volume.
2 Shape the dough into a ball. Place on a greased baking sheet and press the dough down in the center to form a ring. Place a small cake pan in the hole to prevent the dough from closing up during cooking.
3 Brush the brioche with egg yolk. Leave briefly in a warm

place to prove, then bake in a preheated oven, 425°F, for about 30 minutes.

Note: The brioche is delicious with butter and jam.

SWISS BREAKFAST BREAD

Makes 8 slices

1oz fresh yeast
1 generous cup lukewarm milk
Pinch of sugar
4 cups hard wheat flour
½ tsp salt
2½ tbsps margarine, melted and cooled
Margarine
1 egg yolk
1 tbsp Emmenthal cheese, grated

1 Make a yeast dough from the yeast, lukewarm milk (reserving 3 tbsps), sugar, flour, salt and margrine. Leave to rise in a warm place.
2 Grease a wide loaf pan. Fill with the dough to a depth of about ½ inch. Shape the remaining dough into eight rolls and place on top of the bread in a double line. Press lightly on, cover and leave to prove in a warm place.
3 Brush the dough with melted

margarine and bake in a preheated oven, 400°F, for about 40 minutes.
4 Mix the egg yolk with the reserved milk and brush over the rolls after 15 minutes. Sprinkle the rolls with the cheese after a further 15 minutes.

Makes 16 servings

1oz fresh yeast
½ cup lukewarm milk
1¼ tbsps sugar
3 cups flour
⅓ cup sugar
Pinch of salt
⅓ cup margarine, melted and cooled
1 egg
Margarine for greasing

WEEKEND BREAD

Makes approximately 16 slices

4 cups flour
1½oz fresh yeast
¾ cup lukewarm milk
¼ cup sugar
1 egg
1 egg white
1 tsp salt
Juice of half a lemon
2½ tbsps raisins
¾ cup almonds, chopped
Margarine for greasing
1 egg yolk

1 Sift the flour into a bowl. Make a well in the center and crumble in the yeast. Add a little of the lukewarm milk and a good pinch of sugar and mix together with a little flour to a thick paste. Leave to rise until the yeast mixture has doubled in volume. Dot the margarine over the flour, add the remaining milk, egg and egg white and mix together thoroughly. Add the salt, lemon juice, raisins and almonds. Mix and knead thoroughly to a smooth dough and leave covered in a warm place until doubled in volume.

2 Shape the dough into a thick roll, reserving a little for decoration. Put into a greased 10-inch loaf pan and leave in a warm place to prove. Cut decorative shapes from the reserved dough and stick them onto the loaf with beaten egg yolk. Brush the whole loaf with egg yolk.

3 Bake in a preheated oven, 400°F, for 40-50 minutes. After about 30 minutes, cover the loaf with foil to prevent the crust burning.

Filling

2 cups ground almonds
¼ cup sugar
1 egg
⅓ cup whipping cream
1 apple
4 tbsps morello cherry jam

Icing

1 egg yolk
¼ cup powdered sugar
2½ tbsps water

1 Crumble the yeast into the lukewarm milk, add the sugar and leave in a warm place until frothy. Put the flour, sugar, salt, margarine and egg into a bowl. Add the frothy yeast and mix everything together well. Knead the dough thoroughly, cover with foil and leave in a warm place until doubled in volume.
2 Mix together the almonds, sugar, egg and whipping cream. Peel and core the apple, grate them and stir into the mixture together with cherry jam.

3 Roll the dough out to a thickness of about ½ inch, to fit a 14-inch loaf pan. Mark the dough into three equal sections. Spread the filling over the middle section. Cut the two outer sections into strips ¾ inch wide and turn into decorative edges, slightly overlapping the filling.

4 Carefully place the slice in the loaf pan and leave in a warm place to prove. Brush the slice with egg yolk and bake in a preheated oven, 350°-400°F, for about 30 minutes.
5 Mix together the powdered sugar and water and thinly coat the almond and cherry slice with this.

SWEDISH YEAST ROUND

Makes approximately 16 servings

1oz fresh yeast
Generous cup lukewarm milk
Pinch of sugar
4 cups flour
1½ tbsps sugar
Pinch of salt
¼ cup margarine, melted and cooled
1 cup white marzipan
1 egg yolk
1½ tbsps powdered sugar
Margarine for greasing
1 egg yolk

1 Crumble the yeast into the lukewarm milk, reserving 3 tbsps. Add a pinch of sugar and leave in a warm place until frothy. Put the flour, sugar, salt and margarine into a bowl, add the frothy yeast and knead the dough well. Leave in a warm place until doubled in volume.
2 Grease a 9½-inch pan with a removable base and line with dough to a depth of about ½ inch.
3 Knead together the marzipan, egg yolk and powdered sugar. Roll it out and lay it over the dough. Make a thick coil with half the remaining dough and arrange it around the outside edge of the marzipan, like a frame.
4 Shape the remaining dough into eight rolls and place these inside the dough frame. With kitchen scissors, make a few nicks or swirls on top of the rolls. Cover and leave in a warm place for 15 minutes to prove.

5 Brush the rolls with melted margarine and bake in a preheated oven, 400°F for about 40 minutes. Mix the egg yolk with the reserved milk and brush over the bread after 20 minutes.

STUFFED BUN PLAIT

Makes approximately 15 slices

1oz fresh yeast
½ cup lukewarm milk
3 cups flour
⅓ cup sugar
1½ tbsps margarine, melted and cooled
Margarine for greasing
Pinch of salt

Filling

1 cup ground almonds
1 cup raisins
⅓ cup sugar
10 tbsps brandy

Icing

¾ cup powdered sugar
1¼ tbsps lemon juice
1¼ tbsps water

1 Crumble the yeast into the lukewarm milk, stir in a pinch of sugar, cover and leave in a warm place until frothy. Put the flour, sugar, margarine, egg

BULLAR

Makes approximately 40 pieces

⅔ cup margarine
1¾ cup milk
1½oz fresh yeast
⅔ cup sugar
8 cups flour
½ tsp salt
7½ tbsps sugar
2 tsps cinnamon
Margarine for greasing
2 egg yolks
Coarse sugar, shredded coconut or flaked almonds

1 Melt the margarine, add the milk and crumble the yeast into it. Stir in the sugar and leave for 5-10 minutes until frothy. Gradually beat in the flour and salt. Knead the dough well, cover and leave in a warm place for about 40 minutes.
2 Mix together the sugar and cinnamon and knead them into the dough.
3 Form the dough into two equal rolls and slice these into ¾-inch-thick rounds. Place on a greased baking sheet and leave to prove for about 30 minutes.

and salt into a bowl, mix in the frothy yeast and knead the dough thoroughly. Cover and leave in a warm place until doubled in volume.
2 Roll out the dough to a rectangle 10 inches x 23½ inches and cut into three equal pieces.
3 Mix the almonds with the raisins, sugar and brandy and spread evenly over each piece of dough. Roll up each piece beginning with the long side. Plait the three rolls together into a round (see illustration) and

put into a greased 8½-inch pan with a removable base.
4 Bake in a preheated oven, 400°F, for abut 30 minutes.
5 Mix the powdered sugar with the lemon juice and water and spread over the hot bun plait.

4 Brush the rounds with egg yolk and sprinkle with coarse sugar, coconut or flaked almonds. Bake in a preheated oven, 425°F, for about 10 minutes.

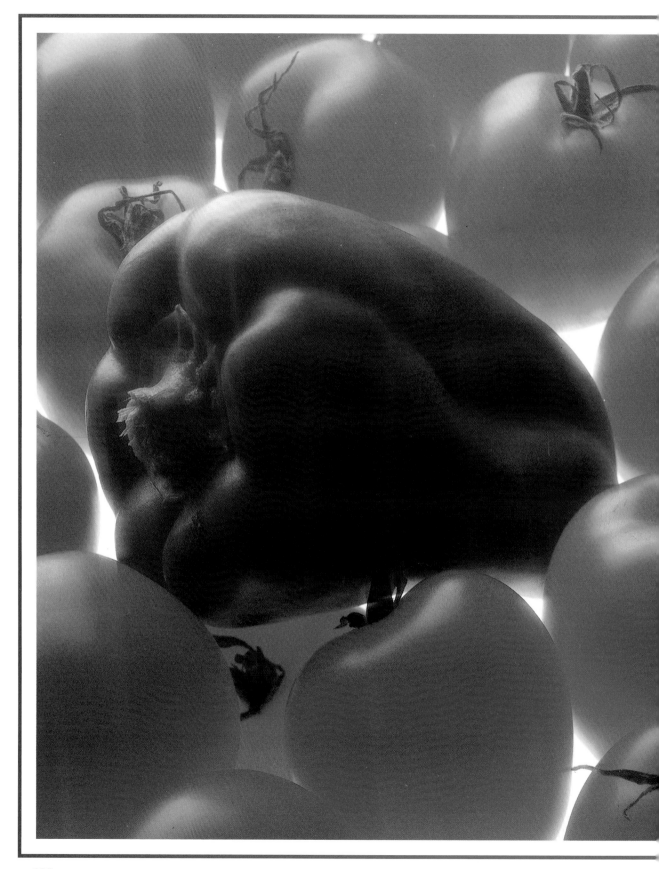

SAVORY SNACKS

Pizzas, quiches and flans can be made in a hundred different ways. This chapter gathers together a few of the most delicious versions from Italy, France and Germany, together with irresistible savory pies, choux, rolls and party snacks.

SALMON QUICHE

Makes approximately 4 servings

2 cups flour
½ cup margarine
4 tbsps water
½ tsp salt
Margarine for greasing

Filling

3 eggs
⅔ cup Philadelphia cheese with herbs
¾ cup light cream
Freshly ground black pepper
Salt
2 cups broccoli flowerets, cooked and drained
2 cups cooked salmon

1 Make a smooth dough from the flour, margarine, water and salt. Chill.

2 Whisk the eggs with the cheese and cream and season with pepper and salt.

3 Roll out the pastry and use to line a 10-inch flan dish, pressing it in firmly. Prick the pastry several times with a fork and bake it blind in a preheated oven, 400°F, for 10 minutes.

4 Fill the flan case with the salmon and broccoli and pour in the cheese mixture. Return the quiche to the oven for a further 30 minutes.

MUSHROOM PIE

Makes 4-6 servings

Pastry

3¼ cups flour
¾ cup margarine
⅓ cup milk
1 egg
1 egg white
Pinch of salt
Pinch of sugar
Margarine for greasing

Filling

¾ cup smoked ham, diced
1 cup onions, diced
3 cups mushrooms, sliced
1 heaped tbsp flour
⅔ cup crème fraîche
2 eggs
Salt, pepper
1 bunch parsley
1 egg yolk
1 tbsp milk for brushing

1 Working quickly, mix together the pastry ingredients and knead to a smooth dough. Chill.

2 Dice the ham and sauté lightly. Dice the onions and color them in a little fat. Slice the mushrooms, add them to the pan and cook gently until almost all the liquid has evaporated. Sprinkle over the flour and leave the mixture to cool. Whisk the crème fraîche with the eggs, season and pour over the mushroom and ham mixture. Wash the parsley, chop and add to the mixture.

3 Roll out a good half of the dough and use to line a well-greased 12-inch pie dish, allowing pastry to overlap the rim slightly. Fill evenly with the mushroom and ham mixture.

4 Roll out the remaining dough to cover the pie. Dampen the pastry edges and press them together firmly to seal. Trim and make two diagonal cuts in the top of the pie, folding the pastry back slightly, to show the filling.

5 Cut out decorative mushroom shapes from the pastry trimmings. Mix the egg yolk with the milk, brush a little onto the base of the pastry mushrooms and stick them onto the pie. Brush the pie with the egg yolk and milk.

6 Bake in the center of a preheated oven, 400°F, for about 40 minutes.

Note: This pie may be served hot or cold.

QUICHE RAMEE

Makes approximately 4 servings

2 cups flour
1 cup margarine
Pinch of salt
1 egg

Filling

⅔ cup crème fraîche
2 eggs
Pinch of pepper
½ cup smoked ham, diced
½ cup soft cheese with
mushrooms, crumbled

1 Make a smooth dough from the pastry ingredients and set aside in the refrigerator to chill.
2 Reserving a little for decoration, use the pastry to line a greased 10½-inch flan dish, pinching it up well around the edge. Bake blind in a preheated oven, 400°-425°F, for about 15 minutes.
3 Thoroughly mix together the crème fraîche, eggs and pepper and pour into the flan case. Spread the diced ham and the crumbled cheese evenly over.
4 Cut four decorative rounds from the reserved pastry and arrange them attractively on top.
5 Return the quiche to the oven for a further 15 minutes.

ASPARAGUS QUICHE

Makes 4-6 servings

1½lbs asparagus
Salt, Pinch of sugar

Flan Case

2 cups flour
½ tsp salt
½ tsp mixed herbs
½ cup margarine
1 egg yolk
3¾ tbsps water
Margarine for greasing

Filling

1 cup creamed cottage cheese
3 eggs, 1 egg white
½ cup whipping cream
Salt, pepper
½ cup shrimp

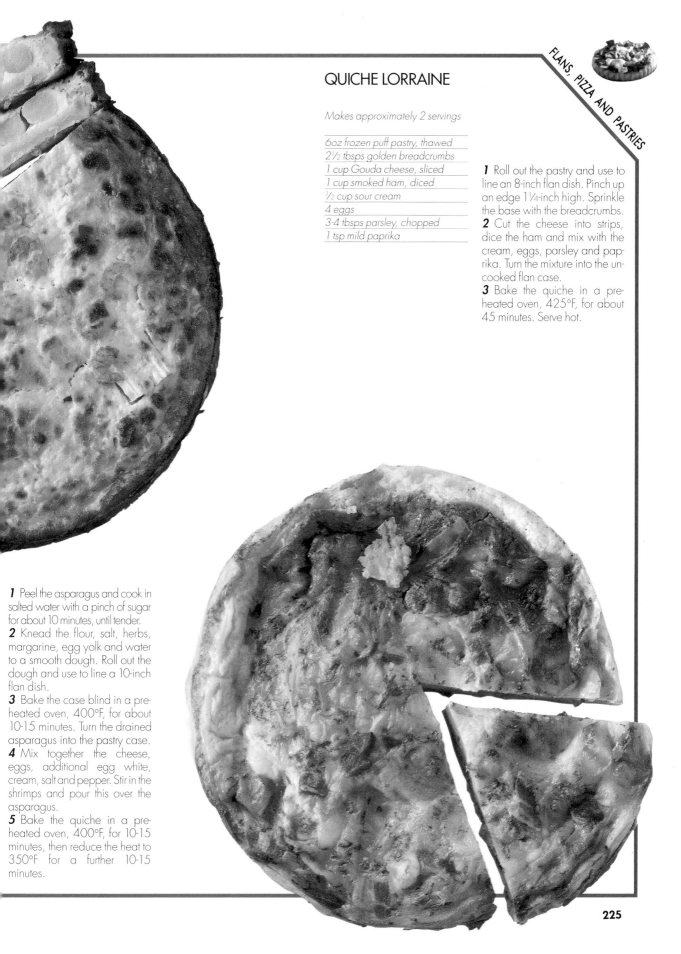

QUICHE LORRAINE

Makes approximately 2 servings

6oz frozen puff pastry, thawed
2½ tbsps golden breadcrumbs
1 cup Gouda cheese, sliced
1 cup smoked ham, diced
½ cup sour cream
4 eggs
3-4 tbsps parsley, chopped
1 tsp mild paprika

1 Roll out the pastry and use to line an 8-inch flan dish. Pinch up an edge 1¼-inch high. Sprinkle the base with the breadcrumbs.
2 Cut the cheese into strips, dice the ham and mix with the cream, eggs, parsley and paprika. Turn the mixture into the uncooked flan case.
3 Bake the quiche in a preheated oven, 425°F, for about 45 minutes. Serve hot.

1 Peel the asparagus and cook in salted water with a pinch of sugar for about 10 minutes, until tender.
2 Knead the flour, salt, herbs, margarine, egg yolk and water to a smooth dough. Roll out the dough and use to line a 10-inch flan dish.
3 Bake the case blind in a preheated oven, 400°F, for about 10-15 minutes. Turn the drained asparagus into the pastry case.
4 Mix together the cheese, eggs, additional egg white, cream, salt and pepper. Stir in the shrimps and pour this over the asparagus.
5 Bake the quiche in a preheated oven, 400°F, for 10-15 minutes, then reduce the heat to 350°F for a further 10-15 minutes.

MINI PIZZA WITH CREAM CHEESE

Makes approximately 4 servings

4oz pizza dough mix
10 small tomatoes
½ cup mushrooms
½ each red, yellow and green peppers
12 olives
1 chilli pepper
1¼ tbsps vegetable oil
Salt, pepper

Oregano
⅔ cup Philadelphia cheese with herbs
Fresh marjoram

1 Make up the pizza dough mix according to the packet instructions. Scald, skin and slice the tomatoes. Wash and slice the mushrooms. Deseed, trim and dice the pepper halves. Slice the olives and the chilli pepper.
2 Sauté the mushrooms and peppers in hot oil for 5 minutes.

Season with salt, pepper and oregano.
3 Divide the dough into four servings and roll it out into thin rounds. Spread the sautéed vegetables over the dough together with the chilli and olives. Decorate with the tomatoes and leave to rise in a warm place for a short while.
4 Bake in a preheated oven, 400°F, for 10-15 minutes. Top with dollops of cream cheese, sprinkle with marjoram and bake for a further 5 minutes.

HAM AND VEGETABLE PIZZA

Makes 3-4 servings

2 cups green and red peppers
1 onion
2½ tbsps vegetable oil
½ cup zucchini, sliced
Salt, pepper
8oz package pizza dough mix
2 tomatoes, sliced
1oz sliced salami
10 black olives
2½oz cooked ham
1 tsp oregano
½ cup mozzarella cheese
⅓ cup Gouda, grated
1 tbsp Parmesan, grated

1 Cut the peppers into strips and the onions into rings and sauté for 10 minutes in the hot oil. Add the sliced zucchini, season with salt and pepper and sauté for a further 5 minutes.
2 Make up the pizza dough mix according to the instructions on the packet and work to a smooth dough.
3 Knead the dough well with floured hands, roll it out and use to line a greased 9½-inch pizza pan or flan dish, pinching up a good edge.
4 Spread the vegetable mixture over the dough, arrange the tomato slices on top. Twist the salami into little cones and top with an olive. Arrange the ham in a fan shape on the tomatoes and decorate with the salami. Season with pepper, salt and oregano. Slice the mozzarella cheese and arrange over everything. Sprinkle the pizza with the grated Gouda and Parmesan.
5 Bake in a preheated oven, 400°F, for about 30 minutes, then increase the heat to 425°F for a further 10 minutes.

HERB QUICHE

Makes 4-6 servings

10oz package frozen puff pastry, thawed
Margarine for greasing
1 each red, green and yellow peppers
5 thin leeks
5 medium onions
1 cup bacon
1 cup cooked ham
6 eggs
¾ cup whipping cream
⅔ cup Philadelphia cheese with mixed herbs
Salt, pepper
Nutmeg
Marjoram
1 egg yolk

1 Roll the pastry out and use to line a greased 13-inch flan dish. Prick the pastry several times with a fork.

2 Cut the peppers into quarters, trim, deseed, wash and dice. Cut the leeks in half lengthwise, wash and slice. Chop the onions. Cut the bacon and ham into thin strips.

3 Blanch the peppers and leek in boiling salted water for 1 minute. Place the bacon in a saucepan over a high heat for a few minutes. Add the ham, peppers, leek and onions and sauté for 5 minutes. Fill the flan case with this mixture to ¾ inch below the top.

4 Using a balloon whisk, beat together the eggs, cream, ⅓ cup of the cream cheese, salt, pepper, nutmeg and marjoram and pour this over the vegetable mixture.

5 Bake in a preheated oven, 350°F, for about 80 minutes.

6 Mix the remaining cheese with the egg yolk and spread over the quiche after 1 hour.

Note: The final cheese and egg yolk mixture may be heated and served separately with the hot quiche.

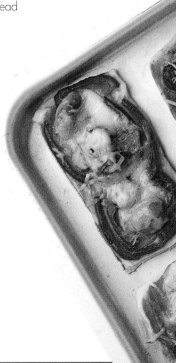

PARTY PIZZA

Makes approximately 12 servings

4 cups flour
1 cup margarine
Scant ¾ cup water
2½ tsps vinegar
2½ tsps salt
Margarine for greasing

Topping
6 tomatoes
2 onions
1 green and 1 red pepper, trimmed and deseeded
1 7½oz can mushrooms
Packet of sliced pepperoni

7oz Gouda, thinly sliced
Ketchup
Thyme, mixed herbs, oregano
Salt, paprika
3½oz salami, sliced
½ cup cheese, grated

1 Knead the flour, margarine, water, vinegar and salt to a smooth dough and chill for 1 hour.

2 Slice the onions and tomatoes, and cut the peppers into thin strips. Drain the mushrooms and cut in half if necessary. Cut the Gouda slices into triangles.

3 Roll out the dough to a thickness of about ¼ inch and cut into rectangles 2½ inches x 4 inches. Place these on a greased baking sheet. Prick each one several times with a fork, spread them thickly with ketchup and sprinkle with herbs.

4 Top with different combinations of the tomato, onion, pepperoni, peppers and mushrooms. Season. Top with the Gouda triangles, or sprinkle with the grated cheese.

5 Bake in a preheated oven, 400°-425°F, for about 20 minutes. Serve immediately.

TOMATO FLAN

Makes 3-4 servings

Pastry
2 cups flour

½ cup margarine

1 egg

Salt, pepper, oregano

Topping
1½lbs small tomatoes

Salt, pepper, oregano

1 small onion

1 triangle cheese spread

9 tbsps milk

4 eggs

1 tbsp paprika

Sugar

1 Quickly knead the pastry ingredients together, and chill for about 30 minutes. Roll out thickly and use to line a lightly-greased 8½-inch flan dish. Press the edge up well, then trim neatly to 1½ inches high. Bake the pastry blind in a preheated oven, 425°F, for about 15-20 minutes.

2 Scald and skin the tomatoes and arrange them on the pastry case. Season well with salt, pepper and oregano. Finely chop the onions and sprinkle them between the tomato slices.

3 Over a low heat, mix the cheese spread with 3 tbsps of the milk, add the remaining milk and the eggs. Whisk together well. Season with the paprika, salt, pepper, sugar and a little oregano and pour the mixture into the flan.

4 Return to the oven for 30-40 minutes. Turn off the heat and leave the flan in the oven for a further 5 minutes. Take out and leave to stand for 10 minutes before serving.

SHRIMP AND ASPARAGUS ENVELOPES

Makes approximately 10 servings

10oz package frozen puff pastry, thawed
1 cup shrimp
3½oz can asparagus
½ cup almonds, chopped
⅔ cup Philadelphia cream cheese with herbs
1¼ tbsps fine breadcrumbs
Salt, pepper
1¼ tbsps chopped fresh dill
1¼ tbsps water
1 egg yolk, beaten

1 Roll out the pastry and cut into 6-inch squares.

2 Carefully mix the shrimp with the asparagus, almonds, cheese and breadcrumbs. Season with salt, pepper and the dill.

3 Divide the mixture between the pastry squares. Brush the pastry edges with the water and fold the squares into triangles. Press the edges together firmly to seal.

4 Place the triangles on a baking sheet, brush with the beaten

egg yolk and bake in a preheated oven, 400°F, for about 20 minutes.

SMOKED SALMON PASTRIES

Makes 10 servings

10oz package frozen puff pastry, thawed
2oz smoked salmon
1 large onion
3½oz cucumber
2 tsps capers
1 tsp horseradish
1 egg yolk

1 Chop the smoked salmon, dice the onion and cucumber and mix with the capers and horseradish.

2 Roll out the pastry and use a pastry wheel to cut out ten 4-inch squares.

3 Place a little of the filling in the center of each square. Dampen the pastry edges with water and fold the squares into envelopes. Press the edges firmly together to seal. Rinse a baking sheet in cold water and arrange the pastries on it.

4 Mix the egg yolk with a dash of water and brush this over the pastries. Bake in a preheated oven, 425°F, for 10-15 minutes.

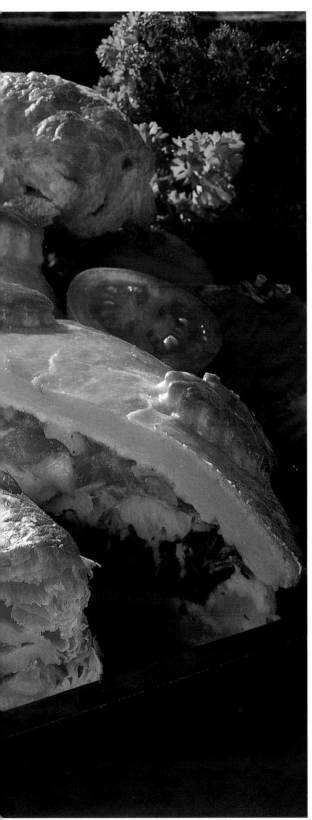

TRIESTE FISH PIE

Makes approximately 4 servings

Pastry

2 cups flour
Pinch of salt
⅓ cup margarine
1 egg
4 tbsps water

Filling

4 tomatoes
1 onion
1 clove of garlic
½ fresh chilli pepper
6 anchovy fillets
Mixed dried herbs
Oregano
15oz frozen spinach
Salt, pepper
Margarine for greasing
13oz fish fillets, fresh or frozen
Vinegar
1 egg yolk, beaten

1 Working quickly, make a smooth dough from the pastry ingredients. Knead lightly and chill for at least 1 hour.

2 Scald, skin, deseed and chop the tomatoes. Chop the onions, garlic, chilli pepper and anchovy fillets. Sauté these ingredients in margarine until any liquid has almost evaporated. Season with the dried herbs and oregano. Leave to cool.

3 Cook the spinach according to the instructions on the package, allowing any liquid to evaporate completely, then season with dried herbs, salt and pepper. Grease a 10-inch round or oval ovenproof dish and turn in the spinach.

4 Sprinkle the fish fillets with vinegar, season with salt and pepper and lay them on top of the spinach. Spread the savory tomato mixture over the fish.

5 Roll out the pastry to a thickness of about ⅛ inch and use to top the pie, pressing the pastry down well onto the rim of the dish to seal. Brush with the egg yolk and prick the pastry several times with a fork. Cut out decorative shapes from the pastry trimmings and use to decorate the pie. Bake in a preheated oven, 425°F, for about 40 minutes.

EMMENTHAL SLICES

Makes 4-6 servings

2½ cups flour
¾oz fresh yeast
½ cup lukewarm milk
Pinch of sugar
1 tbsp margarine, melted and cooled
Pinch of salt
Margarine for greasing
German mustard
8oz Emmenthal cheese, cut into 12 slices
½ cup streaky bacon, diced and cooked

1 Sift the flour into a bowl, make a well in the middle and crumble in the yeast. Mix with a little of the lukewarm milk and a pinch of sugar and flour. Leave in a warm place until frothy. Add the remaining milk, the margarine and a little salt. Mix well and knead to a smooth dough. Leave in a warm place until doubled in volume. Roll out the dough and use to line a greased baking sheet.
2 Spread mustard thinly over the dough, cover with the sliced cheese and sprinkle with the bacon.
3 Leave in a warm place to prove. Bake in a preheated oven, 425°F, for about 30 minutes. Cut into slices to serve.

ONION FLAN

Makes approximately 4 servings

Pastry
2 cups flour
½ cup margarine
1 egg
Pinch of baking powder
Pinch of salt
Margarine for greasing

Topping
⅔ cup bacon, diced
¼ cup margarine
2lb onions, finely chopped
¾ cup sour cream
2 eggs
2½ tbsps flour
Salt
Caraway seeds

1 Make a short dough from the pastry ingredients and use to line a greased 10-inch flan dish. Pinch the edge up well.
2 Color the diced bacon in the margarine; add the finely chopped onions and sauté.
3 Whisk together the sour cream, eggs, flour, salt and caraway seeds to taste. Add the onions and pour the mixture into the uncooked flan case. Bake in a preheated oven, 350°F, for about 60 minutes.

SALAMI ROLL

Makes approximately 4 servings

¾oz fresh yeast
½ cup milk
Pinch of sugar
2 cups flour
Salt
1½ tbsps margarine, melted and cooled
7oz salami, skinned and thinly sliced
1 egg, separated
Margarine for greasing

1 Make a yeast dough from the yeast, lukewarm milk, sugar, flour, salt and margarine. Leave in a warm place until well risen.
2 Roll out the dough to a rectangle. Cover it with thin slices of salami, then sprinkle with oregano. Brush the dough edges with the egg white; roll up the dough and place on a greased baking sheet. Leave in a warm place to prove.
3 Mix the egg yolk with a little water and brush over the salami roll. Score the top of the roll with a sharp knife. Bake in a preheated oven, 400°F, for about 40 minutes.

HERRING AND MUSHROOM FLAN

Makes 2 servings

Dough

1 cup flour
¼oz fresh yeast
Salt
2½ tbsps lukewarm milk
1 tbsp margarine, melted and cooled
1 egg

Filling

3oz can of pickled herrings
4oz can of mushrooms
1 onion
2oz red pepper, skinned
Pepper
½ cup Gouda cheese, grated
Chives

1 Make a yeast dough from the dough ingredients. Leave in a warm place until well risen. Roll out the dough and use to line a greased 8-inch flan dish.
2 Drain the herrings, slice the mushrooms, and cut the onions into rings and the pepper into thin strips. Arrange these ingredients attractively over the flan base. Sprinkle with freshly ground black pepper and grate the cheese over. Leave in a warm place to prove.
3 Bake in a preheated oven, 425°F, for 25-30 minutes. Sprinkle with chopped chives and serve hot.

DECORATIVE VEGETABLE FLAN

Makes approximately 6 servings

Pastry

2 cups flour
1 egg
½ cup margarine
5 tbsps cold water
Pinch of salt

Filling

1½lbs leeks
4-5 medium tomatoes
2 cups zucchini
1 small cauliflower
¼ cup margarine
½lb pork sausagemeat
4 tbsps sour cream
Pepper
Nutmeg
Salt
3 eggs
⅔ cup sour cream
1¼ tbsps cornstarch
2 tbsps Emmenthal cheese, grated

1 Make a dough from the pastry ingredients and knead until smooth. Chill for 30 minutes. Roll out the pastry and use to line a 9-inch flan dish.

2 Bake the pastry case blind in a preheated oven, 400°F, for 20-25 minutes. Leave to cool.

3 Meanwhile, wash and trim the vegetables. Slice the tomatoes and zucchini, cut the cauliflower into flowerets and finely chop the leeks. Lightly sauté the vegetables in the margarine until just soft.

4 Mix the sausagemeat with the 4 tbsps sour cream. Season with pepper, salt and nutmeg to taste. Spread this over the flan base and arrange the vegetables decoratively on top.

5 Whisk the eggs with the ⅔ cup sour cream. Stir in the cornstarch and season with nutmeg, salt and pepper. Pour this mixture over the vegetables and bake in a preheated oven, 400°F, for 25-30 minutes.

6 Grate the Emmenthal and sprinkle it over the flan. Return it to the oven for a further 5 minutes and serve hot.

CHINESE CABBAGE FLAN

Makes approximately 8 servings

2 cups flour

Pinch of salt

Pinch of baking powder

1 cup margarine

1 cup cottage cheese

Margarine for greasing

Filling

1¾ cups cream cheese

3oz Stilton cheese

3-4 tbsps chopped fresh herbs

⅓ cup sour cream

Pinch of gelatine dissolved in ½ cup water

½ tsp salt

Pepper

6 leaves of Chinese cabbage

Meat stock

3oz Gouda cheese, cut into 3 slices

3 slices cooked ham

Tomatoes, to decorate

1 Mix the flour, salt, baking powder, margarine and cottage cheese to a smooth dough. Knead and chill. Roll out the dough into a square, fold it over and roll out again. Repeat this process three times. Use the dough to line a greased 10-inch spring-release pan and bake blind in a preheated oven, 400°F, for 10 minutes.

2 Mix together the soft cheese, Stilton, herbs, sour cream, gelatine, salt and pepper and spread this over the cooked flan base.

3 Wash the Chinese cabbage leaves and blanch them in meat stock. Drain in a colander. Place two leaves together, overlapping them slightly, and put a slice of Gouda cheese and a slice of ham on top. Roll up tightly. Repeat, to make three rolls in total.

4 Cut the rolls into 1-inch thick slices and arrange these over the cheese mixture in the flan. Decorate with tomato slices. Return to the oven for a further 15-20 minutes.

FESTIVE PORK PIE

Makes approximately 8 servings

1½lbs smoked pork
3 cups flour
½ tsp salt
6¼ tbsps ice water
1 white bread roll
7½ tbsps hot milk
1 onion
1¼ tbsps chopped fresh parsley
½ cup light cream
Salt, pepper, cayenne pepper
Dried basil
Margarine for greasing
1 egg yolk

1 Put the meat into boiling water to just cover. Cook for 45 minutes until tender. Leave to cool in the broth.
2 Using a hand-held electric mixer with a pastry hook and working quickly, make a smooth dough from the flour, salt, margarine and ice water. Chill.
3 Grind the meat. Cut the bread roll into cubes, pour the hot milk over and leave to soak. Mix the meat, bread, onion, parsley, cream, basil and seasonings together well.
4 Roll out two-thirds of the dough and use to line a greased 10-inch flan dish. Prick the base several times with a fork. Spread the filling evenly over. Roll out the remaining dough and use to top the pie, pressing the edges together well. Prick the top with a fork several times. Cut a ½ inch hole in the center.
5 Mix the egg yolk with a little water and brush over the pie to glaze. Cut a few decorative shapes from the pastry trimmings, attach and brush with egg yolk.
6 Bake in a preheated oven, 400°F, for about 60 minutes. Serve hot.

Note: This pie is also good cold, jellied. Dissolve 6 sheets of gelatine in ¾ cup of the cooking liquid from the meat. Pour into the cold pie through the hole and leave to set.

LEEK FLAN

Makes approximately 6-8 servings

Pastry

2½ cups flour
Salt
⅔ cup margarine
1 egg

Filling

5lb leeks

PARTY PIES

Makes approximately 16 pies

2 cups flour	
1 cup margarine	
1 cup low fat creamed cottage cheese	
Salt	

Filling

1 cup mixed ground beef and pork	
1 slice white bread	
1 small green pepper, chopped	
½ cup Emmenthal cheese, diced	
1 egg, separated	
Pepper	
2½ tbsps water	

1 Put the flour, salt, margarine and cheese on a pastry board. Mix the ingredients with a palette knife and knead quickly to a smooth dough. Chill.

2 Mix together the meat, white bread, chopped pepper, diced cheese and egg white and season with pepper and salt.

3 Roll out the dough and cut into 4½-inch rounds. Put one tablespoonful of the filling on half of each pastry round. Mix the egg yolk and water, brush this over the pastry edges and fold the pies up. Press the edges together with a fork to seal.

4 Arrange on a baking sheet, brush with egg yolk and bake in a preheated oven, 400°-425°F, for about 20 minutes.

¼ cup margarine
Salt
2 cups smoked ham, diced
1 cup crème fraîche
4 eggs
½ cup grated cheese
Pepper, nutmeg
Margarine

1 Make a short dough from the pastry ingredients. Knead and chill for 30 minutes.

2 Meanwhile, wash and drain the leeks and slice them into rings. Gently sauté them in 1 tbsp of the margarine for 15 minutes. Season with salt, and drain again.

3 Roll out the pastry and use to line a 12-inch flan dish, pinching up an edge of 1 inch. Bake the pastry case blind in a preheated oven, 400°F, for about 20 minutes.

4 Dice the ham, and lightly brown in the remaining margarine. Spread the ham over the flan case and place the leeks on top. Beat together the crème fraîche, eggs and cheese, season with salt, pepper and nutmeg and pour over the leeks.

5 Dot the flan with the extra margarine and return to the oven for about 30 minutes.

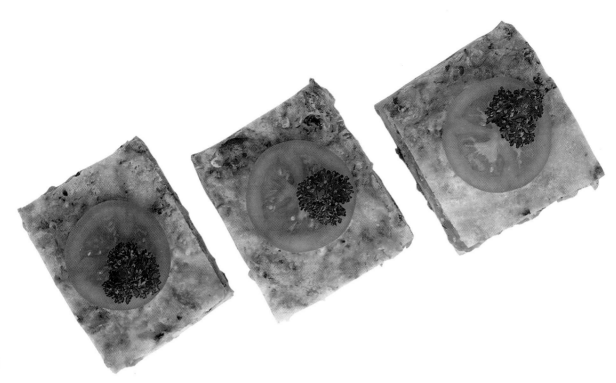

TOMATO AND ONION FLAN

Makes approximately 6 servings

½oz fresh yeast
½ cup lukewarm milk
1 tsp sugar
2 cups flour
Pinch of salt
½ cup margarine, melted and cooled
Margarine for greasing

Topping

3lb tomatoes
1lb onions
¼ cup margarine
1 sprig each fresh basil, parsley, oregano, or 1 tsp dried herbs
Salt, pepper
3 eggs
¾ cup light cream
½ cup Emmenthal cheese, grated

1 Crumble the yeast into the milk, add a pinch of sugar and leave, covered, in a warm place until frothy. Mix together the flour, sugar, salt and melted margarine, add the frothy yeast, mix together well and knead to a smooth dough. Cover and leave in a warm place until doubled in volume. Knead again.
2 Roll out the dough on a floured board and put into a greased baking sheet, pressing the edges well into the sides. Leave in a warm place to prove.
3 Scald, peel and deseed the tomatoes. Reserve 1 or 2 for decoration and cut the rest into quarters or eighths. Slice the onions thinly and sauté them in the margarine. Chop the herbs, add them to the onions and season with salt and pepper.
4 Arrange the tomatoes over the pastry base. Spread with the cooled onion mixture. Whisk the eggs and cream together and pour evenly into the flan.

5 Bake in a preheated oven, 400°F, for 25 minutes, placing the flan on a low shelf for the first 15 minutes. Remove the flan, sprinkle with cheese and replace in the center of the oven, cooking for a further 10 minutes.
6 Decorate with the reserved tomatoes, sliced, and a little chopped parsley and serve hot or cold.

GENTLEMAN'S SAVORY FLAN

Makes approximately 4 servings

Pastry

2 cups flour
½ cup margarine
½ tsp salt
1 egg
Margarine for greasing

Topping

2 onions
1 tbsp margarine

7½oz can mushrooms, drained
Curry powder
Fresh parsley, to taste
2 tbsps fine breadcrumbs
1½ cups sausagemeat
½ cup thin slices of ham
1 cup tomatoes
1 cup peppers
Oregano
1 cup Gouda cheese, sliced and cut into strips

1 Make a short dough from the pastry ingredients. Chill.

2 Meanwhile, slice onions into rings and sauté in the margarine. Add the mushrooms and sauté until tender, then season to taste with curry powder. Chop the parsley and add it to the pan.

3 Grease a 10½-inch flan dish. Roll out the pastry and use to line the dish. Sprinkle the breadcrumbs over the pastry case, spread with the sausagemeat, and top with the onion and mushroom mixture and the sliced ham. Wash the tomatoes and peppers, slice thinly and arrange on the flan. Sprinkle with oregano.

4 Bake the flan in a preheated oven, 425°F, for 10 minutes. Decorate with a lattice of cheese strips and bake for a further 15 minutes.

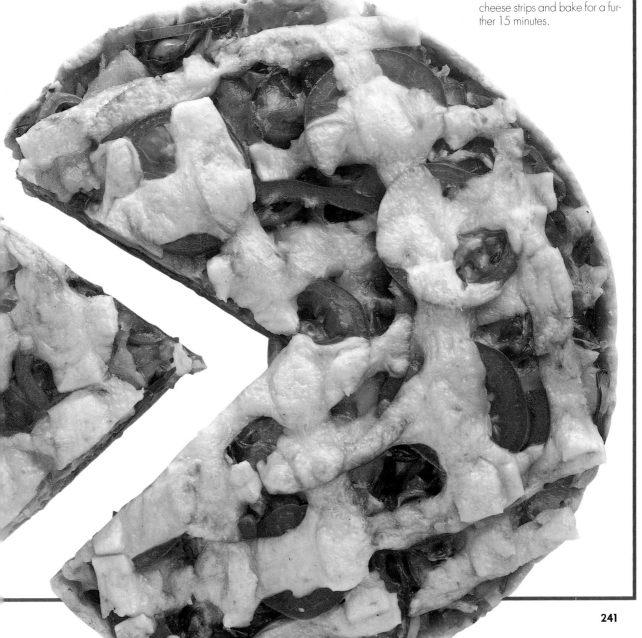

CHEESE PUFFS

Makes approximately 4 servings

2 cups flour
2 good pinches of baking powder
1 cup well-chilled margarine
1 cup low fat creamed cottage cheese
Pinch of salt
1 cup Gouda cheese, coarsely grated
1 egg yolk, beaten

1 Sift the flour with the baking powder, and dot with flakes of margarine. Add the drained cheese and knead quickly to a smooth dough. Chill for at least 30 minutes.
2 Roll out the dough into a long, narrow strip, fold the short sides into the middle and roll out the pastry again, towards the open side. Repeat this process 3-4 times, chilling for 15 minutes between each stage.
3 Roll out the dough for the final time and cut into eight squares. Pile the cheese onto four of the

squares. Cut out a flower shape from the center of each of the other four squares. Top the cheese squares with these decorative squares, pressing the outer edges together firmly, to seal.
4 Brush with the beaten egg yolk and bake in a preheated oven, 425°F, for about 20 minutes.

PUFF PASTRY PIROSHKI

Makes 10 servings

10oz frozen puff pastry, thawed
1 onion, chopped
Margarine
4oz can mushrooms, drained and sliced
Salt, pepper
Fresh parsley, chopped
1 egg yolk, beaten

1 Soften the chopped onions in the margarine, add the mushrooms and sauté briefly. Season with salt and pepper and add the parsley. Remove from the heat and add a little of the egg yolk.

2 Roll out the puff pastry, cut it into squares and spread these with the mushroom mixture. Fold the pastry diagonally to form triangles. Brush the edges with water and press together firmly, to seal.

3 Place the triangles on a baking sheet rinsed in cold water, and prick each one several times. Brush with the remaining egg yolk and bake in a preheated oven, 425°F, for 20 minutes.

CHICKEN AND TURKEY LIVER TERRINE

Makes 12-16 servings

1 onion
1 apple
1/3 cup margarine
1 2/3 cups turkey liver
2/3 cup cooked chicken
1/3 cup bacon
1 egg yolk
8 tbsps light cream
4 tbsps cognac
2-3 tsps salt
Freshly ground black pepper
Pinch of ground cloves
Mixed herbs
10 pistachios
Meat extract
5 tbsps Madeira
3 sheets gelatine
Bay leaves and green peppercorns, to decorate

1 Chop the onion, grate the apple and sauté both in the margarine. Leave to cool. Put 1/2 cup of the turkey liver, the chicken and bacon through the grinder twice. Mix this with the egg yolk, cream and cognac and season with salt, spices and herbs. Dice the remaining liver and add to the mixture with the pistachios.
2 Press the mixture into an ovenproof terrine and cover tightly with foil. Place the terrine in a baking dish of hot water and cook in a preheated oven, 300°-350°F, for about 1¾ hours.
3 Place a plate with a weight on top over the cooked terrine and leave to cool. Reserve any juices that are pressed out and skim these of fat.
4 Add a little water to the reserved terrine juices to make them up to 1 cup and flavor with the meat extract, salt, pepper and Madeira. Stir this liquid into the previously soaked and dissolved gelatine. As soon as the mixture starts to set, pour it over the terrine. Decorate with bay leaves and green peppercorns.

VEAL PIE

Makes approximately 8 servings

2 cups flour
1 tsp mixed dried herbs
Salt
2 cups creamed cottage cheese
2 cups margarine
Margarine for greasing
Breadcrumbs

Filling

2 onions
1 red and 1 green pepper
1/2 cup mushrooms
Margarine
Pepper, salt
2 hard-boiled eggs
2 cups lean veal, ground
1 egg
1 bread roll, soaked in water
Marjoram

1 Mix together the flour, herbs and salt on a pastry board. Place the cheese and margarine on top and cut them in with a palette knife. Working quickly, mix everything together and knead to a smooth dough. Chill.
2 Grease a long loaf pan and sprinkle it with breadcrumbs.
3 Dice the onions and peppers finely, slice the mushrooms and sauté these vegetables in margarine for 5 minutes. Season and leave to cool.
4 Chop the hard-boiled eggs. Make a stuffing with the ground veal, raw egg, squeezed-out bread roll, salt, pepper and marjoram.
5 Roll out the dough and use to line the pan, leaving an overlap at the top edge. Spread half the chopped eggs on the dough, then cover evenly with half the meat mixture.
6 Spread the vegetable mixture over, cover with the remaining meat, and finish with a layer of the remaining chopped egg. Fold the overlapping dough over the top of the pie. Brush the edges with a little water and press them together, to seal.
7 Bake the pie in a preheated oven, 400°F, for about 50 minutes. Serve hot or cold.

COLD TURKEY AND HAM PIE

Makes 15-20 servings

Pastry

4 cups flour
1 cup margarine
1 tsp salt
3 tbsps water
1 egg
Margarine for greasing

Filling

2 cups cooked turkey breast
1 cup cooked ham
2 tbsps chopped fresh parsley
1/2 tsp dried sage
6 hard-boiled eggs

To Finish

1 egg yolk
12 sheets gelatine
1 cup chicken stock
6 tbsps brandy
Grated zest of 1/2 lemon
3 tbsps lemon juice
Salt, freshly ground black pepper

1 Make a smooth dough from the pastry ingredients. Chill.
2 Roughly dice the turkey and ham and mix with the herbs.
3 Roll out about two-thirds of the pastry to a thickness of 1/8 inch and use to line a greased ·12-inch loaf pan. Put half the meat filling into the pie. With the back of a spoon, make a hollow along the center of the filling.
4 Peel the eggs, slice a little off each of the ends to flatten and arrange them in a line along the channel. Cover with the remaining meat filling.
5 Roll out the remaining dough and use to cover the pie. Press the edges together well to seal. Cut a small hole for steam to escape.
6 Mix the egg yolk with a little water and brush over the top of the pie. Cut decorative shapes from the pastry trimmings, fix on top of the pie and brush with egg yolk.
7 Bake in a preheated oven, 350°F, for about 75 minutes. Leave to cool in the pan.
8 Soak the gelatine. Drain it and dissolve it in the hot chicken stock. Add the brandy, lemon zest and juice. Season well with salt and pepper. Pour through the hole into the cold pie. Leave to set in the refrigerator.

ZINGY BREAD ROLLS

Makes 8 rolls

½ cup smoked bacon, diced
1 level tbsp margarine
2 cups flour
3 tsps salt
Good pinch of mustard powder
⅓ cup margarine
½ cup Gouda cheese, grated
1 egg
½ cup milk
Margarine for greasing
Flour
Milk

1 Sauté the bacon in the margarine until colored. Leave to cool.
2 Mix together the flour, baking powder, salt and mustard powder on a pastry board. Dot with margarine and cut this in with a palette knife. Add the grated cheese, reserving 1 tbsp, the bacon and the egg, mixed with milk. Mix everything together well and knead to a smooth dough.
3 Shape the dough into eight balls and place these close together in a circle, in a cake pan with a removable base.
4 Brush a little milk over the sides and tops of the rolls, sprinkle them with the remaining cheese and bake in a preheated oven, 350°-400°F for about 30 minutes.

SAVORY LOAF WITH HERBS

Makes approximately 8 servings

1 red pepper
2 onions
1 large pickle
½ cup margarine
4 eggs
4 cups low fat creamed cottage cheese
⅓ cup semolina
½ cup ham, diced
1 bunch each fresh dill, parsley, chives
1 packet of watercress, chopped
Salt, pepper, paprika
Garlic
Margarine for greasing

1 Dice the pepper, onions and pickle and sauté in 1 tbsp of the margarine. Leave to cool.
2 Cream the remaining margarine until light, then gradually beat in the eggs. Squeeze the cheese in a cloth to drain, and add to the egg mixture together with the semolina, ham, herbs, watercress and the onion mixture. Season with salt, pepper and paprika.
3 Turn into a well-greased loaf pan and smooth the top.
4 Bake in a preheated oven, 350°F for about 80 minutes.

Note: This loaf may be served hot or cold.

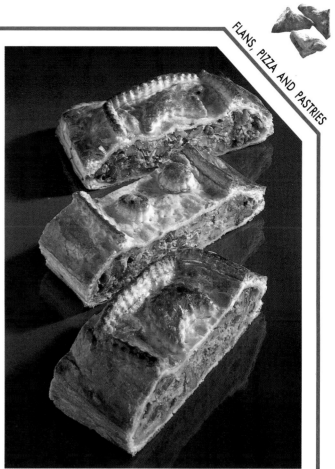

HAM AND TOMATO FLAN

Makes approximately 4 servings

1 cup flour	
Salt	
½ cup margarine	
1 egg	
Margarine for greasing	

Topping

1 lb tomatoes	
½ cup smoked ham, diced	
1 onion, finely chopped	
2 eggs	
½ cup milk	

1 Put the flour and salt onto a pastry board, dot with the margarine and cut this in with a palette knife. Make a well in the center of the mixture and drop in the egg. Mix in, and knead to a smooth dough.

2 Use to line an 8½-inch flan dish, pinching up the edges well. Bake blind in a preheated oven, 400°-425°F, for about 10 minutes.
3 Slice the tomatoes, arrange them in the flan case, and season with salt and pepper. Sprinkle over the ham and onion. Beat the eggs with the milk, season with salt and pepper and pour over.
4 Return the flan to the oven for a further 30-40 minutes.

AMERICAN CHEESE PIE

Makes approximately 4 servings

10oz package frozen puff pastry, thawed	
1 cup Gouda or Camembert cheese, cubed	
½ cup walnuts, chopped	
2 tbsps cranberries	
¼ cup currants	
½-1 tsp salt	
2 egg whites	
1 egg yolk, beaten	

1 Roll out the pastry to a thickness of ⅛ inch. Divide into two equal rectangles, prick with a fork and set aside.
2 Mix together with the walnuts, cranberries, currants and salt. Whisk the egg whites until stiff and fold them in.
3 Rinse a baking sheet in cold water, put one puff pastry rectangle on it and spread with the cheese mixture, leaving ½ inch clear around the edges. Dampen the edges, place the second rectangle on top, and press the edges together well, to seal. Brush the pie with egg yolk. Decorate with the pastry trimmings, cut into shapes.
4 Bake in a preheated oven,

450°-475°F, for about 20 minutes.

SALAMI CROISSANTS

Makes approximately 20 croissants

1¾ cups flour
1 cup creamed cottage cheese
⅔ cup margarine
Pinch of salt
Margarine for greasing

Filling

1 cup sliced salami, diced
1 small onion, finely chopped
1 cup cottage cheese
2 tbsps light cream
Pepper, paprika
Egg yolk, beaten

1 Sift the flour onto a pastry board. Squeeze the cottage cheese in a cloth to drain, and place it on the flour together with the margarine and salt. Cut in, using a palette knife. Mix well and knead quickly to a smooth dough. Chill.
2 Mix the salami and onion with the cheese and cream, and season with pepper and paprika.
3 Roll out the dough to a thickness of ¼ inch. Using a pastry wheel, cut out 6-inch squares and divide these into triangles. Put a little filling on each triangle, roll it up and twist into a croissant shape, then place on a greased baking sheet.

4 Brush the croissants with egg yolk and bake in a preheated oven, 425°F, for 15-20 minutes.

Variation:

Roll out half the dough into a circle, cut out rounds to fit cupcake pans, spread with the filling and use the remaining dough to make lids. Bake for 35 minutes.

GROUND MEAT PIES

Makes approximately 15 pies

1oz fresh yeast
1 cup lukewarm milk
Pinch of sugar
4 cups flour
Salt
Grated zest of ½ lemon
2 eggs
1level tbsp margarine, melted and cooled
Margarine for greasing

Filling

2 cups mixed ground pork and beef
1 level tbsp margarine
1 tsp curry powder
1 small red pepper, diced
1 cup tomatoes, peeled and chopped
6 tbsps red wine
1 tbsp gravy powder
½ tsp paprika
Salt, pepper
2 egg yolks, beaten

1 Crumble the yeast into the lukewarm milk, and stir in a little sugar and flour. Cover and leave in a warm place for about 10 minutes, until frothy. Put the flour, salt and lemon zest into a bowl, add the frothy yeast, eggs, egg yolk and margarine. Knead to a smooth dough and leave, covered, in a warm place until doubled in volume.
2 Brown the meat in the margarine, then stir in the curry powder. Add the diced pepper and chopped tomatoes to the meat. Mix well and stir in the red wine and gravy powder. Simmer until nearly all the liquid has evaporated. Season well with salt, pepper and paprika.
3 Knead the dough again and roll out to a thickness of ¼ inch. Cut out 4½-inch rounds. Spread half with the filling mixture and cover with the remaining pastry rounds. Press the edges together well, to seal.
4 Put the pies on a greased baking sheet, brush with beaten egg yolk and bake in a preheated oven, 425°F, for about 15 minutes.

SAVORY HAM PUFFS

Makes about 20 servings

2 cups flour
1 tsp baking powder
Ketchup
½-1 tsp salt
1 cup low fat creamed cottage cheese
1 cup margarine

Filling

1 cup cooked ham, finely diced
2 small onions, grated
2 tbsps chopped fresh parsley
Good pinch of paprika

1 Squeeze the cheese in a cloth to drain. Working quickly, make a dough from the flour, baking powder, 1 tsp of the ketchup, salt, cheese and margarine, and chill for 1 hour. Roll out the pastry into a rectangle about ½ inch thick, fold the two ends over each other and roll out again to the original size. Repeat the process, rolling in the opposite direction, then chill the pastry for 15 minutes.
2 Mix the ham, onions and parsley, and season generously with paprika.
3 Roll out the pastry to a thickness of ¼ inch. Cut out 4-inch squares or circles, and spread them thinly with ketchup. Place a little of the filling on top.
4 Brush the pastry edges with a little water, fold the puffs into triangles or croissant shapes, seal the edges and decorate the tops with shapes cut out of the pastry trimmings.
5 Rinse a baking sheet in cold water and line with wax paper. Put the puffs onto it and bake in a preheated oven, 425°F, for about 10 minutes. Serve hot with ketchup.

CHEESE BALLS

Makes approximately 20 pieces

¾ cup milk
¼ cup margarine
Salt
4 eggs
1¾ cups flour
5 tbsps light cream
½ cup grated cheese
Margarine for greasing
Flour

1 Bring the milk to the boil with the margarine and salt. Remove from the heat and pour in the sifted flour in a stream. Put back on a low heat and cook, beating continuously, until the mixture shrinks away from the sides of the pan in a ball.
2 Beat 1 of the eggs in immediately. Leave to cool slightly, then beat in the remaining eggs one by one, followed by the cream and cheese.
3 Use a wet teaspoon to drop little mounds of the mixture onto a greased and floured baking sheet and bake in a preheated oven, 400°-425°F, for 30-35 minutes, until golden.

Note: These are good served with fricassees or stews.

CHEESE HATS

Makes approximately 30 pieces

2 cups flour
1 egg
Salt
⅔ cup margarine
¾ cup cheese spread with smoked ham
1 egg yolk, beaten

1 Working quickly, make a pastry dough from the flour, egg, salt and margarine; knead and chill in the refrigerator for 1 hour. Roll out thinly and cut out 2-inch rounds.
2 Divide the cheese between the pastry rounds. Pull up the pastry around the cheese and press the edges together well to form three-cornered hats.

Brush with a little beaten egg yolk.
3 Bake in a preheated oven, 400°F, for 15-20 minutes.

CHEESE PASTRY SNAILS

Makes approximately 60 snails

2 cups flour
Salt
½ cup margarine
½ cup philadelphia cream cheese with herbs
1 egg yolk

1¼ tbsps water
Caraway seeds
Margarine for greasing

1 Using a palette knife, cut the margarine and cheese into the flour and salt. Working quickly, knead the mixture into a smooth dough.
2 Roll out the pastry to a thickness of about ¼ inch and cut into 4-inch-long strips with a pastry wheel.

3 Beat the egg yolk with the water, brush this over the dough and sprinkle it with caraway seeds. Roll up the strips into snail shapes and put on a greased baking sheet.
4 Bake in a preheated oven, 400°-425°F, for 12-15 minutes.

HAM ONION AND HERB BITES

Makes approximately 40 pieces

2 cups flour
1 tsp baking powder
1 cup low fat creamed cottage cheese
1 cup margarine
⅓ cup smoked ham, diced
1 bunch each fresh parsley, dill and chives, chopped
1 small onion, very finely chopped
Good pinch of pepper
½ level tsps salt
Margarine for greasing

1 Knead all the ingredients together well. With floured hands, shape the dough into 2-inch-thick rolls, cut these into ¾-inch-thick slices and shape each slice into a ball.
2 Place the balls on a greased baking sheet and make a small dent in the top of each one with your finger.
3 Bake in a preheated oven, 400°F, for about 20 minutes.

CHEESE AND PEPPER SLICES

Makes approximately 50 slices

2 cups flour
½ cup margarine
1 egg
Salt, pepper
8oz package cheese spread triangles
Margarine for greasing
1 skinned red pepper, thinly sliced
1 egg yolk, beaten

1 Make a short pastry dough from the flour, margarine, egg, salt and pepper. Working quickly, mix it well, knead and chill for 1 hour.
2 Using a hot knife, slice the cheese spread horizontally into thin triangles.
3 Roll out the pastry to a 10-inch square. Place this on a greased baking sheet. Arrange the cheese triangles on top, interspersed with slices of pepper. Brush with egg yolk.
4 Bake in a preheated oven, 450°-475°F for about 20 minutes, until golden. Cut immediately into small rectangles and serve warm.

CARAWAY SEED STRAWS

Makes approximately 35 straws

10oz package frozen puff pastry, thawed
1 egg
Caraway seeds
Salt

1 Roll out the pastry, prick it several times with a tooth pick and cut into strips about ½ inch wide. Lightly beat the egg, brush it over the pastry strips and sprinkle them with caraway seeds and salt.

2 Twist the strips into spiral-shaped straws and leave for 15 minutes on a baking sheet which has been rinsed in cold

water.

3 Bake the caraway seed straws in a preheated oven, 450°-475°F, for about 10 minutes.

PARTY BOATS

Makes 12-14

2 cups flour
Salt
½ cup margarine
1 egg
Margarine for greasing
2 cups cooked shrimp
Parsley, sliced tomatoes, sliced pickle, etc., to decorate

1 Sift the flour and salt onto a pastry board, dot with the margarine and cut it in with a palette knife. Make a well in the center of the mixture, drop in the egg and work everything quickly together to a smooth dough. Cover and chill.

2 Roll out the pastry and use to line greased boat molds. Bake in a preheated oven, 400°-425°F, for about 20 minutes. Turn out of the molds and leave to cool.

3 Shortly before serving fill the boats with chopped shrimp and decorate attractively.

SAVORY STICKS

Makes approximately 30 sticks

1 cup flour
⅓ cup potato flour
2½ level tsps baking powder
1 tsp salt
1 tbsp margarine
2 egg whites
1¼ tbsps milk
1 egg yolk for brushing
Poppy seeds, sea salt or caraway seeds
Margarine for greasing

1 Sift the flour, potato flour, baking powder and salt onto a pastry board, dot with the margarine and cut it in with a palette knife. Lightly whisk the egg whites with the milk. Make a well in the center of the mixture, put in the egg and milk and mix everything quickly to a dough.
2 Roll out the pastry immediately and cut into strips, ⅝ inch x 6 inches. Mix the egg yolk with a little water, brush it over the pastry strips and sprinkle them with the poppy seeds, sea salt or caraway seeds.
3 Twist the strips into spirals and place them on a greased baking sheet.
4 Bake in a preheated oven, 350°-400°F, for 10-15 minutes.

CHEESE WAFFLES

Makes 10-15 waffles

1 cup margarine
4 eggs
Pinch of salt
8¾ tbsps lukewarm water
1¼ cups flour
¾ cup buckwheat flour
1¼ tsps baking powder
½ cup Gouda cheese, grated
Paprika
Pepper
Vegetable oil for greasing

1 Cream the margarine, eggs and salt until light and fluffy. Gradually add the water and flour, sifted together with the baking powder. Add the grated cheese and season.
2 Heat the waffle iron and brush it with vegetable oil. Put about 1 tbsp of the mixture onto the iron and cook for about 3 minutes until golden brown. Repeat until the mixture has been used up.

HAM CROISSANTS

Makes approximately 12 croissants

1oz fresh yeast
½ lukewarm milk
1¼ tsps sugar
3 cups flour
Salt
¼ cup margarine, melted and cooled
1 egg, beaten
Margarine for greasing

Filling

2 egg whites
5oz smoked ham, thinly sliced
15oz can pineapple chunks, finely chopped
2 egg yolks, beaten

1 Crumble the yeast into the milk and stir in a pinch each of sugar and flour. Cover and leave in a warm place for about 5-10 minutes, until frothy. Put the flour, sugar, salt, margarine and egg into a mixing bowl, add the frothy yeast, mix and knead to a smooth dough. Cover with foil and leave in a warm place until doubled in volume. Thoroughly knead dough a second time.

2 Roll out the dough to a thickness of ¼ inch. Using a pastry wheel, cut out about twelve triangles measuring 5½ inches from corner to corner. Brush each with a little egg white, and top with a piece of ham and some of the pineapple. Roll up the triangles and twist them into croissant shapes.

3 Cover the croissants and leave in a warm place to prove. Brush the croissants with the egg yolk and bake them in a preheated oven, 400°F, for about 20 minutes.

SWISS CHOUX GOUGERES

¾ cup water
⅓ cup margarine
½ tsp salt
1½ cups flour
4 eggs
1 tsp baking powder
2 triangles of cheese spread
⅓ cup Emmenthal, grated
Margarine for greasing
Flour
Egg yolk
Chopped watercress, to garnish

1 Bring the water, margarine and salt to the boil. Remove from the heat and beat in all the flour. Return to the heat and beat the mixture until it shrinks away from sides of the saucepan in a ball.

2 Beat one of the eggs into the hot mixture, add the cheese spread cut into pieces and ¼ cup of the grated Emmenthal cheese. Beat in the remaining eggs one at a time. Leave to cool.

3 Spoon the mixture into an icing bag fitted with a plain round nozzle. Pipe mounds of the mixture onto a greased and floured baking sheet. Mix the egg yolk with a little water and brush it over the pastries.

CHOUX PASTRY BUNS WITH CHEESE

Makes approximately 20 buns

¾ cup water
1½ tbsps margarine
Salt
Nutmeg
1 cup flour
2 eggs
2 triangles of cheese spread
1¼ tsps baking powder
Margarine for greasing
Flour

Filling

3 triangles cheese spread with herbs
1 hard-boiled egg, chopped
Evaporated milk
2½ tsps chopped fresh herbs

1 Bring the water, margarine and a little salt and nutmeg to the boil. Off the heat, beat in all the flour at once. Return the mixture to the heat and beat continuously until the mixture shrinks away from the sides of the saucepan in a ball.

2 Beat one of the eggs and the cheese spread into the hot mixture. Leave to cool. Beat in the second egg and the baking powder.

3 Using two teaspoons, drop spoonfuls of the mixture onto a greased and floured baking sheet. Bake in a preheated oven, 450°-475°F, for about 25 minutes. Use scissors to cut off the tops of the buns as soon as they are removed from the oven.

4 Mix the herbed cheese spread with the chopped egg, evaporated milk and fresh herbs and use to fill the buns.

Sprinkle them with grated cheese.

4 Bake in a preheated oven, 425°F, for 25-30 minutes. Garnish the finished gougères with the watercress and serve hot.

INDEX